Sustainable Development Goals Series

The **Sustainable Development Goals Series** is Springer Nature's inaugural cross-imprint book series that addresses and supports the United Nations' seventeen Sustainable Development Goals. The series fosters comprehensive research focused on these global targets and endeavours to address some of society's greatest grand challenges. The SDGs are inherently multidisciplinary, and they bring people working across different fields together and working towards a common goal. In this spirit, the Sustainable Development Goals series is the first at Springer Nature to publish books under both the Springer and Palgrave Macmillan imprints, bringing the strengths of our imprints together.

The Sustainable Development Goals Series is organized into eighteen subseries: one subseries based around each of the seventeen respective Sustainable Development Goals, and an eighteenth subseries, "Connecting the Goals", which serves as a home for volumes addressing multiple goals or studying the SDGs as a whole. Each subseries is guided by an expert Subseries Advisor with years or decades of experience studying and addressing core components of their respective Goal.

The SDG Series has a remit as broad as the SDGs themselves, and contributions are welcome from scientists, academics, policymakers, and researchers working in fields related to any of the seventeen goals. If you are interested in contributing a monograph or curated volume to the series, please contact the Publishers: Zachary Romano [Springer; zachary.romano@springer.com] and Rachael Ballard [Palgrave Macmillan; rachael.ballard@palgrave.com].

Dong Guo · Peng Zhou

Beating Financial Swords into Developmental Plowshares

From Weapon to Wagon

Springer

Dong Guo
China Development Bank
Beijing, China

Peng Zhou
Cardiff Business School
Cardiff University
Cardiff, UK

ISSN 2523-3084 ISSN 2523-3092 (electronic)
Sustainable Development Goals Series
ISBN 978-981-95-5151-4 ISBN 978-981-95-5152-1 (eBook)
https://doi.org/10.1007/978-981-95-5152-1

This Springer imprint is published by the registered company Springer Nature Singapore Pte Ltd.
The registered company address is: 152 Beach Road, #21-01/04 Gateway East, Singapore 189721, Singapore

Preface

> They shall beat their swords into plowshares, and their spears into pruning hooks; nation shall not lift up sword against nation, neither shall they learn war anymore. (Isaiah 2:4, Old Testament)
>
> Forging swords and halberds into farm tools, letting oxen and horses roam in the wild bush. (The School Sayings of Confucius)

Ancient wisdoms from the West and the East have different focuses but share the idea of "beating swords into plowshares." However, humanity has gradually deviated from this concept in modern times. Global competition and confrontation have led countries to wield financial weapons against each other, forgetting that the original mission of finance is development. Imagine a historian in the distant future being asked to summarize the first half of the twenty-first century in three keywords. She might well say—it is a time of changes, a time of conflicts, and a time of challenges.

Changes. Recent decades have been marked by rapid and profound changes across various aspects of society, technology, and the environment. Advancements in technology, such as the rise of the internet, social media, artificial intelligence, and automation, have fundamentally transformed how people communicate, work, and live. Additionally, globalization has intensified, leading to increased interconnectedness among countries, cultures, and economies. Furthermore, climate change has become increasingly urgent, driving changes in energy policies, environmental regulations, and public awareness. Overall, these changes have been pervasive and have set the stage for further transformations in the years to come. Specifically, finance plays a crucial role in driving economic transformations and technological advancements. Investment in research and development, innovation, and infrastructure is often fueled by financial resources. Financial markets facilitate the allocation of capital to businesses and projects that drive growth and adaptation to changing market conditions. In this sense, finance can be a "plowshare."

Conflicts. Despite advancements in diplomacy and peacekeeping efforts, conflicts have remained prevalent today. Regional tensions, political unrest, and ideological divisions have culminated in numerous conflicts around the globe, including the Russia-Ukraine War, Palestine-Israel Conflict, and China-US Trade War. Issues such as terrorism, civil wars, and territorial disputes have caused humanitarian crises and significant loss of life. Moreover, economic disparities and competition for resources have exacerbated tensions between nations and within societies. These conflicts have posed significant challenges to international stability and security, highlighting the complexities of navigating geopolitical landscapes in the modern era. Economic sanctions and financial restrictions are often used as tools of coercion and diplomacy in geopolitical conflicts, imposing economic costs and exerting pressure on adversaries. Financial institutions may also become entangled in conflicts by operating in jurisdictions with weak regulatory oversight or facilitating illicit transactions, contributing to the perpetuation of conflicts and undermining efforts at peacebuilding and conflict resolution. As a result, finance can also be a "sword."

Challenges. Changes and conflicts have presented unprecedented challenges that span political, economic, social, and environmental realms. Technological advancements, while offering immense opportunities, have also raised concerns about privacy, cybersecurity, and job displacement. Healthcare systems have grappled with pandemics and the emergence of new infectious diseases, testing preparedness, and response capabilities. Additionally, environmental degradation, including climate change, pollution, and biodiversity loss, poses existential threats to the planet and future generations. Addressing these multifaceted challenges requires concerted efforts and innovative solutions from governments, businesses, and civil society to ensure a sustainable and equitable future. Finance is central to addressing many of the challenges facing societies in the twenty-first century, including economic inequality, climate change, and global health crises. Wealth disparities and financial exclusion can exacerbate social tensions and undermine social cohesion, posing challenges to inclusive economic growth and development. Sustainable finance initiatives, such as impact investing and green finance, aim to mobilize capital toward environmentally sustainable and socially responsible projects, addressing climate change and promoting sustainable development. Moreover, financial mechanisms such as insurance and disaster risk financing play a critical role in mitigating the impact of natural disasters and pandemics, enhancing resilience and preparedness in the face of unforeseen challenges. Seeing these positive possibilities, our ambition for this book is to explore various ways of "Beating Financial Swords into Developmental Plowshares."

In this book, we emphasize the critical role of finance in adapting to changes, exacerbating conflicts, and tackling challenges, as finance is a powerful tool that can be wielded for both good and evil purposes. The wisdom summarized in this book can be beneficial for policymakers, businesses, and civil society actors who are seeking to navigate complex global challenges and foster sustainable, inclusive development.

Beijing, China — Dong Guo
Cardiff, UK — Peng Zhou

Competing Interests The authors have no competing interests to declare that are relevant to the content of this manuscript.

Contents

Abbreviations

ABM	Agent-Based Model
ADF	Adjusted Dickey-Fuller
AIC	Akaike Information Criterion
ARCH	Autoregressive Conditional Heteroskedasticity
ARRC	Alternative Reference Rate Committee
BBA	British Bankers' Association
BTC	Bitcoin
CCC	Constant Conditional Correlation
CCP	Clearing Counterparties
CDF	Cumulative Distribution Function
CMU	Capital Markets Union
CNY or RMB	Chinese Yuan or Renminbi
CoVaR	Conditional VaR
CPSS	Committee on Payment and Settlement Systems
CSDR	Central Securities Depository Regulation
DBS	Debt-for-Blue Swap
DCC	Dynamic Conditional Correlation
DHS	Direct Holding System
DLT	Distributed Ledger Technology
DNCS	Debt-for-Nature and Climate Swaps
DSGE	Dynamic Stochastic General Equilibrium
ECB	European Central Bank
EGT	Evolutionary Game Theory
ESG	Environment, Social, Governance
ESS	Evolutionarily Stable Strategy
ETS	Emissions Trading System
EU	European Union
EUA	European Union Allowance
EUR	Euro
FFR	Federal Funds Rate
FMI	Financial-Market Infrastructure
Forex	Foreign Exchange
FRN	Floating Rate Note
FSOC	Financial Stability Oversight Council
GARCH	Generalized Autoregressive Conditional Heteroskedasticity
GB	Green Bond

GBP	Great Britain Pound
GVAR	Global VAR
HE	Hedging Effectiveness
HW	Hedging Weight
ICC	International Currency Circulation
IHS	Indirect Holding System
IMF	International Monetary Fund
IOSCO	International Organization of Securities Commissions
IRF	Impulse Response Function
JPY	Japanese Yen
LIBOR	London Interbank Offered Rate
LPR	Loan Prime Rate
MCMC	Markov Chain Monte Carlo
MGARCH	Multivariate ARCH
MLF	Medium-term Lending Facilities
OCA	Optimal Currency Area
OTC	Over The Counter
P2P	Peer-to-Peer
PBoC	People's Bank of China
QE	Quantity Ease
RCEP	Regional Comprehensive Economic Partnership
RRR	Reserve Requirement Ratio
SDG	Sustainable Development Goal
SEC	Securities and Exchange Commission
SEPA	Single European Payments Area
SOFR	Secured Overnight Financing Rate
TGARCH	Threshold GARCH
THS	Transparency Holding System
TVP-VAR	Time Varying Parameter VAR
UK	United Kingdom
US	United States
USD	US Dollar
VaR	Value at Risk
WTI	West Texas Intermediate Light Crude Oil
VAR	Vector Autoregression
WTO	World Trade Organization
YOY	Year-On-Year
ZLB	Zero Lower Bound

List of Figures

List of Tables

1 General Introduction

Finance is the backbone of modern economic systems. However, there has been a long history of debate over whether financial development contributes to economic growth (Keynes, 1930; Schumpeter, 1912). Many argue that finance can promote growth by facilitating transfer from traditional non-growth sectors to more productive sectors. This is termed as the **supply-leading** view (Zhang & Zhou, 2021). Nevertheless, not everyone shares the same opinion. Levine (2001) points out that the supply-leading view reverses the causality. It is economic growth that creates the demand for financial services—where enterprise leads, finance follows. In this **demand-following** view, financial development is not a cause, but a result, of economic growth. Therefore, excessive finance can even have a negative effect on growth as demonstrated by the inverse-U relationship in Fig. 1.1.

As the world becomes increasingly complex and interconnected, finance stretches far beyond traditional confines, influencing not only economic outcomes but also international relations and environmental strategies. So, the debate on the role of finance should go beyond the optimal quantity of financial activities and investigate the right direction of financial development—whether finance is used as a constructive tool or a destructive weapon. Inspired by Kranzberg's Law of Technology, we propose a similar Law of Finance: "*Finance is neither good nor bad; nor is it neutral.*" It is a *choice.*

Financial systems and instruments, such as credit markets, derivatives, and stock exchanges, are not inherently "good" or "bad." They can promote growth, innovation, and wealth creation by efficiently allocating resources and providing capital for businesses and individuals. However, the same financial tools, when misused or poorly regulated, can contribute to inequality, market bubbles, economic crises, and geopolitical conflicts. For example, during the COVID-19 pandemic, financial markets and central banks played a crucial role in stabilizing economies. Rapid responses by central banks, such as cutting interest rates, purchasing government securities, and providing liquidity, helped prevent a deeper financial collapse and provided critical relief to businesses and households. But these same financial mechanisms also brought risks. With low interest rates and expanded liquidity, speculative investments surged, leading to inflated asset prices and increased inequality. Mortgage-backed securities played a central role in the 2008 financial crisis when used irresponsibly. Thus, finance, as a tool, is only as constructive or destructive as its application.

Nevertheless, finance cannot be considered "neutral" either because its use always influences economic, environmental, and social structures, often with significant, lasting consequences. Financial systems are embedded within society, shaping issues like income distribution, environmental sustainability, and access to the international market. For instance, green finance

D. Guo and P. Zhou, *Beating Financial Swords into Developmental Plowshares*,
Sustainable Development Goals Series, https://doi.org/10.1007/978-981-95-5152-1_1

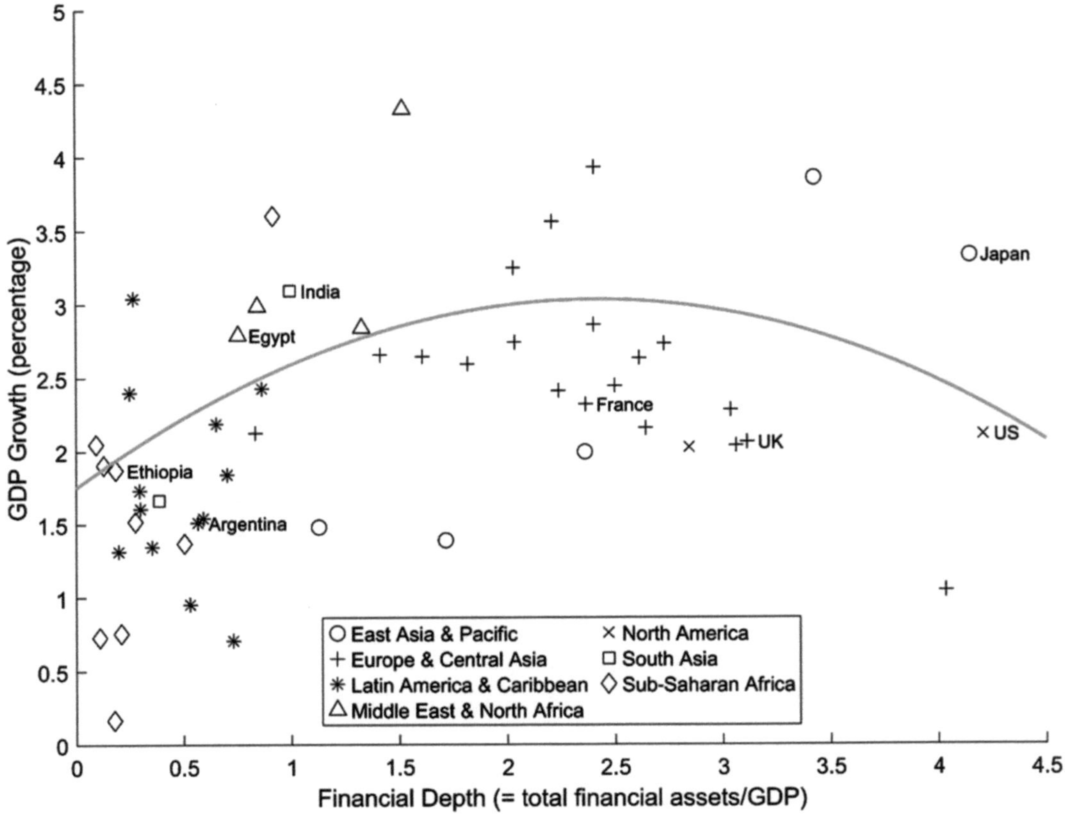

Fig. 1.1 The inverse-U relationship between financial development and economic growth. *Notes* Penn World Table 10. Data points are annual average growth rates and financial depth for 52 countries of 7 regions for 70 years (1950–2019). Financial depth is defined as the value of the total financial assets (including bank credit, private bond, public bond, stock market, and foreign debt) relative to GDP

has emerged as a positive force, providing essential funding for environmentally sustainable projects such as renewable energy and conservation efforts. By channeling capital into initiatives that align with climate goals, green finance supports progress on issues like emissions reduction and biodiversity protection. Nevertheless, if poorly regulated, green finance can also give rise to "greenwashing," where financial products are labeled as sustainable without genuine environmental impact, potentially undermining public trust and diverting resources from truly impactful projects. Similarly, financial sanctions demonstrate finance's profound influence on the international community. When targeted appropriately, sanctions can serve as a powerful tool to discourage aggressive actions, such as violations of international law, by limiting access to capital markets and trade. These sanctions can also have unintended consequences, such as harming ordinary citizens by reducing access to essential goods. This dual impact emphasizes that financial sanctions, while instrumental in diplomatic strategy, must be carefully managed to avoid collateral damage.

Therefore, the effects of finance depend critically on how and where it is used. In countries with robust regulatory frameworks, finance can stabilize economies and promote sustainable growth, acting as a constructive "wagon" or "plowshare." In contrast, in contexts where financial markets are subject to speculations or exploitations, finance can become a destructive “weapon” or “sword” contributing to economic inequality and geopolitical instability. Financial systems should be evaluated in specific socio-economic contexts, considering how they interact with existing economic structures and international dynamics. To achieve this aim, the book is structured into two parts and five themes, each dissecting crucial contexts of finance in the modern world.

Part I: Challenges

- Theme A: Systemic Changes and Monetary System. Celebrate finance’s pivotal role in mitigating rare disasters such as COVID-19 (Chap. 2), promoting regional trade (Chap. 3), and maintaining financial stability (Chap. 4).
- Theme B: Political Conflicts and Financial Sanctions. Treat finance as a destructive weapon that can exacerbate political tensions, examined through both bilateral (Chap. 5) and multilateral (Chap. 6) paradigms.
- Theme C: Environmental Challenges and Sustainable Finance. Unveil finance’s constructive potential in fostering sustainable practices through green bonds (Chap. 7), blue bonds (Chap. 8), and carbon trading (Chap. 9).

Part II: Policies

- Theme D: Monetary Policy. Introduce a new monetary policy tool—medium-term rate (Chap. 10), a new policy target—international currency circulation (Chap. 11), and a new policy mechanism—currency flowback (Chap. 12).
- Theme E: Financial Infrastructure. Highlight the strategic use of disruptive technologies—asset tokenization (Chap. 13) and reinforce the foundation of the modern financial system—treasury markets (Chap. 14).

The logical relationships between the two parts and the five themes are illustrated by the following conceptual framework in Fig. 1.2. PART I discusses *descriptive analysis* of challenges in the economy, society, and environment, while PART II focuses on *prescriptive analysis* of policies to address these challenges. There are multi-way causal relationships among these themes and parts.

In PART I, we start with the smallest circle (economy), where finance can serve as a useful tool. Then, we discuss the derived use of finance as a weapon in political conflicts within the extended circle (society). The largest circle (environment) provides natural resources for, and imposes limits

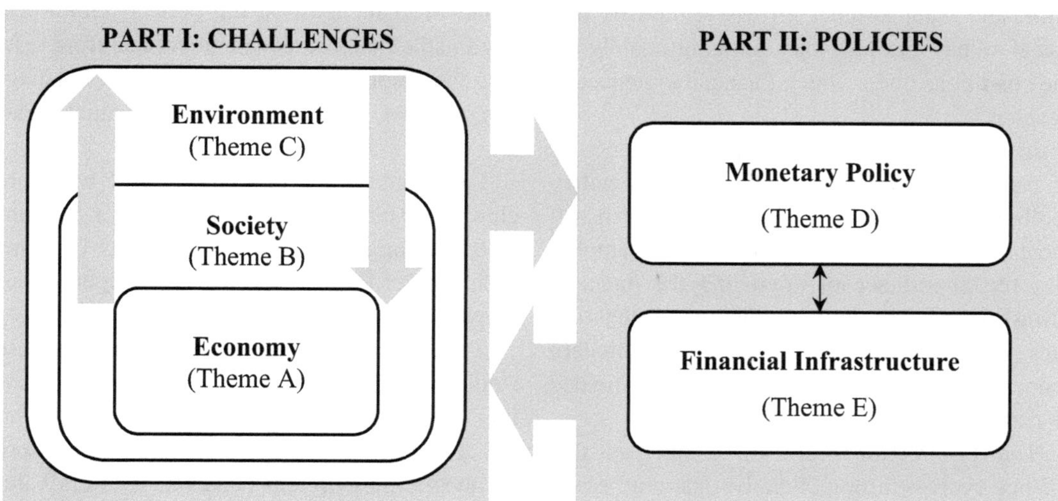

Fig. 1.2 The conceptual framework of the book

Table 1.1 Mapping the chapters with SDGs

Chapter	Focus	SDGs
Chapter 2	Resilience in monetary policy and response to rare disasters	SDG3: Good Health and Well-being SDG8: Decent Work and Economic Growth SDG10: Reduced Inequalities
Chapter 3	Enhancing trade stability through anchor currency selection	SDG17: Partnerships for the Goals
Chapter 4	Examining cryptocurrency regulation and stability	SDG9: Industry, Innovation, and Infrastructure
Chapter 5	Comparative analysis of economic sanctions' effectiveness	SDG16: Peace, Justice, and Strong Institutions SDG17: Partnerships for the Goals
Chapter 6	Strategic coordination and impact of multilateral sanctions	SDG16: Peace, Justice, and Strong Institutions SDG17: Partnerships for the Goals
Chapter 7	Green finance as a tool for stability and sustainability	SDG7: Affordable and Clean Energy SDG12: Responsible Consumption and Production SDG13: Climate Action
Chapter 8	Financing sustainable ocean use through blue bonds	SDG12: Responsible Consumption and Production SDG13: Climate Action SDG14: Life Below Water
Chapter 9	Carbon trading for emission reductions and climate goals	SDG7: Affordable and Clean Energy SDG12: Responsible Consumption and Production SDG13: Climate Action
Chapter 10	Developing stable benchmarks for economic resilience	SDG9: Industry, Innovation, and Infrastructure
Chapter 11	Currency circulation as a policy target for stability	SDG17: Partnerships for the Goals
Chapter 12	Repatriation of foreign-held currency assets for stability	SDG9: Industry, Innovation, and Infrastructure
Chapter 13	Blockchain applications in financial markets	SDG9: Industry, Innovation, and Infrastructure
Chapter 14	Comparing treasury market structures for stability	SDG9: Industry, Innovation, and Infrastructure SDG17: Partnerships for the Goals

on, economic and social activities. The inner-to-outer flow captures finance's widening influence, while the outer-to-inner arrows remind us that social values and planetary limits ultimately set the conditions under which financial systems can develop.

In PART II, we have two interdependent sets of policies. We first enrich the monetary policy toolbox by introducing non-conventional instruments, targets, and mechanisms. Then, we emphasize the importance of upgrading the financial infrastructure with the latest disruptive technologies. Moreover, as the foundation for modern monetary policy, treasury markets are also treated as part of the financial infrastructure.

The bi-directional arrows remind us that finance evolves through iterative learning: crises and social conflicts reveal design flaws; policy experimentation addresses them; and the success or failure of each experiment reshapes the next round of challenges. In the book's framework, sustainable financial development therefore rests on a continuous dialogue between empirical diagnosis (Part I) and institutional innovation (Part II).

Furthermore, the chapters of this book are closely linked with the United Nation's Sustainable Development Goals (SDGs). Table 1.1 maps each chapter to relevant SDGs, highlighting our emphasis on finance as a constructive force.

Through rigorous analysis and insightful case studies, this book not only navigates the complexities of finance but also illuminates its dual potential to act as both a force for good and a tool of division in different contexts. It offers valuable resources for policymakers, financial experts, and scholars, providing them with a deep understanding of how finance can address global challenges and foster sustainable, inclusive development.

References

Keynes, J. (1930). *The great slump of 1930*, The Nation & Athenæum.

Levine, R. (2001). International Financial Liberalization and Economic Growth. *Review of International Economics, 9*(4), 688–702.

Schumpeter, J. (1912). *Theorie der wirtschaftlichen entwicklung*. Dunker & Humblot.

Zhang, B., & Zhou, P. (2021). Financial development and economic growth in a microfounded small open economy model. *The North American Journal of Economics and Finance, 58*, Article 101544.

Part I
Challenges

This Part of this book investigates the role of finance in managing three interconnected global challenges: systemic shifts in monetary systems, political conflicts influenced by financial sanctions, and environmental sustainability through green finance. The chapters analyze how finance can either stabilize or destabilize economies in response to global crises, including rare disasters, geopolitical tensions, and climate change pressures.

The first theme, "Systemic Changes and Monetary System," covers how monetary systems respond to internal and external shocks. The global financial crisis and the COVID-19 pandemic revealed the limitations of conventional monetary policy, emphasizing the need for hybrid approaches that combine interest rate adjustments with unconventional tools. Chapter 2 explores these tools through the case of China, showing how targeted liquidity support stabilizes key sectors in crises. Chapter 3 evaluates anchor currencies within the Regional Comprehensive Economic Partnership (RCEP) area, assessing whether the US dollar, Chinese yuan, or Japanese yen is most suited for stability in regional trade. The analysis highlights the growing role of the yuan, which offers resilience in volatile trade conditions. Chapter 4 addresses the impact of cryptocurrencies on financial stability, noting their role as alternative assets during periods of monetary uncertainty.

The second theme, "Political Conflicts and Financial Sanctions," focuses on financial sanctions as a modern economic weapon. Chapter 5 contrasts trade and financial sanctions, demonstrating that financial sanctions are more precise yet potentially destabilizing, as illustrated in the case of Russia. Chapter 6 explores the dynamics of co-sanctions and counter-sanctions, where multilateral sanction regimes may weaken as geopolitical alliances shift, emphasizing the complexity of maintaining sanctions over time.

The third theme, "Environmental Challenges and Sustainable Finance," presents green finance as a constructive force for addressing environmental issues. Chapter 7 discusses green bonds as hedges against market volatility, showing that they offer relative price stability and are effective in risk management. Chapter 8 introduces blue bonds, focusing on marine conservation financing and sustainable ocean use, while Chapter 9 evaluates carbon trading's effectiveness in incentivizing emission reductions. These chapters underscore finance's constructive potential in fostering resilience to environmental threats through sustainable instruments.

Together, these themes illustrate how finance, through deliberate and targeted approaches, can either mitigate or magnify the impact of modern global challenges. Each chapter provides actionable insights for policymakers, emphasizing that finance, while often a source of division, holds powerful potential for constructive development.

Systemic Changes and Monetary System

Modern financial activities are conducted within national, regional, and global monetary systems. The robustness of these monetary systems is critical to financial stability and economic stability, safeguarding against various systemic changes due to external or internal shocks. This theme is divided into three chapters, each discussing a different aspect of currency use: the role of fiat currencies in tackling rare disasters, the role of anchor currencies in enhancing regional trade, and the role of cryptocurrencies in ensuring financial stability.

Chapter 2 explores responses to rare economic shocks, using COVID-19 as a case study. It highlights China's hybrid monetary approach, combining targeted liquidity with moderate interest policies, which balanced economic support and inflation control. The chapter suggests central banks consider adaptable tools to address extreme events effectively.

Chapter 3 assesses anchor currencies within the RCEP, finding the Chinese yuan increasingly suitable due to China's growing economic influence. Adopting the yuan as a regional anchor could enhance stability in Asia, offering a buffer against external shocks linked to the dollar.

Chapter 4 investigates Bitcoin's role as an alternative asset amid uncertain monetary conditions, noting its appeal for diversification but also its volatility. The chapter calls for balanced regulatory frameworks to manage cryptocurrencies' risks while enabling innovation.

Overall, Theme A highlights finance's constructive potential in building resilience through robust, adaptable currency policies, aligning with the book's focus on finance as a tool for economic stability and sustainable development.

Political Conflicts and Financial Sanctions

This theme examines the role of finance as a strategic tool wielded by global powers in geopolitical conflicts and the maintenance of hegemony. As global powers confront complex political challenges, financial sanctions have become a preferred mechanism over traditional trade sanctions due to their targeted impact on monetary systems and financial infrastructure. This theme's two chapters examine financial sanctions in both bilateral and multilateral contexts, highlighting the dynamics of interdependence and the strategic interplay of sanctions, co-sanctions, and counter-sanctions. It is argued that the sophisticated strategic interdependence inherent in the sanctions game leads to significant resource waste, resources that could otherwise be invested in development and welfare.

Chapter 5 provides an overview of financial sanctions' effectiveness compared to trade sanctions, using the US-Russia conflict as a case study. It examines how financial sanctions influence economic stability by disrupting currency value and market expectations, often triggering capital flight and economic contraction. Despite countermeasures such as currency localization and developing domestic financial infrastructure, target economies still experience significant challenges. This chapter argues that financial sanctions, while impactful, can destabilize global financial systems and exacerbate political tensions.

Chapter 6 expands the discussion to multilateral sanctions involving the US, the EU, and Russia, illustrating the complex interdependence in co-sanctioning arrangements. Using an evolutionary game-theory model, the chapter highlights how coordination challenges and divergent interests, especially within the EU, weaken sanctions' efficacy. The findings suggest that co-sanctioning strategies are most effective when aligned with each participant's economic and political constraints, yet such arrangements often create long-term instability and resource inefficiencies.

Overall, Theme B emphasizes the dual role of finance in supporting political agendas while also threatening global stability. These insights reinforce the book's theme by illustrating how finance, through careful coordination and strategic alignment, can serve as a constructive tool for managing international conflicts more effectively.

Environmental Challenges and Sustainable Finance

This theme addresses finance's role in tackling environmental challenges by focusing on sustainable instruments like green bonds, blue bonds, and carbon trading. As climate change and environmental degradation become more urgent, sustainable finance emerges as a critical tool for supporting eco-friendly initiatives while promoting financial stability.

Chapter 7 explores green bonds, which fund environmentally beneficial projects such as renewable energy and sustainable land use. These bonds show promise not only as sustainable investments but also as safe-haven assets during financial crises. The chapter's findings suggest that green bonds effectively hedge against market risks, especially in times of economic instability, highlighting their dual value for investors and policymakers seeking both stability and environmental progress.

Chapter 8 introduces blue bonds, which support marine-focused sustainability efforts, including biodiversity conservation and pollution control. By examining the development of blue finance, particularly debt-for-blue swaps, this chapter shows how these bonds help indebted nations invest in ocean conservation while addressing fiscal challenges. It underscores the potential for blue bonds to drive economic growth and sustainability in maritime-dependent economies.

Chapter 9 examines carbon trading, focusing on the relationship between carbon prices and commodities like oil and gold. It finds that carbon trading can contribute to emission reductions, effectively turning environmental impact into a financial asset. Policy insights include the need for integrated carbon market frameworks to enhance stability and support a low-carbon economy.

Together, these chapters illustrate how finance, through green finance and carbon trading, can constructively address environmental challenges, aligning with the book's theme of finance as a positive force for sustainable development.

2 Rare Disasters and Fiat Currency

Abstract

COVID-19 exposed the limits of conventional monetary policy and forced central banks to improvise. This chapter gauges the relative effectiveness of three policy archetypes—price-based interest rate cuts, quantity-based liquidity injections, and China's hybrid "structural" mix—through a Dynamic Stochastic General Equilibrium (DSGE) model calibrated to the Chinese economy. Simulations show that when shocks drive policy rates toward the zero lower bound, pure interest rate measures provide little support. Unconventional liquidity facilities, widely employed in the US and Europe, better stabilize output but raise longer-term inflation risk. China's structural approach—combining targeted credit lines, reserve-requirement adjustments, and modest rate moves—delivers the most balanced outcome, cushioning activity without igniting excessive price pressures. Policy lessons are threefold. First, rare disasters call for adaptable hybrid instruments that can channel funds to stressed sectors while preserving overall financial discipline. Second, credibility matters: governments must shore up confidence yet avoid crowding-out market signals. Finally, because extreme shocks propagate quickly across borders, coordinated frameworks among major central banks are essential for containing spillovers and safeguarding sustainable recovery.

Keywords

Monetary policy · Rare disaster · Pandemic

Classification:

SDG3 · SDG8 · SDG10

2.1 Introduction

The COVID-19 pandemic presents an unprecedented challenge to the balance between public health and economic growth. Since the outbreak in 2019Q4, strict containment measures were implemented by the Chinese government including lockdown, large-scale mobility restrictions, social distancing, and a fortnight quarantine for international travelers (IMF, 2021). Following these administrative reactions, the Chinese economy contracted by 6.8 percent in 2020Q1 year-on-year (National Bureau of Statistics of China, 2021). These extreme and decisive measures worked well for the pandemic in 2020Q1, so the government has gradually removed mobility and activity restrictions within the country from mid-February 2020. Despite some new hotspots after June 2020, the economy has returned to normal and the real GDP growth bounced back to 3.2 percent in 2020Q2 year-on-year and continued to recover by 4.9 and 6.5 percent in Q3 and Q4, resulting in a 2.3 percent annual growth in 2020 (National Bureau of Statistics of China, 2021). China is one

D. Guo and P. Zhou, *Beating Financial Swords into Developmental Plowshares*, Sustainable Development Goals Series, https://doi.org/10.1007/978-981-95-5152-1_2

of a few countries with a quick recovery from the pandemic. In contrast, the US and most European countries underwent much higher infection rates and worse economic interruptions (Goodell & Huynh, 2020). Take the US as an example, the real GDP shrank by 3.5 percent in 2020 (Bureau of Economic Analysis, 2021). What caused the differences? What is the role of monetary policy? Can the central bank do better to mitigate a rare disaster like the pandemic? As the vaccine rolling out from 2021, the world is expected to return to normal, marking the end of the first half of the battle against the pandemic. The second half of the battle has a different theme, i.e., quick recovery rather than shock buffering. Based on the data up to 2020Q4, this chapter attempts to analyze the contribution of unconventional monetary policy in China at the early stage of the pandemic. This experience provides a valuable lesson for policymakers in the future.

As early as January 2020, a sophisticated mix of monetary policy instruments were implemented to buffer the negative shock to the economy and to safeguard the financial market stability in China. Unlike the Fed which reduced the Federal Funds Rate (FFR) to an extreme level of 0–0.25%, the People's Bank of China (PBoC) still stuck to a macroprudential principle to maintain the effectiveness of Loan Prime Rate (LPR) and Reserve Requirement Ratio (RRR). Apart from these two conventional price-mechanism instruments, PBoC also developed unconventional quantity-mechanism instruments like Medium-term Lending Facilities (MLF). Throughout 2020, key measures taken by PBoC include:

a. Open market operations such as reverse repos and MLF were used to inject liquidity to the money market.
b. An earmarked package of RMB 1.8 trillion was released to support manufacturers of medical supplies and daily necessities, micro-, small- and medium-sized firms, and the agricultural sector.
c. The 7-day and 14-day reverse repo rates were reduced by 30 bps, while the 1-year MLF rate and targeted MLF rate were respectively cut by 30 and 20 bps.
d. Targeted RRR was decreased by 50–200 pbs for large- and medium-sized banks meeting the inclusive financing criteria to support micro-, small-, and medium-sized enterprises.
e. The interest rate on excess reserves was reduced from 72 to 35 bps.
f. A policy banks' credit of RMB 350 billion was provided to micro- and small-sized enterprises.
g. New instruments were introduced (RMB 400 billion) to support lending to micro- and small-sized enterprises, including a zero-interest "funding-for-lending" scheme.
h. Deadlines of loan payments are extended, and restrictions for online loans were eased for small businesses and households.

These measures, both conventional and unconventional, can be categorized into the following matrix. Different from the 2008 global financial crisis when the policy mix of PBoC focused on reducing the LPR and the RRR, liquidity injections and earmarked policy measures play a major role in mitigating the COVID-19 pandemic (Funke & Tsang, 2020).

	Non-earmarked Tools	Earmarked Tools
Quantity Mechanisms	a	b, f, g, h
Price Mechanisms	c, e	d

Similarly, monetary policies in developed economies also responded in a radical fashion. However, a specific challenge to central banks is the Zero Lower Bound (ZLB) of short-term interest rate, given that the Taylor rule is the mainstream choice in normal times. Unconventional monetary policy instruments are then developed during the COVID-19 pandemic. For example, additional liquidity was injected by the Federal Reserve in the US using diverse facilities including Commercial Paper Funding Facility, Money Market Mutual Fund Liquidity Facility, Paycheck Protection Program Liquidity Facility, etc. In the EU, a new liquidity facility PELTRO was introduced in 2020M5 to respond to the extra liquidity demand in the market. Bank of England in the UK launched COVID Corporate Financing Facility, which, together with the Coronavirus Business Interruption Schemes, provided £330 billion of loans to buffer the pandemic shock.

COVID-19 is a "once-in-a-century pandemic" (Gates, 2020), so it can be regarded as a rare disaster. Like the global financial crisis, world wars, natural disasters, a rare disaster is featured by its small probability but huge damage to the real economy (Barro, 2006). Early studies on rare disaster concentrate on financial markets, where asset prices are explained by introducing disaster risks and Markov processes (Mehra & Prescott, 1988). Most recent literature explores the measure of disaster risk (Manela & Moreira, 2017) and monetary policy responses to mitigate disaster risks (Cortes et al., 2022). There are some preliminary studies on the relationship between monetary policy responses to the pandemic, but most are econometric models without a solid microfoundation (Zhou et al., 2021a, 2021b; Fernandez-Gallardo, 2023). This chapter attempts to combine literature on rare disasters with monetary policy in the context of COVID-19.

In rare disasters like the pandemic, governments face different sets of instruments and ways of implementation, so separate research is needed for abnormal times. Specifically, studies on alternative monetary policy such as quantity rule and structural rule are scanty in mainstream literature. As the first country fighting against the coronavirus, Chinese monetary policy seems to have done a fairly good job with the help of a diverse set of policy mix. As a policy experiment, the experience of China is worth investigating.

Therefore, this chapter has two contributions, one theoretical and one practical. First, unconventional monetary policy rules (such as the quantity rule and the structural rule) are introduced into a dynamic stochastic general equilibrium (DSGE) model to compare with the conventional interest rate rule. This is to see how alternative monetary policy mix can be more effective in a critical time like COVID-19. The estimated model following a Bayesian procedure is then simulated to offer a numerical evaluation of different monetary policy choices. Second, this chapter provides a pragmatic guide for unconventional monetary policy instruments in practice. Academic literature tends to over-simplify the jobs of central banks, usually condensed into one equation such as Taylor rule. However, the complicated environments surrounding monetary policymakers require a comprehensive toolbox of instruments in practice. It is a much more challenging decision than simply setting a policy rate—real-life central bankers must also worry about which rate to set, when to set it, what policy mix should be used, and so on. A practical discussion on the issues is offered to inform these "know-how" questions.

2.2 Literature

Early research on rare disasters mainly focuses on risk premia of financial assets. The introduction of rare disasters in the traditional economic theory has successfully explained many asset pricing and macroeconomic financial puzzles. Barro (2006) calibrates the probability of global disaster events since the twentieth century and points out that the existing of rare disasters can explain many asset pricing puzzles such as high equity premiums, low risk-free interest rates, fluctuations in stock returns, and so on.

After the global financial crisis in 2008, studies of disaster risk have extended to many aspects of the real economy. This chapter mainly focuses on the literature about business cycles and monetary policy regulations. For the literature on business cycles, Gourio (2012) studies disaster risks and real business cycle models and finds that disaster shocks can lead to unemployment, investment reduction, and decline in output and financial asset price. This research proves that disaster shock is an important factor of economic fluctuations. Isore & Szczerbowicz (2017) integrate a time-varying disaster shock in the new Keynesian model. Based on the expected impacts on the real economy, they propose that an increased probability of disasters can affect macroeconomic aggregates and asset prices.

As for the literature on monetary policy, Keen and Pakko (2011) find that the fluctuations of financial market prices caused by hurricanes and other disasters would lead to an increase in speculative short-selling, which can then trigger the Federal Reserve to adopt expansionary monetary policies. The modeling results suggest that under a price-based monetary policy (i.e., Taylor rule), the optimal monetary policy is independent of nominal rigidities. Mechler et al. (2016) point out that the costs caused by sudden disasters are not fully included in the government's rescue budget and lack of price signals. Fiscal policy and monetary policy should be considered together to build an alliance of common interests to pursue synergies, to manage rare disasters, and to speed up recovery. By constructing a new Keynesian DSGE model with disaster factors, Zhou et al., (2021a, 2021b) analyze the dynamic impacts of rare disaster events on China's economy. They find that monetary policy is more effective than fiscal policy.

Our model integrates the two fields of literature (rare disasters and monetary policy) and enriches monetary policy with conventional, unconventional, and China's special measures. The experiment and experience can shed light on future policymaking to counter disasters.

2.3 Model

We adopt a typical DSGE model of China based on Dai et al. (2015). Like any canonical New Keynesian DSGE models, it has consumers, final goods producers, intermediate goods producers, and a central bank (Smets & Wouters, 2007). To incorporate money into the model, we assume a money-in-the-utility function for the household. Nominal frictions are modelled by the Calvo price setting (Calvo, 1983). A distinctive feature of our model is to include a rare disaster shock (e.g., global financial crisis, COVID-19), along with other familiar structural shocks in DSGE literature (e.g., productivity shock, monetary policy shock). The focus of this chapter is monetary policy, so the behavioral assumption of central banks is elaborated to describe different rules. We will begin with the two vital components before describing the standard New Keynesian setup.

2.3.1 Monetary Policy Rules

The most popular one is the interest rate (price) rule, followed by most developed economies like the US and EU. A policy rate (i_t), usually short-term interest rates, is chosen as the instrument to balance between inflation gap ($\pi_t - \pi^*$) and output gap ($\ln y_t - \ln y^*$) around the long-term rate (i^*) with a consideration of interest rate smoothing mechanism. It has been the conventional monetary policy rule of central banks in developed economies since 1980s (Taylor, 1993), which can be written in the following form:

$$1 + i_t = (1 + i_{(t-1)})^{\rho_i^I} (1 + i*)^{1-\rho_i^I} \left(\frac{1+\pi_t}{1+\pi*}\right)^{\rho_\pi^i} \left(\frac{y_t}{y*}\right)^{\rho_\pi^i} exp(\varepsilon_t^I) \quad (2.1)$$

The quantity rule is much older, dating back to the quantity theory of Fisher and Monetarists. Money supply growth (g_t) is treated as the instrument to hit the target inflation (McCallum, 1988) around a long-term money growth rate (g^*). However, Zhang (2009) finds that the McCallum rule cannot capture China's monetary policy well. The PBoC in China also considered output gap when setting the quantity of money supply before 2010s. A typical quantity rule in the literature can be written in the following form:

$$\frac{M_t}{M_{t-1}} = 1 + g_t = (1 + g_{(t-1)})^{\rho_m^M} (1 + g^*)^{1-\rho_m^M} \left(\frac{1+\pi_t}{1+\pi*}\right)^{\rho_\pi^M} \left(\frac{y_t}{y*}\right)^{\rho_y^M} \exp(\varepsilon_t^M) \quad (2.1')$$

The so-called structural rule or hybrid rule is a unique feature of the current Chinese monetary policy (Liu & Zhang, 2010). China has been undergoing a transitional reform from a command system where interest rates are set by the regulators to a market system where interest rates are set by the market. Apart from inflation gap and output gap, the structural rule also reacts to the liquidity gap in money supply growth ($g_t - g^*$). Therefore, the structural rule is basically an augmented Taylor rule because it uses interest rate as the instrument, but the liquidity gap can be filled with the help of other unconventional facilities such as MLF and earmarked loans. The structural rule is:

$$
\begin{aligned}
1+i_t =&(1+i_{(t-1)})^{\rho_i^S}(1+i^*)^{1-\rho_i^S}\\
&\left(\frac{1+\pi_t}{1+\pi*}\right)^{\rho_\pi^S}\left(\frac{y_t}{y*}\right)^{\rho_y^S}\\
&\left(\frac{1+g_t}{1+g*}\right)^{\rho_M^S}\exp(\varepsilon_t^S) \qquad (2.1")
\end{aligned}
$$

All monetary shocks (ϵ_t^I, ϵ_t^M, ϵ_t^S) are assumed to be $i.i.d.N(0, \sigma_{\blacksquare}^2)$, where $\blacksquare = I, M, S$. The three rules are estimated with the rest of the model separately to evaluate which rule can better fit the monetary policy in China. Also note that the potential output y^* is defined as the output level when there are no nominal frictions as in Smets and Wouters (2007).

2.3.2 Rare Disaster Shocks

The probability of falling into the disaster state (Δ_t) is assumed to be time varying rather than constant as in Nakamura et al. (2013). It follows a Markov chain that approximates the following mean-reverting autoregressive process disturbed by a disaster probability shock ϵ_t^Δ.

$$
\begin{aligned}
\ln \Delta_t =&\varphi^\Delta \ln \Delta_{t-1} + (1-\varphi^\Delta)\ln \bar{\Delta} + \varepsilon_t^\Delta,\\
&\text{where } \varepsilon_t^\Delta \sim i.i.d.N(0, \sigma_\Delta^2) \qquad (2.2)
\end{aligned}
$$

Rare disasters can affect the real economy via total factor productivity (TFP), labor supply, and capital accumulation (Gourio, 2012). The TFP is a probability-weighted average between the normal state and the disaster state. In the normal state, productivity (A_t^*) is assumed to be disturbed by a productivity shock ϵ_t^A. In the disaster state, productivity is negatively affected by a damage factor ($0 < d < 1$).

$$
\begin{aligned}
A_t &= (1-\Delta_t)A_t^* + \Delta_t(1-d)A_t^*\\
&= (1-\Delta_t d)A_t^* \qquad (2.3)
\end{aligned}
$$

$$
\begin{aligned}
\ln A_t^* =& \phi^A \ln A_{t-1}^* + \varepsilon_t^A,\\
&\text{where } \varepsilon_t^A \sim i.i.d.N(0, \sigma_A^2) \qquad (2.4)
\end{aligned}
$$

The existence of the two possible states of TFP influences the technological constraint of firms, so the marginal cost function and aggregate output are subject to this uncertainty.

2.3.3 The Rest of the Model

To facilitate communication, we set some notational conventions before rolling out the structural component of the model. The *price* variables are in real terms if lowercases are used and nominal if uppercases are used. The *quantity* variables are defined at the individual or per capita level if lowercase is used and at the aggregate level if uppercase is used. Nevertheless, the population is standardized to 1, so the aggregate quantities are effectively the per capita quantities. The time scripts are defined by when the variable is determined rather than when it takes effect. The optimality conditions and equilibrium conditions of the representative consumer, final goods firm, and intermediate goods firm are derived below.

Consumer. We adopt the assumption of money-in-the-utility (Poilly, 2010) to introduce money into the system. The three utility inputs (consumption c_t, labor n_t, and real money balance $m_t \equiv \frac{M_t}{P_t}$) are separable and featured with relative risk aversion. The representative consumer maximizes the expected sum of discounted future utilities:

$$
\begin{aligned}
&\max_{c_t, n_t, B_t, M_t}, E_0 \Sigma_{t=0}^{\infty}\beta^t\\
&[\frac{c_t^{1-\sigma}}{1-\sigma} - \gamma_n \frac{n_t^{1+\eta}}{1-\eta} + \gamma_m \ln \frac{M_t}{P_t}],\\
&\text{subject to } P_t c_t + [B_t - (1+i_{t-1})B_{t-1}]\\
&\quad + [M_t - M_{t-1}] = W_t n_t + \Pi_t \qquad (2.5)
\end{aligned}
$$

The left-hand side of the budget constraint (2.5) states the outflows. Consumption (c_t) is purchased at the current price of P_t. In addition, the consumer holds her wealth in two ways: B_{t-1}

is the (nominal) bond balance determined in period $t-1$ but held during period t with a predetermined nominal interest rate i_{t-1}; M_{t-1} is the money balance determined in period t but held during period t with no interest but essential for transactions. Changes of the two stocks are sources of outflows. The right-hand side states the inflows, including (nominal) labor income ($W_t n_t$) and dividend income (Π_t). The optimality conditions consist of two intratemporal conditions and an intertemporal condition.

$$MRS_{l,c} \equiv \frac{\psi_n n_t^{\eta}}{c_t^{-\sigma}} = W_t, \quad \text{where } W_t \equiv \frac{W_t}{P_t} \tag{2.6}$$

$$MRS_{m,c} \equiv \frac{\psi_n m_t^{-1}}{c_t^{-\sigma}} = \frac{i_t}{1+i_t}, \quad \text{where } m_t \equiv \frac{M_t}{P_t} \tag{2.7}$$

$$MRS_{c,c'} \equiv \frac{c_t^{-\sigma}}{\beta \mathrm{E}_t[c_{t+1}^{-\sigma}]} = \frac{1+i_t}{1+\mathrm{E}_t[\pi_{t+1}]}, \quad \text{where } \pi_t \equiv \frac{P_{t+1}-P_t}{P_t} \tag{2.8}$$

Note that in the last condition, we can define the (gross) real interest rate as $1+r_{t+1} \equiv \frac{1+i_t}{1+\pi_{t+1}}$. The reciprocal is therefore the one-period ahead Stochastic Discount Factor (SDF), which will be used in the intermediate goods producer's problem later. In general, the SDF can be defined for any τ periods ahead:

$$\Lambda_{t,\tau} \equiv \frac{\beta \mathrm{E}_t[c_{t+1}^{-\sigma}]}{c_t^{-\sigma}} \tag{2.9}$$

Final Goods Firm. Assuming perfect competition, the final goods firm maximizes its profit:

$$\max_{y_t \cdot y_\tau(j)} P_t y_t - \int_0^1 Q_t(j) x_t(j) dj,$$

$$\text{subject to } \left(\int_0^1 \mathrm{x_t(j)}^{\frac{s-1}{s}} \mathrm{dj}\right)^{\frac{s}{s-1}}$$

The production function employs a continuum of intermediate goods $x_t(j)$ to produce the final goods y_t with a constant elasticity of substitution ($s \geq 1$). The optimality condition is the demand function for intermediate goods:

$$x_t(j) = \left(\frac{Q_t(j)}{P_t}\right)^{-s} y_t \tag{2.10}$$

Intermediate Goods Firm. An intermediate goods firm j in monopolistic competition faces a Calvo-type nominal rigidity (degree of stickiness is ϕ) while maximizing its sum of discounted future profits. Following the tradition in the New Keynesian models, we split this optimization problem into two steps to facilitate the illustration. The first stage achieves **technical efficiency** by minimizing the total costs for given output (assuming a normal state):

$$\min_{n_t(j), k_{t(j)}} TC_t \equiv P_t(w_t n_t(j) + r_t k_t(j)),$$
$$\text{subject to: } x_t(j) = A_t k_t(j)^a n_t(j)^{1-a} \tag{2.11}$$

The optimality conditions can be combined to obtain the optimal input ratio $\frac{k_t(j)}{n_t(j)} = \frac{\alpha}{1-\alpha}\frac{w_t}{r_t}$. Make use of this resulting condition and the production function to substitute out the two inputs in the objective function (TC), resulting in the minimized cost function:

$$TC_t^* = \frac{P_t}{A_t}\left(\frac{w_t}{1-\alpha}\right)^{(1-\alpha)}\left(\frac{r_t}{\alpha}\right)^{\alpha} x_t(j)$$

Therefore, the minimized marginal cost function is:

$$MC_t^* = \frac{P_t}{A_t}\left(\frac{w_t}{1-\alpha}\right)^{(1-\alpha)}\left(\frac{r_t}{\alpha}\right)^{\alpha} \tag{2.12}$$

In the case of $\alpha = 0$ (which will be assumed later), the minimized (nominal) marginal cost function becomes linear in wage: $MC_t^* = \frac{P_t}{A_t} w_t$.

The second stage is to choose the optimal output level $x_t(j)$ and the optimal resetting price

$Q_t(j)$ to achieve **economic efficiency** by maximizing the sum of discounted, expected (real) profits in the contingency that $Q_t(j)$ is fixed:

$$\max_{x_t(j), Q_t(j)} \quad E_t \Sigma_{\tau=0}^{\infty} \phi^{\tau} \Lambda_{t,\tau} \frac{\Pi_{t+\tau}(j)}{P_{t+\tau}}$$

subject to the market demand function [10].

The discount factor is defined by (2.9) and the probability of fixing the price up to period τ ahead is ϕ^{τ}. The profit is defined using the minimized marginal cost function (2.12):

$$\Pi_t(j) \equiv Q_t(j) x_t(j) - MC_t^* x_t(j) \qquad (2.13)$$

The optimal reset price $Q_t(j)$ determined at period t but may be fixed for many periods ahead can be solved:

$$Q_t(j) = \frac{s}{s-1} \left(\frac{E_t[\Sigma_{\tau=0}^{\infty} \phi^{\tau} \beta^{\tau} c_{t+\tau}^{-\sigma} P_{t+\tau}^{s-1} y_{t+\tau} MC_{t+\tau}^*]}{E_t[\Sigma_{\tau=0}^{\infty} \phi^{\tau} \beta^{\tau} c_{t+\tau}^{-\sigma} P_{t+\tau}^{s-1} y_{t+\tau}]} \right)$$

If $\phi = 0$, we go back to the flexible price case (Dixit & Stiglitz, 1977) where the optimal reset price is equal to the mark-up $\frac{s}{s-1}$ multiplied by MC_t^*. Further operations can make (2.14) usable for programming. First, use the symmetry of monopolistic competition to drop the subscript j. Second, the equation can be rewritten in the recursive form:

$$Q_t = \frac{s}{s-1} \frac{Z1_t}{Z2_t} \qquad (2.14)$$

$$Z1_t = c_t^{-\sigma} P_t^{s-1} y_t MC_t^* + \phi \beta E_t[Z1_{(t+1)}] \qquad (2.15)$$

$$Z2_t = c_t^{-\sigma} P_t^{s-1} y_t + \phi \beta E_t[Z2_{(t+1)}] \qquad (2.16)$$

There are three types of equilibrium conditions. First, the market clearing condition, i.e., supply is equal to demand. Second, the no-arbitrage condition, i.e., the returns to alternative uses of the same resources must be equal. Third, the competition condition, i.e., there are no new entry or exit of firms due to zero profit or barriers. Essentially, these three types of conditions are about the same thing—there are no changes in quantity, on price, or on agents in equilibrium.

In the final goods market, competition drives the profit of final goods firms to zero, resulting in the equilibrium price of final goods (output):

$$P_t^{1-s} = \int_0^1 Q_t(j)^{1-s} dj$$

Based on the solution (2.14) to the key variable (Q_t), we can then rewrite the equilibrium aggregate price (2.17) in a recursive form. To do this, note that the aggregate price at a particular point in time t is a weighted average of past price level (P_{t-1}) and current reset price (Q_t). Since the proportion of reset prices is $1-\phi$, we can separate this proportion from the integral of (2.17).

$$P_t^{1-s} = (1-\phi) Q_t^{1-s} + \phi P_{t-1}^{1-s} \qquad (2.17)$$

The market clearing condition of the final goods requires that:

$$y_t - c_t \qquad (2.18)$$

In the intermediate goods market, for simplicity, the capital is assumed away (or fixed) in our analysis so $\alpha = 0$, the production function (2.11) becomes $x_t(j) = A_t n_t(j)$, and the minimized marginal cost function (2.12) becomes $MC_t^* = \frac{P_t w_t}{A_t}$. This does not affect the generality because intertemporal transfer of economic resources can be done via the financial market (B_t). According to the no-arbitrage condition, physical investment and financial investment should achieve the same return and effect. One of them is redundant if there is no friction.

In addition, the market clearing condition equates with the supply (2.11) and demand (2.10) of particular goods. Integrate over j to derive the equilibrium condition at the aggregate level.

$$y_t = \frac{A_t n_t}{v_t}, \quad \text{where} \quad v_t \equiv \int_0^1 \left(\frac{Q_t(j)}{P_t} \right)^{-s} dj \qquad (2.19)$$

If $s > 1$, then $v_t > 1$ which describes the price dispersion due to monopolistic power (Carvalho & Schwartzman, 2015). It can also be rewritten in recursive form to facilitate coding. Use P_{t-1} as the deflator, we have:

$$v_t = (1-\phi)q_t^{-s} + \phi(1+\pi_t)^s v_{(t-1)}, \quad \text{where } q_t \equiv \frac{Q_t}{P_t} \tag{2.20}$$

To summarize, the model can be described by 14 Eqs. (2.1), (2.2), (2.3), (2.6), (2.7), (2.8), (2.12), (2.14), (2.15), (2.16), (2.17), (2.18), (2.19), (2.20) for 14 endogenous variables: i_t (or $r_t \equiv \frac{1+i_t}{1+\pi_t} - 1$), Δ_t, A_t, n_t, M_t (or $m_t \equiv \frac{M_t}{P_t}$), c_t, MC_t (or $mc_t \equiv \frac{MC_t}{P_t}$), Q_t (or $q_t \equiv \frac{Q_t}{P_t}$), $Z1_t$ (or $z1_t \equiv \frac{Z1_t}{P_t^s}$), $Z2_t$ (or $z2_t \equiv \frac{Z2_t}{P_t^{s-1}}$),$P_t$ (or $\pi_t \equiv \frac{P_t}{P_{t-1}} - 1$), W_t (or $w_t \equiv \frac{W_t}{P_t}$), y_t, v_t. There are four structural shocks (productivity shock ϵ_t^A, disaster probability shock ϵ_t^Δ, disaster damage shock ϵ_t^D, and monetary shock $\epsilon_t^\blacksquare$ where $\blacksquare = I, M, S$).

To solve the stochastic, dynamic system of equations, it is necessary to transform all the equations so that only stationary variables are included. There are three possible reasons for non-stationarity, technology (due to the trend in A_t), population (due to the trend in n_t), and nominal price (due to the trend in P_t). Given that our model is a short-run business cycle model, we can simply treat A_t and n_t as stationary (the cyclical component). The conclusions are the same if a deterministic trend is assumed. Nominal variables can be deflated by P_t or a function of P_t. Note that P_t per se is replaced by inflation (π_t).

2.4 Calibration

Most structural parameters are well documented in empirical literature. The prior means in Table 2.2 are based on studies in existing literature (Angeloni et al., 2015). The disaster-related parameters in China are based on a recent paper in Zhou et al., (2021a, 2021b). According to Gourio (2012) and Nakamura et al. (2013), the average probability of entering disaster state is 0.72% per quarter, φ^Δ is 0.9, σ_Δ is 2.8, and the damage d is equal to 20%.

To closely link our model with the Chinese economy during the pandemic, we estimate the key parameters using a standard Bayesian procedure (the Metropolis–Hastings algorithm). Macroeconomic data on HP-filtered real GDP per capita, inflation rate, nominal interest rate, and M2 growth (1980Q1–2020Q4) are used as observables. There are four structural shocks in the model to ensure the identification condition. The impulse response functions in the analysis are simulated based on the estimated/calibrated parameters in Table 2.2. Other simulation results such as variance decomposition and historical forecast errors are omitted from the analysis.

2.5 Analysis

We first discuss the dynamic effects of the COVID-19 disaster shock and policy responses of the three monetary policy rules. We focus on the simulated impulse response functions of the key macroeconomic variables following a typical disaster shock (one standard deviation of the shock) are shown in Fig. 2.1.

A typical disaster shock can produce significant negative effects on output as shown in the upper-left panel. Like most DSGE models, the response has a hump shape due to the adjustment costs and price/wage rigidity, and the impact reaches the peak in about a quarter after the shock. The half-life of the shock is about six months, but the effect is very persistent. It vanishes after 16 quarters or 4 years. A main cause of the negative output gap is due to the rise in supply-side cost (lower-right panel) due to the increased labor costs during the disaster. Among the three monetary policy choices, the conventional price-based rule has the worst effect in defending the economy from disaster shock, mainly because of the ineffectiveness when the ZLB is hit. The unconventional quantity-based rule (QE) adopted by the US and Europe, on the contrary, generates the most effective defense against shock. The structural rule (in China) lies in the middle because it is

Table 2.1 Bayesian parameter estimation

Symbol	Definition	Prior Mean	Distribution	Posterior Mean	95% Highest Density Interval	
σ	Coefficient of Relative Risk Aversion	1.000	Normal	0.9303	0.7430	1.1106
β	Subjective discount factor	0.990	Calibrated			
γ^n	Utility weight of leisure	1	Calibrated			
γ^m	Utility weight of money	1	Calibrated			
η	Elasticity of labor supply	1	Normal	4.7918	3.8560	5.7513
ϕ	Nominal rigidity	0.50	Calibrated			
s	Elasticity of substitution of factors	10	Calibrated			
ρ^i	Reaction coefficient to interest rate	0.800	Beta	0.8131	0.8034	0.8217
ρ^π	Reaction coefficient to inflation gap	1.500	Beta	1.5380	1.5183	1.5532
ρ^y	Reaction coefficient to output gap	0.125	Beta	0.1496	0.1383	0.1608
ρ	AR coefficient of disaster probability	0.684	Beta	0.7156	0.7008	0.7290
P^*	Average probability of disaster	0.01	Calibrated			
d	Damage of disaster to TFP	0.10	Calibrated			
σ^A	Productivity shock standard deviation	0.01	Inv. Gamma	0.0033	0.0028	0.0038
σ^S	Monetary shock standard deviation	0.01	Inv. Gamma	0.0008	0.0002	0.0014
σ^P	Disaster shock standard deviation	0.01	Inv. Gamma	0.0004	0.0003	0.0005

a combination of both price- and quantity-based instruments.

The inflation pressure rises after the expansionary monetary policy under all three variants (the upper-right panel of Fig. 2.1). Nevertheless, the quantity-based rule and the structural rule can lead to an overshooting reaction (deflation) after about a year. This is because the inflation pressure will trigger a higher interest rate (as shown in the upper-right panel), which then depresses the price level to a lower level. Again, the eclectic structural rule lies in the middle between the conventional and unconventional monetary policy rules.

As an eclectic counter-cyclical approach, the structural monetary policy strikes a good balance between output gap and inflation gap by combining the advantages of the price-based and quantity-based rules. As evidenced in 2020Q1, the Chinese economy recovered fairly quickly back to normal with the help of both structural monetary policy and the strict quarantine policy. In what follows, we compare the three monetary policy rules and their effects during the pandemic between the US and China based on the simulated impulse responses of the two countries in different stages of the pandemic. It can shed light on future monetary policymaking and crisis management for future rare disasters.

At the beginning of the pandemic, the Fed in the US followed the conventional price-based rule. In fact, the FFR was about to rise to curb the emerging inflation pressure in 2019Q4. The outbreak of COVID-19 canceled out the need for an interest hike, but the Fed did not engage in any further action either in 2020Q1. As the pandemic swept the US completely in 2020Q2, the urgent

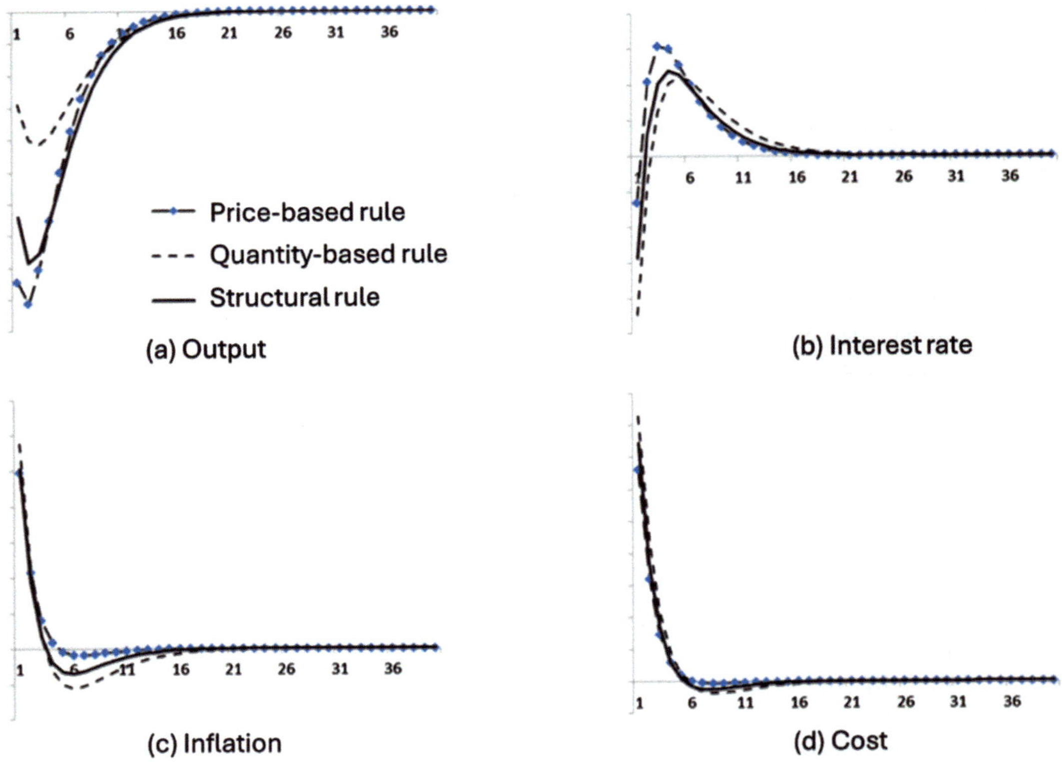

Fig. 2.1 Comparison of impulse response functions

need to protect public health and to reduce the output gap made the Fed reduce FFR substantially. However, due to the panic in the financial market, the stock market crashed and hit the circuit breaker thresholds four times. In response, the Fed cut FFR twice in a short time by 150bps, the interest rate level effectively gets to the ZLB. The conventional price-based monetary policy rule became ineffective. As shown in the impulse responses (upper panel), disaster shock has a very different magnitude of negative impact on the economy. Once the pandemic enters the worst stage, both the price-based and quantity-based rules become ineffective by 2020Q3.

In contrast, China underwent similar experience in 2020Q1. By the end of February 2020, the coronavirus had spread to the entire country. In the first two months of 2020, the industrial output fell by 13.5% year-on-year and the fixed investment fell by 24.5% year-on-year. As shown in the lower panel of Fig. 2.2, the impulse responses in the first stage of the pandemic are the same for the US and China. Nonetheless, the Chinese government quickly imposed a much stricter quarantine policy compared to the US, it resulted in a quick clearance of COVID-19 cases at the cost of a plunge in output. At the same time, to mitigate the damage, the central bank in China (PBoC) implemented a sophisticated mix of structural monetary policies to, on the one hand, provide timely support to the most impacted enterprises and individuals, and on the other hand, avoid over issuance of money to the public. The advantage of targeted support of the structural rule (e.g., earmarked tools) optimally reduced the inflation pressure, which was seen in the US and Europe. After stabilizing the economy and the pandemic, China entered the recovery stage in 2020Q3, and all conventional policies are effective again under the quasi-normal conditions. Despite lasting uncertainties and persistent costs due to the pandemic, the economy had successfully survived the knock-on effect of the disaster shock with a smoother transition compared to the US. If we only focus on

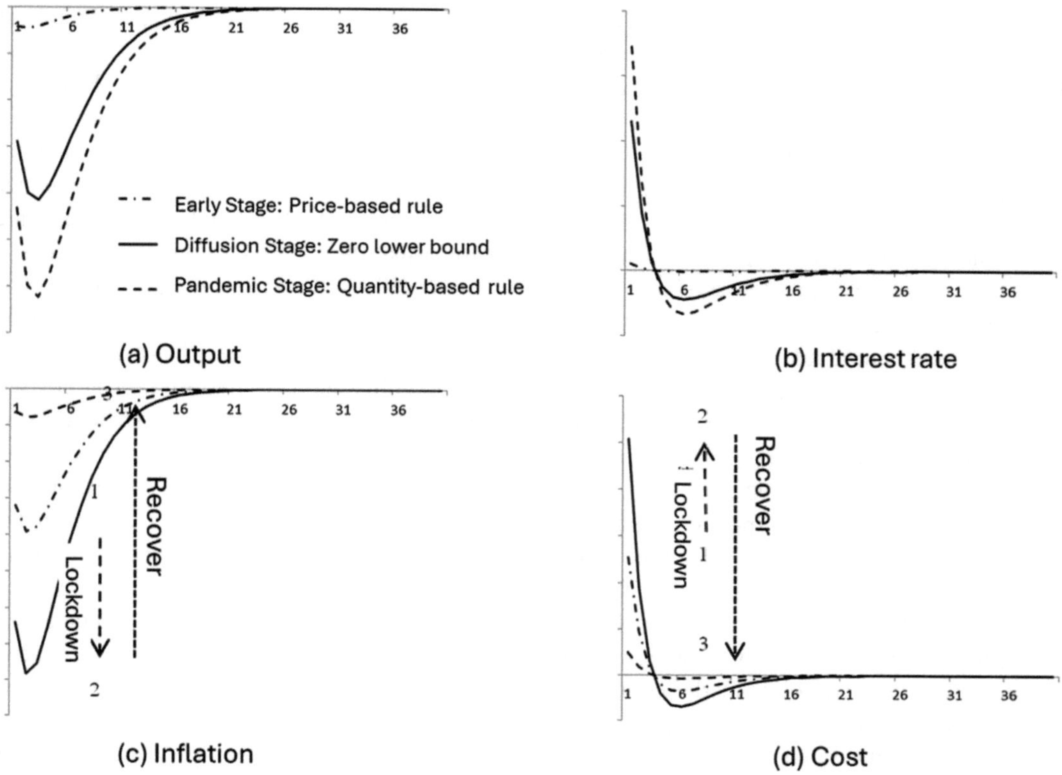

Fig. 2.2 Impulse response functions of different stages

the first year of the pandemic (2020), the economic performance of China (a growth rate of 2.3%) was exceptional compared to the US (a growth rate of -3.4%). This contrast entails some reflections on how rare disasters can be managed better by timely administration and structural monetary policy.

2.6 Conclusion

The pandemic will eventually pass, but the possibility of rare disasters always exists, exposing the urgent need to improve economic resilience to unpredictable shocks. Using the US and China as examples, this chapter compares three monetary policy mechanisms in defending the economy against the COVID-19 pandemic. The key conclusion is that the structural rule strikes a better balance between the output gap and the inflation gap by using earmarked monetary tools. In rare disasters like the pandemic, these targeted monetary mechanisms can accurately mitigate the impact on the most affected agents in the economy without causing significant inflation.

Based on the estimated DSGE model, this chapter simulates and analyzes the economy's responses following the rare disaster shock of the COVID-19 pandemic. Focusing on the experience of the first year of the pandemic, we propose the following policy implications:

First, it is advisable to enhance the credibility of the central bank, implement prudent monetary policies, effectively use structural policy tools such as the new LPR mechanism, and avoid extremely aggressive monetary policies. According to past experiences with disasters and economic recessions, combined with the simulation results of this chapter, we recognize that ample liquidity is crucial for market stability and economic recovery post-shock. Furthermore, price-based monetary policy tools are limited in their ability to defend the economy against disasters. When the COVID-19 pandemic struck in

2020Q1, developed economies relied too heavily on the low-cost, conventional price-based rule. A deeper reason for the ineffectiveness of the price-based rule is the lack of confidence in central banks. Although the quantity-based rule is effective, it induces significant side effects like inflation and distorts financial market signals by flooding the economy with excessive money. Therefore, monetary authorities should also rebuild market confidence through price guidance and targeted support. The structural rule in China proved effective in stabilizing the market without much distortion in price levels, and the economy recovered more quickly once market confidence in the monetary system was restored.

Second, the role of government in managing rare disasters is crucial, but the role of the market is essential. The early stages of the COVID-19 pandemic in China demonstrated the importance of a powerful government in providing public health protection and restoring market confidence. However, this does not imply that the government should replace the market. In fact, the later stages of the COVID-19 pandemic in China saw many distorted behaviors in implementing the zero COVID policy. Market-based activities were severely hampered, and the marginal cost of imposing strict track-and-control measures escalated as the coronavirus evolved into highly contagious variants. Simultaneously, the marginal benefits of the zero COVID policy diminished as the new variants became less life-threatening. The strict quarantine policy might be optimal if China were the only country in the world. Nonetheless, in a global context, such a policy is not sustainable and is expected to converge to a general equilibrium (Nash equilibrium), where individuals attempt to coexist with COVID. Individuals must learn to protect themselves based on their own cost–benefit analysis rather than relying solely on government protection and enforced control. This approach allows self-interested, well-informed individuals to make their own optimal choices on the trade-off between the economy and health after the government has mitigated the initial impacts of the disaster. The virus can evolve, and so can individuals and markets. Post-pandemic, new tools in both public finance and private finance are expected to emerge to hedge against future rare disasters. For example, in the US during Hurricane Katrina and in Japan during the nuclear leakage, both government funds and insurance compensations played important roles. China's insurance industry was underdeveloped in covering rare disasters like the COVID-19 pandemic, necessitating significant government intervention. The difference in market maturity explains why China needed a centralized approach to manage rare disasters unlike the US. Yet, a powerful government can also hinder market development from the outset. The relationship between the government and the market resembles a parent–child dynamic. We believe that decentralizing power from the government to the market is a matter of "when," not "whether."

Third, addressing economic fluctuations caused by rare disasters requires cooperation and coordination both within and across countries. To ensure the effectiveness of monetary policy, coordination with different government sectors and cooperation with international counterparts are necessary. From the experience of central banks worldwide, activating counter-cyclical adjustments of monetary policy is a systematic task that requires alignment among core decision-makers, major government departments, market regulators, and key market stakeholders to achieve policy objectives. To avoid excessive interventions that could have economy-wide impact, the LPR mechanism was applied in coordination with consistent administrative management, fiscal policy, industrial policy, bank regulation policy, and others. Moreover, given the global impact of the COVID-19 pandemic, central banks implemented various counter-cyclical monetary policies targeting their countries' specific goals. Major economies such as China, the US, the EU, the UK, and Japan should build monetary coordination mechanisms to reduce the negative spillover effects of extreme domestic monetary policies. Disruptions in the international financial markets and trade can also exacerbate disaster impacts through exchange rate channels.

References

Angeloni, I., Faia, E., & Lo Duca, M. (2015). Monetary policy and risk taking. *Journal of Economic Dynamics and Control, 52*, 285–307.

Barro, R. J. (2006). Rare disasters and asset markets in the twentieth century*. *The Quarterly Journal of Economics, 121*(3), 823–866.

Bureau of Economic Analysis. (2021). Principal federal economic indicators. Suitland, MD: Bureau of Economic Analysis.

Calvo, G. A. (1983). Staggered prices in a utility-maximizing framework. *Journal of Monetary Economics, 12*(3), 383–398.

Cortes, G. S., Gao, G. P., Silva, F. B. G., & Song, Z. (2022). Unconventional monetary policy and disaster risk: Evidence from the subprime and COVID–19 crises. *Journal of International Money and Finance, 122*, Article 102543.

Carvalho, C., Schwartzman, F.F., (2015). Selection and monetary non-neutrality in time-dependent pricing models. *Journal of Monetary Economics, 76*, 141–156. https://doi.org/10.1016/j.jmoneco.2015.09.002

Dai, L., Patrick, M., & Zhou, P. (2015). A DSGE model of China. *Applied Economics, 47*(59), 6438–6460.

Dixit, A. K., & Stiglitz, J. E. (1977). Monopolistic competition and optimum product diversity. *The American Economic Review, 67*(3), 297–308.

Fernandez-Gallardo, A. (2023). Preventing financial disasters: Macroprudential policy and financial crises. *European Economic Review, 151*, Article 104350.

Funke, M., & Tsang, A. (2020). The People's bank of China's response to the coronavirus pandemic: A quantitative assessment. *Economic Modelling, 93*, 465–473.

Gates, B. (2020). Responding to Covid-19 — A once-in-a-century pandemic? *New England Journal of Medicine, 382*(18), 1677–1679.

Goodell, J. W., & Huynh, T. L. D. (2020). Did Congress trade ahead? Considering the reaction of US industries to COVID-19. *Finance Research Letters, 36*, Article 101578.

Gourio, F. (2012). Disaster risk and business cycles. *American Economic Review, 102*(6), 2734–2766.

IMF. (2021). *IMF and COVID-19: Policy Responses to COVID-19*. International Monetary Fund.

Isoré, M., & Szczerbowicz, U. (2017). Disaster risk and preference shifts in a New Keynesian model. *Journal of Economic Dynamics and Control, 79*, 97–125.

Keen, B. D., & Pakko, M. R. (2011). Monetary policy and natural disasters in a DSGE model. *Southern Economic Journal, 77*(4), 973–990.

Liu, L.-G., & Zhang, W. (2010). A New Keynesian model for analysing monetary policy in Mainland China. *Journal of Asian Economics, 21*(6), 540–551.

Manela, A., & Moreira, A. (2017). News implied volatility and disaster concerns. *Journal of Financial Economics, 123*(1), 137–162.

McCallum, B. T. (1988). Robustness properties of a rule for monetary policy. *Carnegie-Rochester Conference Series on Public Policy, 29*, 173–203.

Mechler, R., Mochizuki, J., & Hochrainer-Stigler, S. (2016). "Disaster risk management and fiscal policy: narratives, tools, and evidence associated with assessing fiscal risk and building resilience. *Policy Research Working Paper*, 7635.

Mehra, R., & Prescott, E. C. (1988). The equity risk premium: A solution? *Journal of Monetary Economics, 22*(1), 133–136.

Nakamura, E., Steinsson, J., Barro, R., & Ursúa, J. (2013). Crises and recoveries in an empirical model of consumption disasters. *American Economic Journal: Macroeconomics, 5*(3), 35–74.

National Bureau of Statistics of China. (2021).*Annual GDP Accounting Instructions of China*. National Bureau of Statistics of China.

Poilly, C. (2010). Does money matter for the identification of monetary policy shocks: A DSGE perspective. *Journal of Economic Dynamics and Control, 34*(10), 2159–2178.

Smets, F., & Wouters, R. (2007). Shocks and Frictions in US business cycles: A Bayesian DSGE approach. *American Economic Review, 97*(3), 586–606.

Taylor, J. B. (1993). Discretion versus policy rules in practice. *Carnegie-Rochester Conference Series on Public Policy, 39*, 195–214.

Zhang, W. (2009). China's monetary policy: Quantity versus price rules. *Journal of Macroeconomics, 31*(3), 473–484.

Zhou, B., Zhang, Y., & Zhou, P. (2021a). Multilateral political effects on outbound tourism. *Annals of Tourism Research, 88*, Article 103184.

Zhou, H., Yu, M., Li, J., & Qin, Q. (2021b). Rare disasters, exchange rates, and macroeconomic policy: Evidence from COVID-19. *Economics Letters, 209*, Article 110099.

References

3 Regional Trade and Anchor Currency

Abstract

This chapter evaluates currency-anchoring options for the Regional Comprehensive Economic Partnership (RCEP), the world's largest trading bloc formed in 2020 by 15 Asia–Pacific economies. Using a time-varying parameter VAR calibrated to bilateral trade data, we compare the US dollar (USD), Chinese yuan (CNY), and Japanese yen (JPY) with respect to trade-weighted volatility and marginal effects on intraregional flows across crisis episodes. Results show that the USD's stabilizing power has waned since the 2008 global financial crisis—a decline intensified by the 2018–19 US–China tariff dispute and the COVID-19 shock—while dollar-denominated volatility spills over even to dyads that exclude the US. The CNY now delivers superior value stability and trade-creation effects, mirroring China's expanding share of regional output. The JPY, once dominant, trails the yuan except in corridors closely linked to Japan and South Korea. Policy implications are twofold. First, selecting a regionally embedded anchor—likely the CNY—can lower transaction risk, strengthen supply-chain resilience, and advance South-South financial integration. Second, targeted measures such as enhanced yen-settlement facilities could revive JPY relevance and diversify the monetary ecosystem, thereby boosting RCEP's collective capacity to absorb external shocks.

Keywords

Anchor currency · Regional trade · Currency war

Classification:

SDG17

3.1 Introduction

Fifteen Asian countries signed the Regional Comprehensive Economic Partnership (RCEP) in November 2020. The trade deal, promoted by ASEAN for years, will create the most populous economic region in the world, accounting for about 30 percent of global GDP. Tariff reductions and financial facilities among the members are estimated to boost the regional trade by $428 billion (Petri & Plummer, 2020). It sends a major signal of multilateral trade integration in contrast to the burgeoning Protectionism in other parts of the world since 2016 (e.g., US-China trade war, Brexit). In fact, RCEP was pushed forward by the sudden withdrawal of the US from a competing trade deal Trans-Pacific Partnership which does not include China (Balistreri & Tarr, 2020).

In global and regional development, economic integration is always accompanied by financial integration (Fry-McKibbin et al., 2018). The US dollar (USD) has been the de facto anchor currency (i.e., which currency to peg) for most

D. Guo and P. Zhou, *Beating Financial Swords into Developmental Plowshares*, Sustainable Development Goals Series, https://doi.org/10.1007/978-981-95-5152-1_3

countries engaging in international trade and investment since the Bretton Wood System. USD is extensively adopted as the medium of exchange and/or as the unit of account for the traded goods and services even if the US is not part of the trade. Nevertheless, the wide use of dollars inevitably leads to excessive volatilities in regional trade volume because USD is susceptible to uncertainties outside the region such as monetary policies in the US (Rey, 2016). As a result, there has been a tendency for regional trade to choose alternative anchor currencies other than dollars (Zhang, 2014). An interesting anecdote of this trend is the currencies adopted in drug trafficking. According to the World Drug Report (United Nations, 2020, Booklet 3), currencies used by drug cartels exhibit a clear regional feature. In the two largest opium production zones, USD dominates the drug trade in Central America (Mexico and Colombia), while euro (EUR) is widely circulated in the Golden Crescent (Iran, Afghanistan, and Pakistan). Ironically but arguably, drug dealers must know the optimal currencies to minimize financial risks in the riskiest international business. More generally, USD is constantly challenged by currencies that are more intensively used in regional trade such as Japanese Yen (JPY) during 1980s (Malliaris, 2002) and EUR during 2000s (Fischer, 2016). Since the global financial crisis, many countries have openly questioned the viability of the dollar-based monetary and financial system in regional trade (Chiţu et al., 2014). For example, an increasing proportion of oil trade is made using other currencies like EUR. Australia signed an agreement to accept CNY in iron ore trade since 2017. CNY-denominated crude oil futures market was launched in 2018 (Ji & Zhang, 2019). Korea and China renewed the $59 billion currency swap in 2020.

The fast economic growth of China and its expanding weight in the regional trade provide a potential for CNY to establish a new currency bloc after the "dollar bloc" and the "euro bloc" (Fischer, 2016). Transaction-level evidence shows that CNY has been increasingly adopted as a vehicle currency in merchandize trade and FDI, but its global use decreases by geographic distance and economic connections (Liu et al., 2019). Thus, the internationalization ambition of CNY should start with East and Southeast Asia. In recent years, CNY is shown to be more closely linked with the ASEAN countries than USD and JPY (Caporale et al., 2018) given that the RCEP trade system has gradually developed into a China-centered regional supply chain. Figure 3.1 shows the growing importance of China in trade within the RCEP region (from 18 to 35%) with a waning share of Japan (from 26 to 14%), especially after the financial crisis.

On the one hand, most intermediate goods produced in RCEP members flow into China, rather than into Japan and the US, for further value-added processes, which form an important part of the global value chain. On the other hand, an increasing proportion of final goods manufactured in RCEP, and the rest of the world are exported to and consumed in China thanks to its growing national income and demand. China has become a crucial connecting point of the two value chains.

In the literature on Optimal Currency Area (OCA), the trade integration within a potential currency bloc is identified as a decisive factor of an anchor currency choice (Fischer, 2016). As shown above, China plays a key part in the RCEP region, but Japan has been a traditional influencer in Asia for decades. In fact, both CNY and JPY are in good positions to challenge the anchor role currently assumed by USD. Moreover, financial assets and liabilities denominated by potential anchor currencies have been increasingly paid attention to in the empirical OCA literature (Meissner & Oomes, 2009). To perform a more comprehensive evaluation of the three candidate currencies, other factors are also considered, such as shock symmetry (Picard & Worrall, 2020) and colony ties (Klein & Shambaugh, 2012). To better understand these factors, remember that an anchor currency is essentially a currency, so it also has three basic functions of money as defined in any undergraduate economics textbook:

(i) Medium of exchange. It can be used in international trade by countries other than the issuer of the anchor currency. The currency with this function is also known

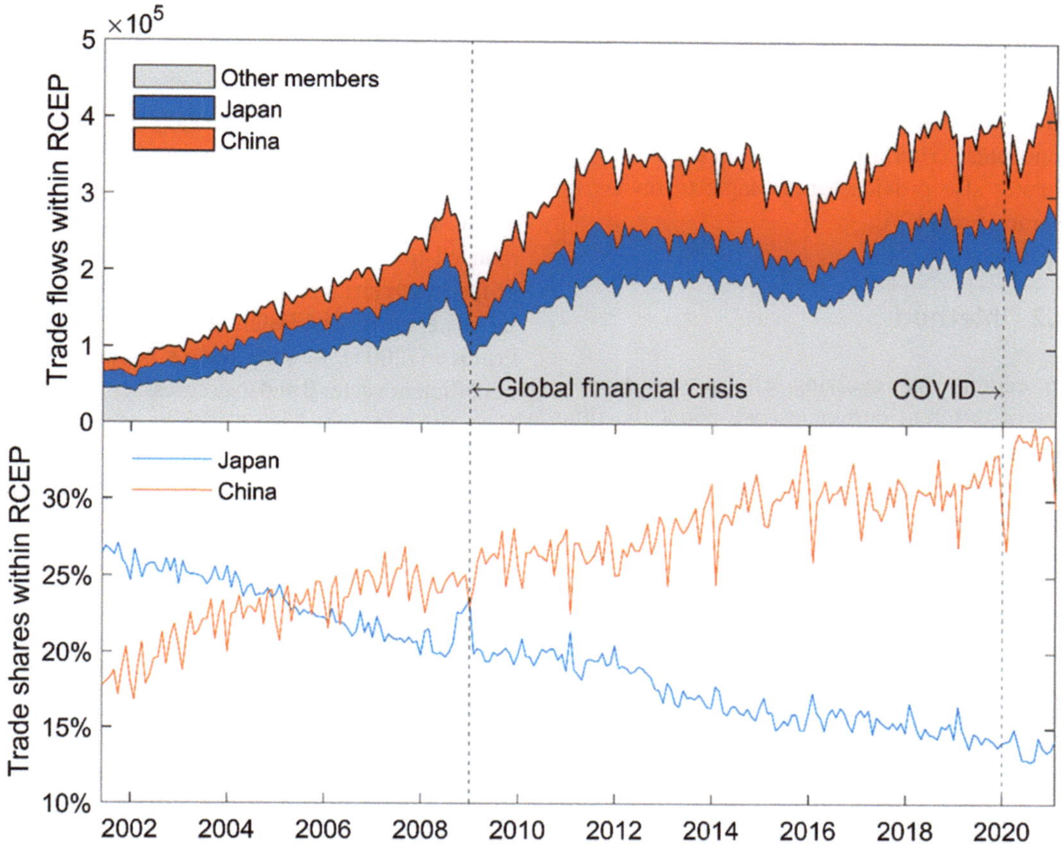

Fig. 3.1 Trade flows within RCEP region. *Source* Wind Data Service. Trade flow is the sum of imports and exports with other members of RCEP

as the vehicle currency (Picard & Worrall, 2020).

(ii) Store of value. It can be used as foreign exchange reserves.

(iii) Unit of account. It can be used to denominate assets and liabilities.

We can group the three functions into two general types. First, as a medium of exchange, the anchor currency needs to be intensively used in the region (measured by the share of regional trade). This is a flow-based criterion focusing on the *intensity* of use (the intensity criterion). In general, a high intensity of use implies a greater effect of that currency on regional trade. Second, to achieve the other two functions, it requires the value of the anchor currency to be relatively stable (measured by the volatility and correlations of shocks). This is a stock-based criterion focusing on the *stability* of value (the stability criterion). Arguably, there seems to be a trade-off between the two criteria. A more intensively used currency is more likely to suffer from uncertainties outside the trade partners, while a stable currency cannot accommodate sizeable capital flows, as illuminated by the "impossible trinity."

An optimal balance between the two criteria depends on various theoretical assumptions, which are beyond the scope of the present paper. Instead, we aim to empirically investigate the competitiveness of USD, CNY, and JPY as the anchor currency for RCEP in terms of the two criteria with the help of a quantitative model. The intended contribution of the paper is both practical and methodological. We explored a very pragmatic issue of the new trade agreement, which can inspire further discussions of financial integration after economic integration. In addition, the two conceptual criteria proposed and applied in this chapter also provide a new angle to review the literature on OCA.

3.2 Method

To capture the evolving effects and volatilities of different currencies, we adopt the time-varying parameter VAR (TVP-VAR) approach in a Bayesian tradition (Primiceri, 2005). It has been applied to empirical studies in international trade and international finance (He et al., 2021). The key advantage of the TVP-VAR model is that it can accommodate both stochastic coefficients and volatilities of the VAR model (Cogley & Sargent, 2005). This is essential for our purpose because the relative roles of the three candidate currencies, USD, JPY, and CNY, are changing over time.

Without losing generality, we remove the means of each series, so that the intercepts can be omitted from the specification. Consider a structural VAR(p) model:

$$Ay_t = B_1 y_{t-1} + \cdots + B_\rho y_{t-\rho}, \quad \text{where } \varepsilon_t \sim (0_k \textstyle\sum) \tag{3.1}$$

$\mathbf{y}_t$ is a $K \times 1$ vector of endogenous variables. It is straightforward to determine the recursive structure of the four variables in the TVP-VAR model. First, influences of currencies depend on their relative importance or shares in the global trade (US > China > Japan), so USD affects CNY, and both affect JPY. Second, prices determine quantities, so the trade flow should be the last variable in $\mathbf{y}_t$. $\mathbf{B}_1$, ..., $\mathbf{B}_p$ are $K \times K$ coefficient matrices. The lower triangle matrix $\mathbf{A}$ with ones on the diagonal effectively assumes recursive causality among the endogenous variables. This is a popular identification strategy in VAR literature. $\boldsymbol{\epsilon}_t$ is a vector of independently distributed structural shocks, so the covariance matrix $\boldsymbol{\Sigma}$ is diagonal. Pre-multiply the inverse matrix $\mathbf{A}^{-1}$ on both sides of Eq. (3.1) to obtain the reduced-form of the VAR model:

$$Y_t = \Gamma_1 Y_{t-1} + \cdots + \Gamma_\rho Y_{\rho-1}, \quad \text{where } \xi_t \sim N(0_k, \Omega) \tag{3.2}$$

where $\boldsymbol{\Gamma}_s \equiv \mathbf{A}^{-1}\mathbf{B}_s$ ($s = 1, \ldots, p$) is the reduced-form coefficients and $\boldsymbol{\Omega} \equiv \mathbf{A}^{-1}\boldsymbol{\Sigma}\mathbf{A}\prime^{-1}$ is the symmetric covariance matrix of reduced shocks $\boldsymbol{\xi}_t \equiv \mathbf{A}^{-1}\boldsymbol{\epsilon}_t$. Following the convention in Primiceri (2005), we stack the pK^2 coefficients in a coefficient vector $\boldsymbol{\beta}$ and the regressors in a matrix $\mathbf{X}_t$ in order to write Eq. (3.2) more compactly:

$$y_t = X_t\prime\beta + \xi_t, \quad \text{where } X_t\prime \equiv I_K \otimes [y_t\prime_{-1} \cdots, y_t\prime_{-\rho}] \tag{3.3}$$

Similarly, the $\frac{K(K-1)}{2}$ parameters in $\mathbf{A}$ and the K parameters in $\boldsymbol{\Sigma}$ can be stacked in two vectors $\mathbf{a}$ and $\mathbf{h}$ where $h_k \equiv \ln\sigma_k^2$ ($k = 1, \ldots, K$). In a general TVP-VAR model, all parameters can change over time, so we should add time scripts for $\mathbf{a}_t$, $\boldsymbol{\beta}_t$, and $\mathbf{h}_t$, which are assumed to follow random walks:

$$a_t = a_{t-1} + \varepsilon_t^a, \quad \text{where } \varepsilon_t^a \sim N\left(\frac{0k(k-1),\ \Sigma^a}{2}\right) \tag{3.4a}$$

$$\beta_t = \beta_{t-1} + \varepsilon_t^\beta, \quad \text{where } \varepsilon_t^\beta \sim N\left(0_{\rho k^2},\ \Sigma^\beta\right) \tag{3.4b}$$

$$h_t = h_{t-1} + \varepsilon_t^h, \quad \text{where } \varepsilon_t^h \sim N\left(0_k,\ \Sigma^h\right) \tag{3.4c}$$

Note that (3.3) is effectively the measurement equation of a state space model, and (3.4) ABC are the transition equations. For simplicity, the covariances among the structural shocks ($\boldsymbol{\epsilon}_t^{\mathbf{a}}$, $\boldsymbol{\epsilon}_t^{\boldsymbol{\beta}}$, $\boldsymbol{\epsilon}_t^{\mathbf{h}}$) are assumed to be zero. The initial conditions specified in Table 3.1 are assumed to follow standard prior distributions in the Bayesian literature (Nakajima, 2011). A different set of priors are

Table 3.1 Prior distributions of initial conditions

	Prior Distribution	Prior Mean	Prior Std. Dev
$\mathbf{a}_0$	Normal	0	1
$\mathbf{\Sigma}_0^{\mathbf{a}}$	Inverse Gamma	10	0.01
$\boldsymbol{\beta}_0$	Normal	0	1
$\mathbf{\Sigma}_0^{\boldsymbol{\beta}}$	Inverse Wishart	10	0.01
$\mathbf{h}_0$	Normal	1	5
$\mathbf{\Sigma}_0^{\mathbf{h}}$	Inverse Gamma	10	0.01

also used to provide a robustness check. The estimation of this model is performed using standard Markov Chain Monte Carlo (MCMC) procedures (Primiceri, 2005).

3.3 Data

The data used to estimate the TVP-VAR model are monthly time series spanning from 2006M2 to 2021M2 (181 months). The value of USD is measured by the USD index relative to a basket of foreign currencies (created by Bloomberg). It provides a good indicator of the strength of USD in the global money market. The value of CNY is (inversely) measured by USD/CNY exchange rate or USD denominated by CNY. A rise in USD/CNY rate means a stronger USD relative to CNY. Similarly, the value of JPY is measured by JPY/CNY exchange rate or JPY denominated by CNY. A rise in JPY/CNY means a stronger JPY relative to CNY. The total trade flows are calculated as the sum of bilateral exports and imports among all member countries within RCEP. To make the data ready for TVP-VAR, monthly percentage changes of exchange rates and year-on-year (YOY) percentage changes of trade flow are used to stationarize the data.

As shown in the descriptive statistics (Table 3.2), JPY witnessed a decline in value (–0.05%) with a high volatility (2.29%), while CNY gained a strong upward trend (0.13%) with a low volatility (0.78%). The USD lies in between JPY and CNY in terms of both mean and standard deviation. In line with Fig. 3.1, there is a secular growth of the trade flow within RCEP (0.57%) mainly attributed to the growth of trade with China. The ADF and KPSS tests show that the stationarized series are all $I(0)$ processes. The correlation matrix in Table 3.2 suggests that CNY has a more significant correlation with the regional trade than USD and JPY.

Figure 3.2 plots the stationarized series $\mathbf{y}_t$, i.e., monthly percentage changes in USD, CNY, JPY, and trade. JPY has the highest volatility especially during the global financial crisis. USD also fluctuates but with relatively constant volatility. CNY used to have a very stable exchange rate pegged to USD even during the financial crisis. The volatility started to rise since August 2015 when the People's Bank of China changed the USD/CNY central parity quoting mechanism (Das, 2019).

3.4 Results

To determine the optimal lag length for the TVP-VAR model, specifications with different lag lengths ($p = 1, \ldots, 4$) are estimated. Most (quarterly) macroeconomic models follow an $AR(1)$ process (Smets & Wouters, 2007), which is equivalent to a lag length of 3 months in a monthly data model. In our case, however, all information criteria (AIC, BIC, and DIC) support $p = 1$ month rather than $p = 3$ months because all information criteria penalize the number of parameters. As shown in Table 3.3, as p rises, the number of parameters grows fast due to the "curse of dimensionality," outweighing the benefits of overparameterization. As a robustness check, we apply a wider range of priors, but the specification of $p = 1$ remains robust.

3.4.1 Posterior Estimation of Parameters

Given the large number of parameters in the TVP-VAR, the common practice in Bayesian literature is not to report the complete estimated model, but to focus on several key structural parameters. We select the contemporaneous effects (i.e., a_{41}, a_{42}, and a_{43} in matrix $\mathbf{A}$) and lagged effects (i.e., β_{41}, β_{42}, and β_{43} in matrix $\boldsymbol{\beta}$) of the three currencies

Table 3.2 Descriptive statistics of stationarized series (monthly percentage change)

	USD index	USD/CNY	JNY/CNY	Trade
No. of Obs	181	181	181	181
Mean	0.0735	0.1258	–0.0476	0.5691
Std. Dev	1.3854	0.7830	2.2868	1.2406
Stationarity				
ADF test	–8.3987***	–7.5003***	–10.2254***	–3.0026***
KPSS test	0.1450*	0.2452**	0.1312*	0.4100***
Correlation				
USD index	1			
CNY/USD	–0.4185***	1		
JNY/CNY	–0.0152	–0.2198***	1	
Trade	–0.0385	0.2417***	–0.0631	1

Table notes significance level, * 10%, ** 5%, *** 1%

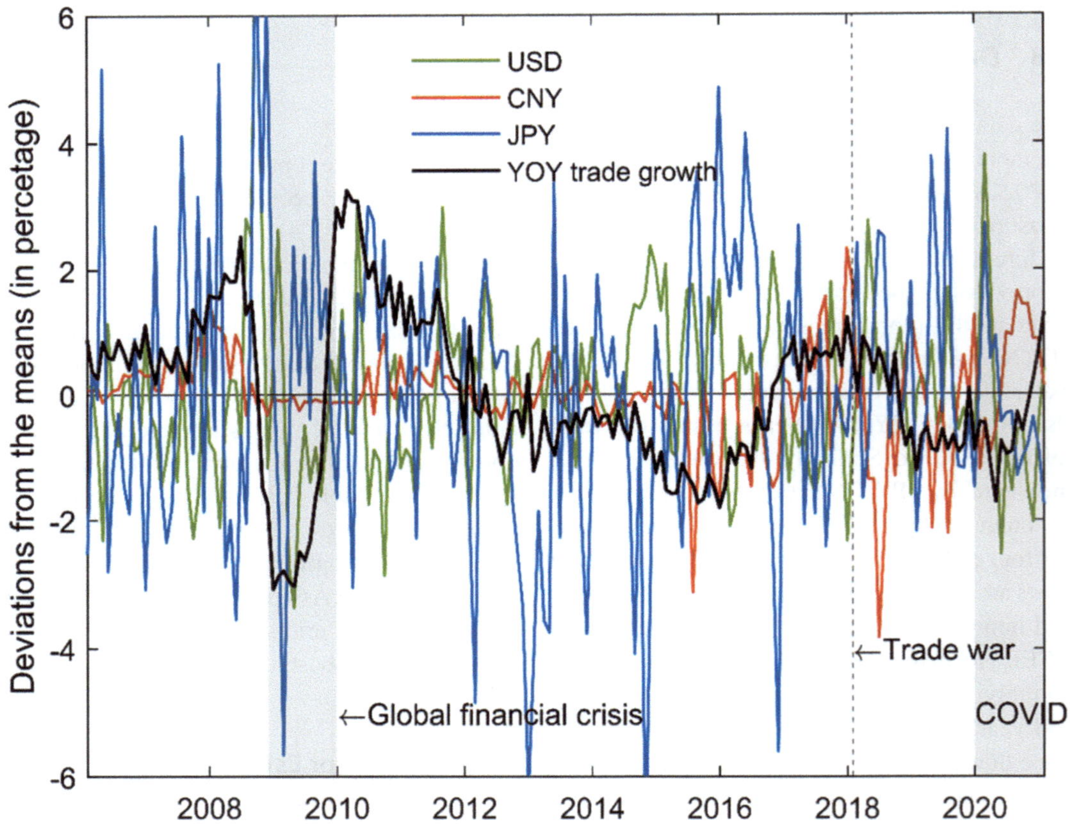

Fig. 3.2 The monthly percentage change of exchange rates and trade flows. *Source* Wind Data Service

on trade. The effects are evolving over time, especially after the global financial crisis and the US-China trade war. For example, during 2008–2009, the sudden depreciation of USD and JPY coincided with a sharp plummet in the regional trade, which is in line with the greater contemporaneous effects (the first column of Fig. 3.3). The trade frictions between the US and China from early 2018 raised the lagged influence of USD and JPY in the RCEP region (the second column of Fig. 3.3),

Table 3.3 Model selection with different lag lengths

p	No. of parameters	AIC	BIC	DIC
1	26	2009.4	1957.4	2070.3
2	42	2838.5	2754.5	3430.9
3	58	4579.4	4463.4	4866.4
4	74	8964.8	8816.8	9274.1

Table notes AIC = Akaike information criterion; BIC = Bayesian information criterion; DIC = Deviance information criterion

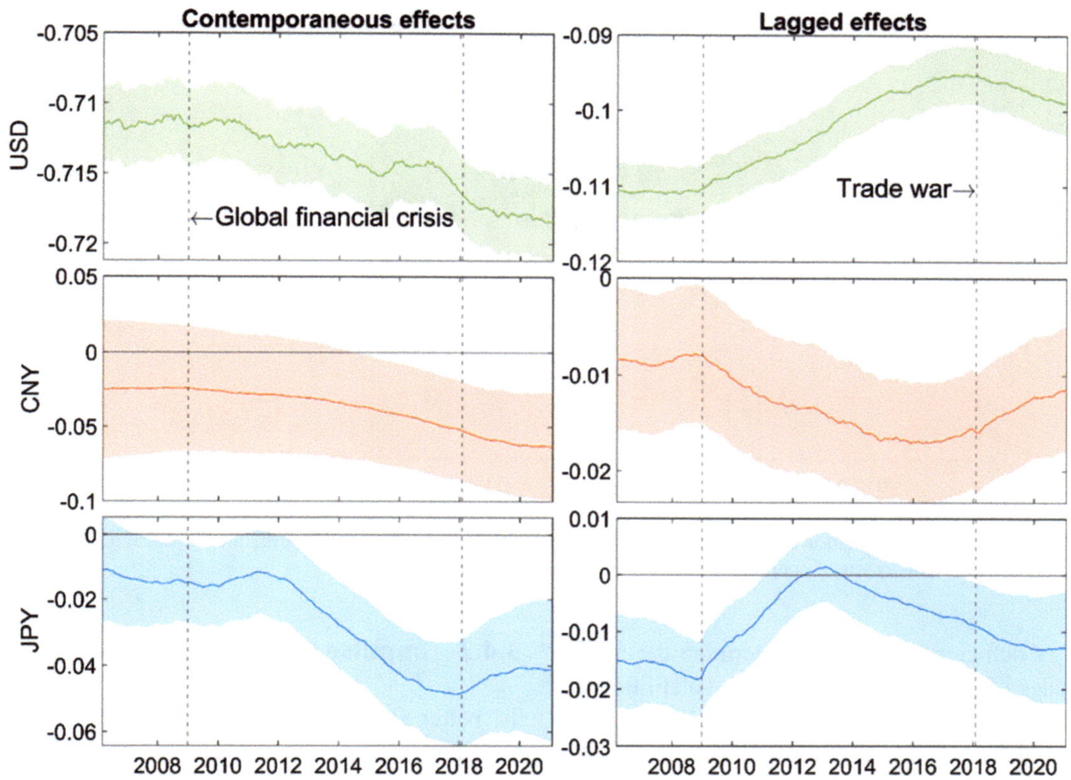

Fig. 3.3 Bayesian estimation of selected time-varying coefficients. *Notes* The shaded areas are Bayesian 95% credible intervals (the counterparts of confidence intervals in frequentist econometrics). The estimation results are robust to a different choice of prior

while reduced the lagged effect of CNY (less negative). It is also noted that the COVID-19 pandemic does not alter the trend after the trade war.

Now turn to the cross-section dimension of Fig. 3.3. The magnitude of influence of USD (both contemporaneous and lagged effects) is always larger than JPY and CNY. As argued earlier, it is unfavorable for a region to adopt an anchor currency with excessive influence and volatility. In contrast, CNY seems to be a good candidate as the anchor currency, since its fluctuations have the smallest impact on the regional trade (the stability criterion) and China accounts for the highest trade share within the RCEP region (the intensity criterion). In fact, JPY has similar attributes in terms of both criteria, but the main competition is between USD and CNY. To see this, there is a clear negative correlation in the (lagged) effects between USD and CNY, which suggests that the influences of USD and CNY wane and wax inversely. This pattern does not exist between USD and JPY or between JPY and CNY.

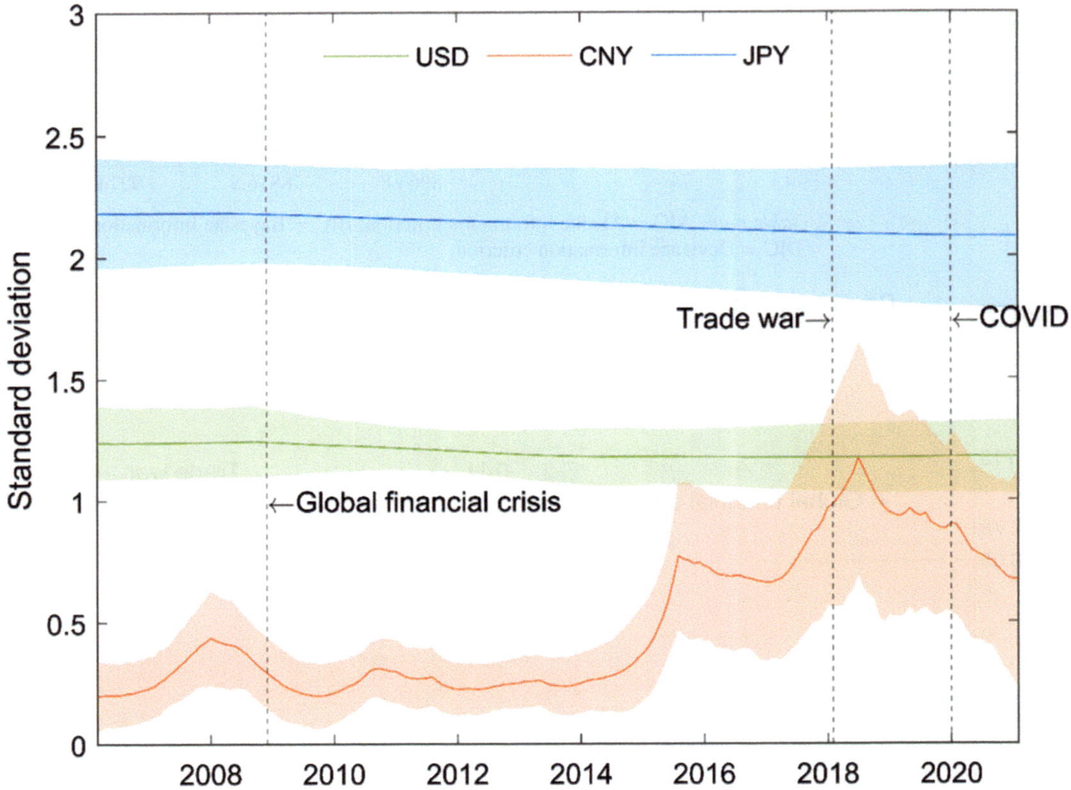

Fig. 3.4 Bayesian estimation of selected time-varying volatilities. *Notes* The shaded areas are Bayesian 95% credible intervals (the counterparts of confidence intervals in frequentist econometrics)

Coefficients (**A** and **β**) determine the magnitudes of effects of shocks, while volatilities ($\mathbf{h}_t$) determine the magnitude of the shocks per se. The estimated standard deviations of the three currencies are plotted in Fig. 3.4. The volatilities of USD and JPY hardly change over the entire sample period, suggesting relatively stable exchange rate regimes in the two countries. The volatility of CNY was very low before 2015, because China maintained a strictly regulated peg to USD. Even after 2015 as the central bank in China allowed for greater forex market freedom, the volatility of CNY is still the lowest among the three currencies despite a temporary surge during the US-China trade war in 2018. This ranking is in line with the descriptive statistics reported in Table 3.2.

3.4.2 Impulse Response Functions

To better summarize the effects of shocks on trade flows, impulse response functions (IRFs) are usually used to combine the estimated coefficients in an intuitive way. However, in the TVP-VAR context, each date is associated with a unique set of IRFs. To parsimoniously demonstrate the time-varying effect of a currency shock on the trade flow, we plot the cumulative effects of IRFs of each month in Fig. 3.5. It measures the total loss of the regional trade (in percentage) due to a positive currency shock (appreciation). For example, if USD appreciates by one standard deviation (1.39% according to Table 3.2), then the regional trade within RCEP will eventually drop by -3.3%

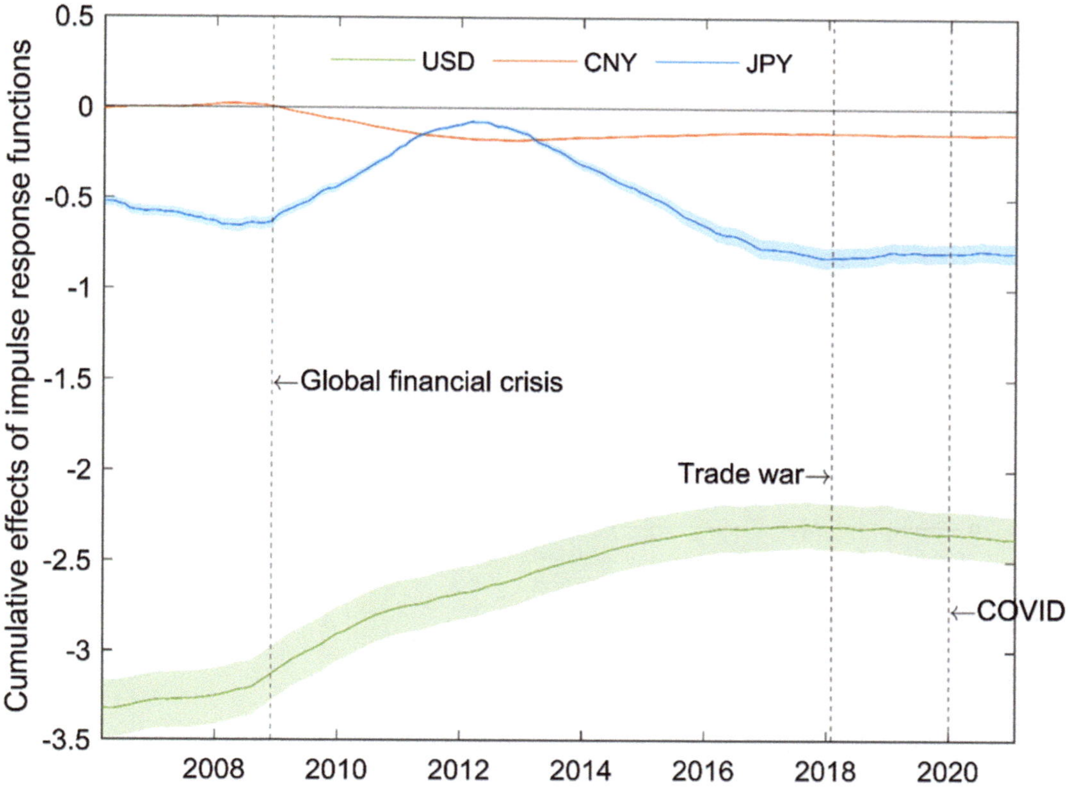

Fig. 3.5 The cumulative impulse response functions of the three currencies on trade. *Notes* The shaded areas are Bayesian 95% credible intervals (the counterparts of confidence intervals in frequentist econometrics)

in 2006 and by -2.4% in 2021. Consistent with the earlier findings, the effect of USD is always bigger than that of JPY, which is then bigger than that of CNY. It confirms the advantage of CNY as a candidate anchor currency in term of the stability criterion because it reduces the uncertainties of a common currency according to the OCA literature (Chari et al., 2020; Eichler & Karmann, 2011; Mundell, 1961).

Moreover, Fig. 3.5 shows a new feature, which was not salient in the coefficient analysis (Fig. 3.3)—the cumulative response of the regional trade to USD decreases over time, while the effects of CNY and JPY seem to increase in a competing fashion. The effect of CNY peaked around 2012, which coincides with the trough of the effect of JPY. To summarize, the declining influence of USD is shared by CNY and JPY, and CNY is the biggest winner.

To better visualize the dynamics of the TVP-VAR system, we plot IRFs of three selected points in time: 2007M1 (pre-crisis), 2009M1 (post-crisis), and 2021M1 (COVID-19 pandemic). Three significant patterns are found in Fig. 3.6. First, the effect of USD on trade gradually diminishes after the global financial crisis. This trend is reinforced during the COVID-19 pandemic. Second, the inverse happens to CNY. During the pandemic, the effect of CNY on trade becomes less persistent compared to the post-crisis period. Third, the effect of JPY declines after the financial crisis and then increases during the COVID-19 period.

It confirms the observations of Fig. 3.5—USD is phasing out while CNY and JPY are weighing in. There are three critical events. The first is the global financial crisis, after which the influence of CNY started to increase. The second is

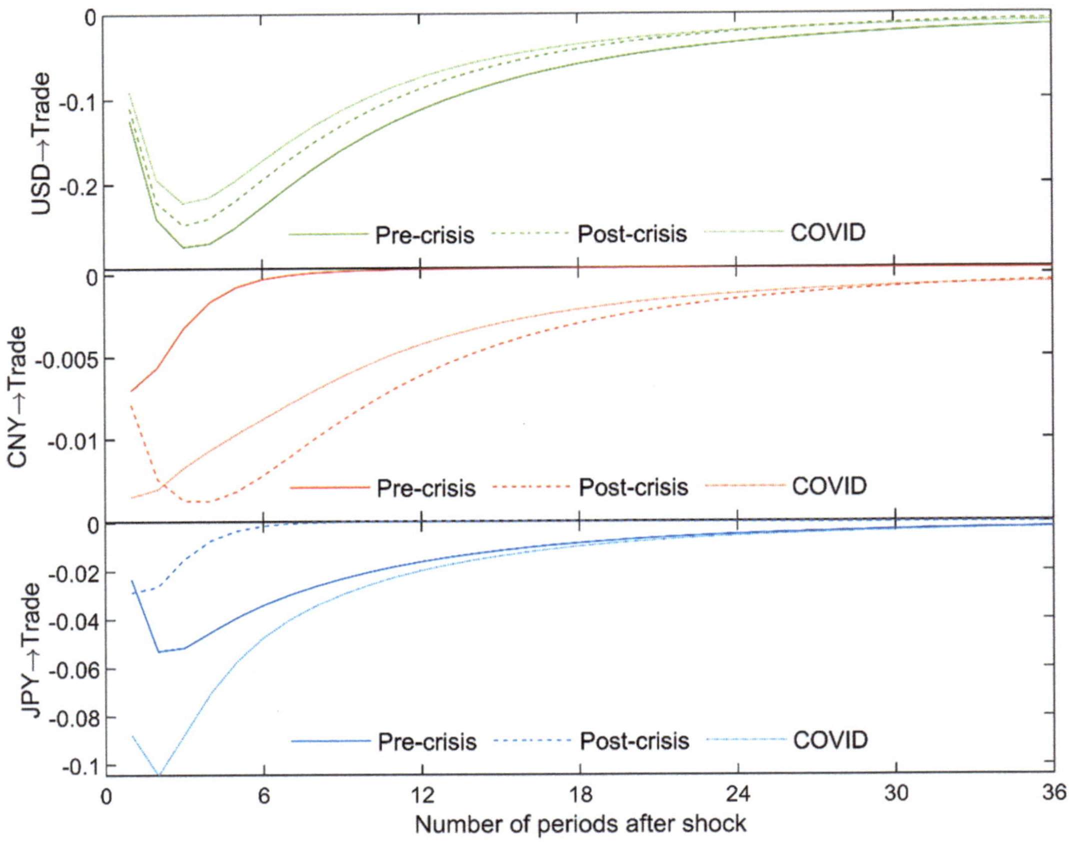

Fig. 3.6 The 6-month ahead trade responses to currency shocks

the US-China trade war since 2018, which weakened CNY but strengthened JPY. The third is the COVID-19 pandemic, during which the influence of USD continued to diminish. Therefore, the timing of RCEP signing up posed both CNY and JPY in good positions against USD in the region.

Compared to JPY, CNY has an additional advantage apart from meeting the flow-based and stock-based criteria. As CNY enters an appreciation cycle in 2020, it makes CNY-denominated assets more attractive since China has a long-term trade deficit within the region. By holding CNY as a reserve currency, RCEP members can indirectly benefit from the fast economic growth within China.

Another practical implication of the model is that using USD as the unit of account in RCEP trade can lead to an exchange rate trap to exacerbate the trade imbalance. For example, if USD appreciates due to causes outside the RCEP region, then the overall trade within the region will drop even if the US is not involved with any of the trade. Furthermore, a stronger USD means a weaker JPY, so the rest of the RCEP will undergo a greater deficit with Japan. This spillover effect of USD unnecessarily disturbs the trade volume and composition if USD is still used as the anchor currency for regional trade. In contrast, the spillover effect of USD through CNY is much weaker because the cumulative effect of CNY on trade is much smaller.

3.5 Conclusion

We summarize and compare the empirical findings in Table 3.4. The influence of USD in the RCEP region is fading away since the global

Table 3.4 Comparison of the three currencies as anchor currency in RCEP

Criterion	Measure	USD	CNY	JPY
Intensity	Trade share	Weak	Strong	Medium
Stability	Contemporaneous effect	Weak	Medium	Strong
	Lagged effect	Weak	Strong	Strong
	Total effect	Weak	Strong	Medium
	Volatility	Medium	Strong	Weak
Reputation	Foreign exchange reserve	Strong	Weak	Medium

Notes Contemporaneous effects and lagged effects are measured by VAR coefficients shown in Fig. 3.3. Total effect is measured by the sums of impulse responses in the first 36 months after shocks shown in Fig. 3.5

financial crisis and the COVID-19 pandemic reinforce this trend. As a result, the benefits of using USD as the anchor currency for the region can no longer justify the excessive uncertainties it induced. Switching from USD to an intramural currency as the anchor currency is both an exogenous opportunity and an endogenous need. It is shown that CNY enjoys a clear advantage in terms of the stability criterion over JPY, but JPY is in a similar position to CNY in terms of the intensity criterion. However, given the historical influences of USD and JPY, there is still a long way for CNY to win a dominant position for the anchor currency in RCEP region.

For the policymakers, we propose the following two practical suggestions based on the empirical findings. First, China is running a trade deficit with RCEP in general, so it is difficult to further promote the intensity of use of CNY in the short run. Therefore, for China, the key strategy lies in the stability criterion to entrench the upper hand over Japan. More attractive CNY-denominated assets, such as the so-called "panda bonds" and FDI, can expand the impacts of CNY. On the contrary, Japan is running a trade surplus with RCEP, so there is room to further increase its proportion in the regional trade. So, Japan's momentum lies in the intensity criterion to compete with China. The choice between CNY and JPY is essentially a competition between flow-based and stock-based benefits.

Second, to pave the path for a new anchor currency (either CNY or JPY), an improved financial infrastructure is due to catch up with the increasing need of international payment and currency settlement. The Chiang Mai Initiative Multilateralization (CMIM) agreement is one of such facilities among ASEAN + 3 members. This regional currency swap arrangement involves a total amount of 240 billion USD to facilitate the regional trade, mostly RCEP members. China and Japan respectively contribute 32% of the capital, forming a duopoly with both cooperation and competition. USD may have temporarily withdrawn, but the game between China and Japan is still on. And the arena is always overshadowed by the uncertainty of a new administration and trade policy in the US.

References

Balistreri, E. J., & Tarr, D. G. (2020). Comparison of deep integration in the Melitz, Krugman and Armington models: The case of The Philippines in RCEP. *Economic Modelling, 85*, 255–271.

Caporale, G. M., Gil-Alana, L. A., & You, K. (2018). Exchange rate linkages between the ASEAN currencies, the US dollar and the Chinese RMB. *Research in International Business and Finance, 44*, 227–238.

Chari, V. V., Dovis, A., & Kehoe, P. J. (2020). Rethinking optimal currency areas. *Journal of Monetary Economics, 111*, 80–94.

Chiţu, L., Eichengreen, B., & Mehl, A. (2014). When did the dollar overtake sterling as the leading international currency? Evidence from the bond markets. *Journal of Development Economics, 111*, 225–245.

Cogley, T., & Sargent, T. J. (2005). Drifts and volatilities: Monetary policies and outcomes in the post WWII US. *Review of Economic Dynamics, 8*(2), 262–302.

Das, S. 2019. China's Evolving Exchange Rate Regime, *IMF Working Papers*, No. 2019/050. https://doi.org/10.5089/9781498302029.001

Eichler, S., & Karmann, A. (2011). Optimum currency areas in emerging market regions: Evidence based on the symmetry of economic shocks. *Open Economies Review, 22*(5), 935–954.

Fischer, C. (2016). Determining global currency bloc equilibria: An empirical strategy based on estimates of anchor currency choice. *Journal of International Money and Finance, 64*, 214–238.

Fry-McKibbin, R., Hsiao, C.Y.-L., & Martin, V. L. (2018). Global and regional financial integration in East Asia and the ASEAN. *The North American Journal of Economics and Finance, 46*, 202–221.

He, F., Lucey, B., & Wang, Z. (2021). Trade policy uncertainty and its impact on the stock market -evidence from China-US trade conflict. *Finance Research Letters, 40*, Article 101753.

Ji, Q., & Zhang, D. (2019). China's crude oil futures: Introduction and some stylized facts. *Finance Research Letters, 28*, 376–380.

Klein, M. W., & Shambaugh, J. C. (2012). *Exchange rate regimes in the modern era*. MIT Press.

Liu, T., Wang, X., & Woo, W. T. (2019). The road to currency internationalization: Global perspectives and chinese experience. *Emerging Markets Review, 38*, 73–101.

Malliaris, A. G. (2002). Global monetary instability: The role of the IMF, the EU and NAFTA. *The North American Journal of Economics and Finance, 13*(1), 72–92.

Meissner, C. M., & Oomes, N. (2009). Why do countries peg the way they peg? The determinants of anchor currency choice. *Journal of International Money and Finance, 28*(3), 522–547.

Mundell, R. A. (1961). A theory of optimum currency areas. *The American Economic Review, 51*(4), 657–665.

Nakajima, J. (2011). Time-varying parameter VAR model with stochastic volatility: An overview of methodology and empirical applications. *Monetary and Economic Studies*, 107–142.

Petri, P. A., & Plummer, M. G. (2020). *East Asia decouples form the United States: Trade war, COVID-19, and East Asia's new trade blocs*. PIIE, Peterson Institute for International Economics.

Picard, P. M., & Worrall, T. (2020). Currency areas and voluntary transfers. *Journal of International Economics, 127*, Article 103390.

Primiceri, G. E. (2005). Time varying structural vector autoregressions and monetary policy. *The Review of Economic Studies, 72*(3), 821–852.

Rey, H. (2016). International channels of transmission of monetary policy and the Mundellian trilemma. *National Bureau of Economic Research*, w21852.

Smets, F., Wouters., R. 2007. Shocks and Frictions in US Business Cycles: A Bayesian DSGE Approach. *American Economic Review 97* (3): 586–606. https://doi.org/10.1257/aer.97.3.586

United Nations. (2020). *World Drug Report*. United Nations.

Zhang, C. (2014). An information-based theory of international currency. *Journal of International Economics, 93*(2), 286–301.

Financial Stability and Cryptocurrency 4

Abstract

We examine how cryptocurrencies interact with state-backed money by tracing Bitcoin's response to monetary shifts in the US and China—today's two largest economies. Employing a Bayesian TVP-VAR estimated by daily data (2013–2019), the study links Bitcoin price and trading volume to (i) the long-term Treasury rate spread between the two countries and (ii) movements in the USD/CNY exchange rate. Results show that a widening spread—especially when Federal Reserve tightening lifts the dollar—raises Bitcoin's price and activity, as investors seek an asset insulated from divergent policy stances. Similarly, a weaker yuan relative to the dollar spurs additional trade in Bitcoin, confirming its appeal as a cross-border substitute for fiat. These patterns illustrate "de-fiatization": cryptocurrencies siphon value from central bank money when policy credibility or convertibility is in doubt. Policy implications follow. First, while blockchain technology can boost efficiency, high volatility demands proportionate supervision and global coordination to forestall systemic risk. Second, balanced frameworks should protect innovation while curbing cybercrime and fraud. Finally, because cryptocurrencies diffuse monetary and even political power, timely regulatory adaptation—not blanket prohibition—offers the best path toward a resilient, inclusive financial architecture.

Keywords

Cryptocurrency · Financial stability · Decentralization

Classification:

SDG9

4.1 Introduction

The white paper released by Facebook about its plan to launch a new cryptocurrency Libra in 2019 triggered instant responses from countries and institutions, including the US, which had an obscure attitude toward cryptocurrency innovations. Hours later, Democratic representative Maxine Waters requested Facebook to stop developing its cryptocurrency Libra. On the same day, the G7 stated that it would establish a high-level forum to examine the risks such currencies pose to the financial system. The development of Bitcoin since 2009 was featured with periodically skyrocketing or plummeting prices; cryptocurrency trading platforms (decentralized exchanges or DEXs) have become a "casino" for risk-seeking speculators. Facebook is now the world's largest supranational business ecosystem benefiting from its huge user group. Its integration with cryptocurrency may signify the birth of the only super digital currency that can shake the position of the world currency (USD) at present. The potential

D. Guo and P. Zhou, *Beating Financial Swords into Developmental Plowshares*,
Sustainable Development Goals Series, https://doi.org/10.1007/978-981-95-5152-1_4

risk caused by the fluctuation of currency values therefore is unmeasurable.

What are the determinants of cryptocurrency price fluctuations? And will the future development of cryptocurrency embrace the characteristics of fiat currencies such as the USD? And most importantly, as the two largest economies in the world, will China and US's monetary policies have spillover effects on cryptocurrency? To answer these research questions, we start with a literature review on the academic literature of policy transmission mechanisms. A two-country open-economy model of cryptocurrency is then presented. Following the theoretical model, we report the empirical results of a time-varying analysis and breakpoint regressions. Next, by trend analysis, the Granger causality test, and breakpoint regressions, we analyze the policy impacts of China and the US's monetary policies on transaction prices and volumes of cryptocurrencies. Impulse response functions of a TVP-VAR model are discussed to quantify the dynamic effects on cryptocurrency.

4.2 Literature

Cryptocurrencies are P2P (Peer-to-Peer) solutions based on cryptography, blockchain, and smart contract technologies, primarily issued and circulated on the internet. Satoshi Nakamoto (2008) operationalized and popularized the concepts of distributed ledger technology (DLT) and blockchain by creating the first cryptocurrency Bitcoin. The integration of finance and computing technology provides a higher level of information symmetry, increases efficiency of transaction settlement (Yin et al., 2025), and reduces the cost of trust (Zhang & Zhou, 2021). Bitcoin has since become the world's most dominant cryptocurrency and served as a potential alternative to fiat currencies (e.g., USD, EUR, JPY).

The features of cryptocurrency spark numerous discussions on whether it meets the economic definition of currency (Raskin & Yermack, 2018). Bitcoin, for example, resembles mainstream currencies, such as the USD, since it was designed as a P2P medium of exchange. In contrast, Bitcoin holds its unusual position by being a "private currency" that is not backed by a sovereign state (Bjerg, 2016). The analysis of Dyhrberg (2016) puts the position of Bitcoin between USD and gold, highlighting its advantages as a medium of exchange and its disadvantages as a store of value. Furthermore, the result from the asymmetric GARCH model supports her argument that Bitcoin provides a hedging capability like gold. On the contrary, Glaser et al. (2014) conclude that Bitcoin users mainly trade with a speculative intention. By comparing the characteristics of Bitcoin, fiat currencies (USD, RMB, EUR, and JPY), and their corresponding treasury bonds, Slawotsky (2020) concludes that Bitcoin-like cryptocurrencies promote "de-dollarization." In contrast, our paper also argues for a "de-fiatization" effect of cryptocurrencies via the crowding-out effect. This is partly caused by exchange rate movements and the negative pressure on government bonds due to interest rate differences.

As an intensively investigated topic, the literature on drivers of the Bitcoin price seems to have reached a more balanced consensus. That is a combination of fundamentals and speculative behaviors. Kristoufek (2015) analyzes four commonly claimed influential factors of the Bitcoin price, including fundamentals, speculation, technology, and the Chinese market. The fundamental factors are found to play a role over the long term, while short-term demands driven by speculation also serve to elevate the short-term price volatility. Hence, he concludes that "*Bitcoin forms a unique asset possessing properties of both a standard financial asset and a speculative one.*"

Furthermore, the media and academic attention on Bitcoin went beyond its speculations and implications. The technological and conceptual advantages have also sparked thoughts and excitement about its development and potential applications. In mid-2010s, China started to explore potential application of blockchain in a more traditional context—Central Bank Digital Currency (CBDC). Guo and Zhou (2023) acknowledge that the central bank's traditional currency issuance will face new challenges in the face of information technology development. And the central bank's issuance of cryptocurrency may point in the direction of future development. They explore the potential of the CBDC from conceptual, technical, and practical dimensions, and make proposals for using blockchain technology to further incorporate technological advancement. Barrdear & Kumhof (2022) analyze a DSGE model calibrated to match pre-crisis US economy and identify several macroeconomic advantages associated with the CBDC, including a sizeable gain in the steady-state GDP, the business cycle stability assisted by a second policy instrument, and the financial stability given certain policy assurance.

Cryptocurrencies are meant to be globally used because the economy is increasingly interconnected globally. At the same time, the literature on traditional monetary policy has also been devoted to explaining how and to what degree one country's monetary policy can have impacts on its global counterparts. A few channels of international monetary policy transmission mechanism are proposed and studied extensively. Miranda-Agrippino and Rey (2022) study financial market friction and find significant monetary policy spillovers from the US to major economies that operate based on floating exchange rates with an established inflation targeting regime. Georgiadis (2015) analyzes the validity of "impossible trinity" in the context of financial globalization using a GVAR (Global VAR) model. He concludes that the flexibility of exchange rate is not only still critical for monetary autonomy under free capital mobility but is also an increasingly important channel for the monetary policy transmission. However, few research attempts to bridge decentralized cryptocurrency and centralized monetary policy in one unified framework despite the substitutability between cryptocurrencies and fiat currencies. This chapter aims to fill this gap.

4.3 Model

VAR models are extensively used in macroeconomic research. Recent extensions from the simple VAR model are mainly developed in two dimensions. First, the progress of the ever-complex economic analysis is frequently stalled by the dimensionality curse—the trade-off between economic coherence and statistical consistency. Pesaran et al. (2004) first propose a relatively practical, yet effective GVAR model that has since been adopted widely particularly in the area of policy analysis and risk evaluations. Second, the economic complications are far beyond a set of linear relationships presented by a VAR model—time series can have multiple structural breakpoints that correspond to economic and policy shifts. To capture these time-varying features, Primiceri (2005) first develops a TVP-VAR model which allows both coefficients and variance–covariance matrix to vary over time. Time-varying coefficients capture the variation in the systemic dynamics of the economy, while time-varying variance–covariance matrix captures the variation in the non-systemic shocks of the economy.

This study contributes to literature in two aspects. First, as world's two largest economies, both China and the US are considered as open economies with policy externalities in the literature. Studies of China and the US' influences on Bitcoin trading have been done in various aspects. Nevertheless, studies from the aspect of joint policy dynamics are rare. This study investigates the joint impacts of monetary policies in China and the US on the Bitcoin trading price and volume. It bridges and enriches the literature on monetary policy and cryptocurrency from an open-economy and multilateral macroeconomic perspective. Second, this study carries out various time-varying analysis to identify underlying structural changes around the steady states. A TVP-VAR model with stochastic volatility is used to explore the roles of systemic and non-systemic changes in Bitcoin trading.

What distinguishes a "two-country open-economy" model from a "small open-economy" model is the extent to which a country's economic and policies influence its counterparts. For example, the Chinese economy has gradually made the transition to a small open economy since 2001 when it joined the WTO (Wei et al., 2023). From 2010, China became the second largest economy after the US, which made the two-country open-economy model more appropriate (Zhang & Zhou, 2021). Moreover, cryptocurrency can be used globally as a substitute for fiat currency, so both China and the US are potentially relevant. In this chapter, we introduce cryptocurrency into a two-country open-economy model and establish the relationship between monetary policy, inflation, exchange rates, and interest rates.

In this context, country A (US) is the leading economy which incorporates cryptocurrency into its money supply alongside its traditional fiat currency. It is assumed that the cryptocurrency is not big enough to impact the economy of country A substantially. Country B (China) represents the counterpart economy, within which the circulation of cryptocurrency is restricted, though the exchange between fiat currency and cryptocurrency is allowed. The structure of the model follows a standard RBC model augmented with money. The economic conditions of country A (denoted by *) consist of:

Aggregate demand:	$y_t^* = AD^*\left(y_{t-1}^*, i_{t-1}^*, e_t\right)$
Aggregate supply:	$y_t^* = AS^*(y_{t-1}^*, \pi_t^* - \pi_{t-1}^*, e_t)$
Money supply:	$m_t^* = MS^*\left(\gamma_t^*, \theta_t^*\right)$
Money demand:	$m_t^* = MD^*\left(p_t^*, y_t^*, i_t^*\right)$

The economic conditions of country B consist of:

Aggregate demand:	$y_t = AD(y_{t-1}, i_{t-1}, e_t)$
Aggregate supply:	$y_t = AS(y_{t-1}, \pi_t - \pi_{t-1}, e_t)$
Money supply:	$m_t = MS(\gamma_t, \theta_t)$
Money demand:	$m_t = MD(p_t, y_t, i_t)$

The relationship between the two countries:

PPP:	$p_t^* = p_t - e_t$
Uncovered IRP:	$e_t = E_t[e_{t+1}] + i_{t+1}^* - i_{t+1}$
Balance of payment:	$e_t = e(y_t, y_t^*, r_t, r_t^*, E_t[e_{t+1}])$
Fisher equation:	$r_t = i_t - E_t\left[\pi_{t+1}\right]$

Following conventional notations, $p_t, y_t, i_t, e_t, \pi_t, \gamma_t, \theta_t, m_t$ denote the price level, output, nominal interest rate, real interest rate, exchange rate, inflation rate, fiat currency, cryptocurrency, and total money supply in country B at time t. Variables with * indicate the counterparts in country A.

After combination and approximation, the log-linearized money demand function of country A can be rewritten as a linear function:

$$m_t^* = m^*\left(y_t^*, i_t^*, E_{t-1}[e_t], e_{t-1}, E_t[e_{t+1}], i_{t+1}^*, i_{t+1}, i_t^*, i_t\right) \quad (4.1)$$

Similarly, the amount of cryptocurrency in circulation can be expressed as:

$$\theta_t^* = \theta^*\left(y_t^*, p_t^*, m_t^*, \gamma_t^*, E_{t-1}[e_t], e_{t-1}, E_t[e_{t+1}], i_{t+1}^*, i_{t+1}, i_t^*, i_t\right) \quad (4.2)$$

The factors can be classified as fundamental factors $F_t\left(y_t^*, p_t^*, m_t^*, \gamma_t^*\right)$, exchange rate factors $X_t\left(E_{t-1}[e_t], e_{t-1}, E_t\left[e_{t+1}\right]\right)$, interest rate factors $R_t\left(i_{t+1}^*, i_{t+1}, i_t^*, i_t\right)$,, and shock factors (ϵ_t). Equation [26] suggests that the monetary policies of two economies play a role in determining the volume of cryptocurrency. It also suggests that cryptocurrency in circulation can be affected by the past and expected exchange rates and interest rates.

In this study, cryptocurrency is denominated in currency A, the total volume of cryptocurrency can be defined simply as: $\theta_t^* = P_t^* Q_t^*$, where P_t^* denotes the price of cryptocurrency denominated in currency A, and Q_t^* denotes the quantity of cryptocurrency in circulation. An empirical model of Q_t^* can be specified with transaction-driven factors, technology-driven factors, security-driven factors, speculation-driven factors, and China-related factors. Note that cryptocurrency shows a substitution effect on fiat currencies implied from the structural equations above, i.e., $corr\left(\theta_t^*, \gamma_t^*\right) < 0$. This is what is termed as "de-dollarization" effect of cryptocurrency in the literature. But this is not the only effect. Given that CNY also has a "de-dollarization" effect on USD in regional trade (Guo & Zhou, 2021), there is a competition between cryptocurrency and CNY as well. It is arguable that cryptocurrency not only promotes de-dollarization but also induces de-fiatization in general. It decentralizes the entire monetary economic system.

4.4 Data

In line with the discussion in the previous session, the empirical model operationalizes the theoretical model to estimate the impact of policy differences on cryptocurrency. Building on that, policy implications are evaluated to mitigate financial risks and strengthen financial stability.

Bitcoin trading price (BTC/USD) and volume are two main indicators for the performance of cryptocurrency. In terms of policy differences, the US-China interest rate (10-year government bonds) spread is used. The exchange rate is defined as the amount of CNY for one unit of USD (USD/CNY). The daily sample is obtained from the Wind Database, ranging from 2013M1 to 2019M6. To match the frequency of other macroeconomic variables, daily data are transformed into monthly data by the average.

The TVP-VAR model with stochastic volatility is a vector autoregressive model with time-varying parameters. It has been widely used in the literature on financial markets to capture continuous evolution of underlying market structures. This is especially evident in the turbulent international financial and money markets of modern times, such as forex and cryptocurrency markets. Hence, the TVP-VAR model is well suited to the purpose of this study as the time-varying factor enables an in-depth analysis of such structural changes. The technical details of the TVP-VAR model can be found in **Method** of Chap. 3.

Figure 4.1 compares Bitcoin price P_t^* against US-China interest spread s_t. After 2017M1, the trend of Bitcoin price and the US-China interest rate spread seem to co-move with each other. The interest rate spread shows neither leading nor lagging position until 2019M1 when the interest rate spread starts to show a leading position against the Bitcoin price. In comparison, the trade volume shows a two-month lag against the interest rate spread, particularly after 2017M11. Similarly, the exchange rate also shows a certain synchronicity with Bitcoin after 2016, but it exhibits more time variations and an alternating parallel-deviating-parallel pattern. For example, the two variables ran in parallel in 2016 and 2018M1-2018M5, while diverging in 2017 and 2018M5-2018M11 (Table 4.1).

Given the complicated lead-lag co-movements, we apply Granger Causality test to all four series. The lag order is set to 2. First, there are bi-directional causalities between the interest spread s_t and Bitcoin price P_t^*, while the causality from s_t to the Bitcoin trade volume Q_t is only unidirectional. Second, there are bi-directional causalities between the exchange rate e_t and Bitcoin price P_t^*, but the causality from e_t to Bitcoin trade volume Q_t^* is only unidirectional. Monetary policy differences between the Fed and the PBoC are the driving force behind fluctuations of Bitcoin trade volume. e_t and Q_t^* are not two divergent indicators; rather, e_t reflects the policy differences between the two economies and acts as a leading indicator of Q_t^*. The results of the Granger causality test are in line with the Interest Rate Parity theory of exchange rates and interest rates since there is a one-way causal relationship between the China-US interest rate difference and the exchange rate, but no reverse causal relationship.

Granger causality tests only verify the short-term relationship between variables. An insignificant result does not rule out the possibility of long-term equilibrium relationship. Johansen cointegration tests are therefore carried out to verify possible long-term causal relations. Both trace tests and maximum eigenvalue tests show the existence of two cointegration vectors. Hence, long-term causal relationships should not be neglected either.

Furthermore, standardized breakpoint tests are used to identify unknown structural breakpoints in the time series (Fig. 4.2). The interest rate difference between the two countries is not substantial to destabilizing the bond markets and the

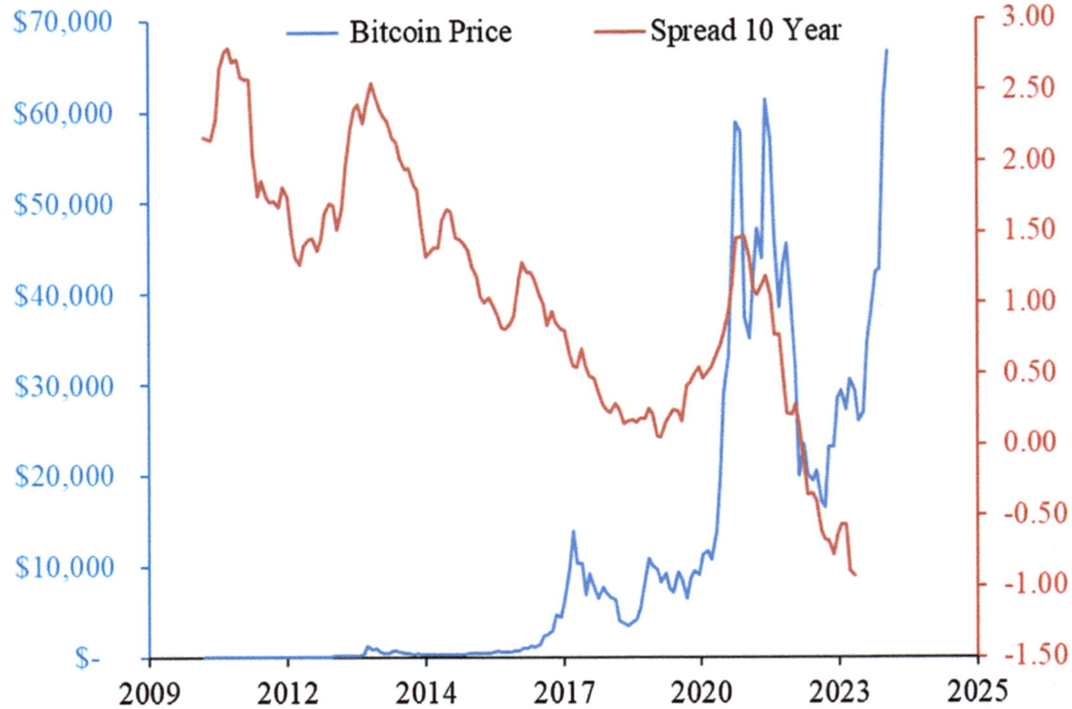

Fig. 4.1 Time plots of key variables used in the empirical model

Table 4.1 Granger causality test results

Null hypothesis H_0	F-test	$\Pr(H_0)$
s_t does not Granger-cause P_t^*	0.57597	0.5623
P_t^* does not Granger-cause s_t	1.30247	0.2722
s_t does not Granger-cause Q_t^*	8.17259	0.0003***
Q_t^* does not Granger-cause s_t	0.0316	0.9689
e_t does not Granger-cause P_t^*	2.20734	0.1103
P_t^* does not Granger-cause e_t	2.09013	0.124
e_t does not Granger-cause Q_t^*	7.94196	0.0004***
Q_t^* does not Granger-cause e_t	0.76728	0.4645

effectiveness of monetary policy regulation. Thus, we can use the China-US interest rate difference as reference for trend comparison, especially the jumping feature of breakpoints.

Four breakpoints are detected in the sample period from 2002M1 to 2019M7. They divide the sample into five phases corresponding to monetary policy differences between the US and China over the global economic cycles (Table 4.2).

Phase 1. Starting from 2001M1, the US economy recovered from the previous recession (the dot-com bubble) and China started to be integrated into the world economy via joining WTO. Both US and China's interest rates were high, and monetary policies were relatively tight to curb the new bubble. Hence, during this period, the policy differences were maintained at a medium–low level.

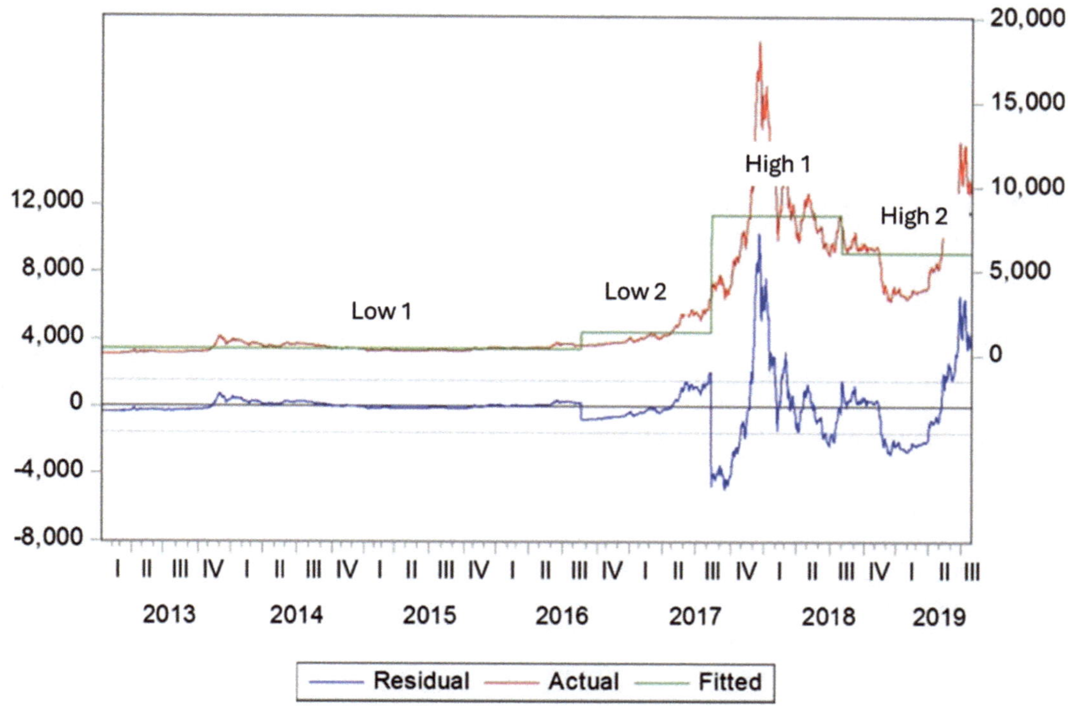

Fig. 4.2 Breakpoints of Bitcoin price

Table 4.2 Monetary policy differences between the US and China

	Difference	Period	Months	Fed policy	PBoC policy	Events
1	Medium–low	2001M1-2005M2	49	Move from tightening to easing	Follow the FED	Recovery after recession
2	Low	2005M3-2007M9	31	Expansionary	Follow the FED	Bubbles
3	Medium	2007M10-2011M6	44	Counter-cyclical	Follow the FED	Global financial crisis
4	High	2011M7-2015M3	44	Quantitative easing	Not following	European debt crisis
5	Medium–high	2015M4-2019M7	47	Raising interest rate, reducing balance sheet	Independent	US: recovery; China: supply-side structural reform

Phase 2. This phase witnessed a global economic boom with the ease of monetary policies. Economic bubbles started to form in this phase in the housing market. The policy differences were at a low level as monetary policies were very consistent across countries.

Phase 3. The global economy plummeted in this phase. The subprime mortgage crisis in 2007 triggered a global financial crisis in 2008. Conventional and unconventional counter-cyclical monetary policies were used all over the world, so this phase is a period of synchronization in monetary policy.

Phase 4. The policy gap between China and the US had started to widen due to different timing and magnitude of monetary policies. The double-dip European debt crisis further reinforced the policy divergence. On the one hand, the Fed and European Central Bank (ECB) adopted unconventional quantitative easing, expanding central bank balance sheet, entering an era of liquidity trap. On the other hand, China turned her attention inward and focused on domestic economic development and policy independence. Its monetary policy deviated from major economies in the world.

Phase 5. Starting from 2015M4, the phase is characterized by a medium–high level of monetary policy divergence. The Fed's policy rate follows a steep-climbing curve from 2016 as the US economy rebounded from the crisis. China's monetary policy continues to decouple from the US and focuses more on the domestic economy. The policy difference is maintained at a relatively high level.

Specifically, the medium–high-level echoes the concept of "US-China interest rate spread comfort zone" proposed by the PBoC. In this zone, there is room for mild policy adjustments without substantially diverging from the US counterpart. The interest rate spread fluctuates around a relatively stable level, so one shall expect that deviations from this level is temporary due to financial market arbitrage. For example, amid the Fed's frequent interest rate hikes, prudent monetary policies were followed in China. There was a significant deviation from the "comfort zone" at the end of 2018 and in the first half of 2019. But soon the Fed decided to cut interest rates due to the pressure on the economy. As a result, the interest rate spread returned to the "comfort zone."

Table 4.2 also shows the four structural breaks of exchange rate during the sample period. Before 2015, the low to medium–low levels of exchange rate coincided with higher levels of interest rate spread. The trend is in line with the conventional economic theory in general. However, the structural break in 2015 occurred during China's exchange rate reform, followed by a period of erratic CNY depreciations. At the meantime, a widening interest rate spread reflects the divergence of monetary policies between the two economies. China's monetary policy remained prudent, while the US underwent several interest hikes to curb the inflation. Conventional open-economy theory can no longer explain the post-2015 exchange rate movements.

The Bitcoin price shows three structural breaks during the sample period from 2013M1. The price was kept at a stable, low level until 2017M8 when the price suddenly soared. In 2018M8, a downward trend of the Bitcoin price level coincided with the "comfort zone" of interest rate spread and the high post-reform exchange rate.

To avoid spurious regressions, all variables are tested for unit root using the ADF (augmented Dickey-Fuller) test. Results from the unit root test suggest stationarity at 1% significance level for all variables. Further tests with and without trend and intercept also confirm the above findings. Finally, to determine the optimal lag length, multiple standards (e.g., LR and AIC) suggest that the optimal lag length is 2.

4.5 Results

Building on the theoretical model and the data description, we apply the TVP-VAR model to analyze the dynamics between monetary policy differences and Bitcoin price/volume.

4.5.1 Posterior Estimation of Parameters

This study adopts common calibrations from Nakajima (2011) who provides a comprehensive overview of TVP-VAR models with stochastic volatility. Given the previous discussion and test results of structural breaks, the time-varying coefficients are set to follow a random walk to ensure that any structural break and permanent change are properly captured. To calculate the parameter posterior distribution, the MCMC (Markov Chain Monte Carlo) method iterates 20,000 times and discards the initial 2,000 samples as the burn-in period (10%).

The null hypothesis of the convergence to the posterior distribution is not rejected for any of the estimates at the 5% significance level. The MCMC iterations converge in all cases. The highest inefficiency factor is around 220, which gives at least $\frac{20000-2000}{220} \approx 82$ uncorrelated samples for the

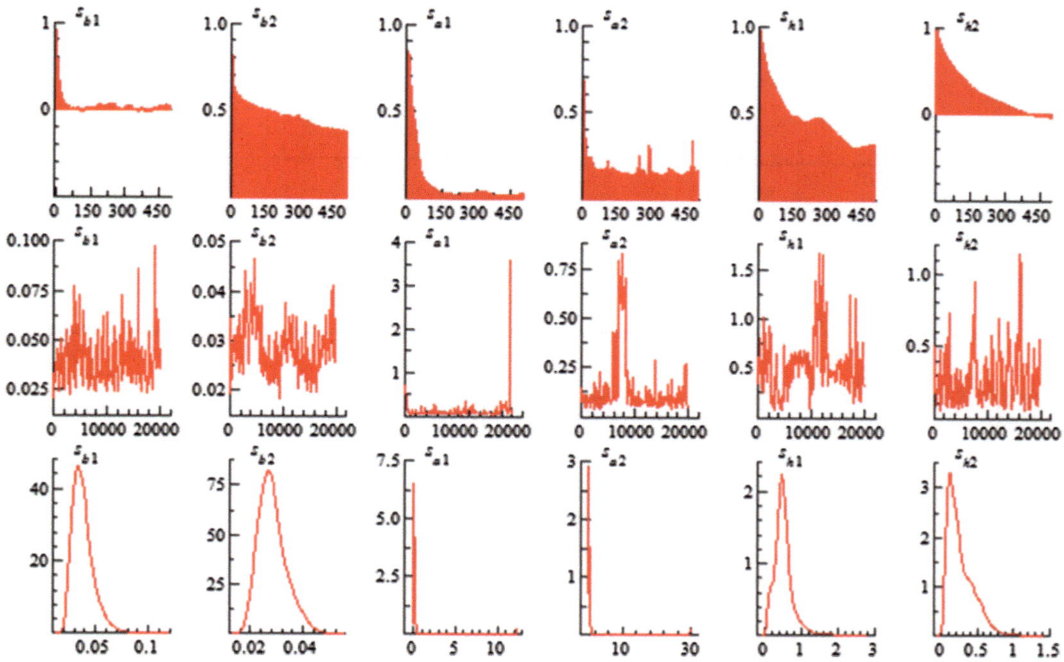

Fig. 4.3 MCMC simulation diagnosis of selected parameters

parameter. Since this study focuses more on identifying time-varying characteristics and less on the precise quantification, the number of uncorrelated samples is sufficient.

Figure 4.3 shows the autocorrelations (top row), sample paths (middle row), and posterior densities (bottom row) of selected parameters. The left panels are the first chain, and the right panels are the second chain. As shown by the declining trends (top), the autocorrelations of the simulations are well removed by MCMC algorithm. The sample paths (middle) converge to white noises, so the estimated parameters are independently distributed. The posteriors (bottom) show that some parameters may be bimodal, but most are normally distributed (Fig. 4.4).

The simulated volatilities of interest rate spread and exchange rate exhibit an upward trend from the end of 2017. On the one hand, the economic recovery in the US signaled the end of quantitative easing and a round of interest rate hikes were implemented to curb overheated investment. However, the trade war between China and the US since 2018 weakened the recovery which eventually forced the Fed to cut interest rate. On the other hand, China continued to strengthen her monetary policy independence but also faced severe domestic and international challenges such as the shortened domestic bond market cycles, de-leveraging, and the trade war with the US. They jointly caused a significant level of high volatility in the interest rate spread. At the meantime, the volatility of the exchange rate was amplified since the exchange rate reform in China—the exchange rate was no longer a monetary policy target and was more influenced by the market force rather than central bank interventions. Coupled with external depreciation pressures, the exchange rate has exhibited excessive volatility since 2018.

The volatility of Bitcoin price and volume surged during the same period. The Bitcoin price skyrocketed first, ending the year of 2017 with a historical high price at 19,891.99 USD. It was then followed by a plunge in 2018, its 10th anniversary, touching a low point at just over 3000 USD before a more gradual rebound in 2019. The Bitcoin trade

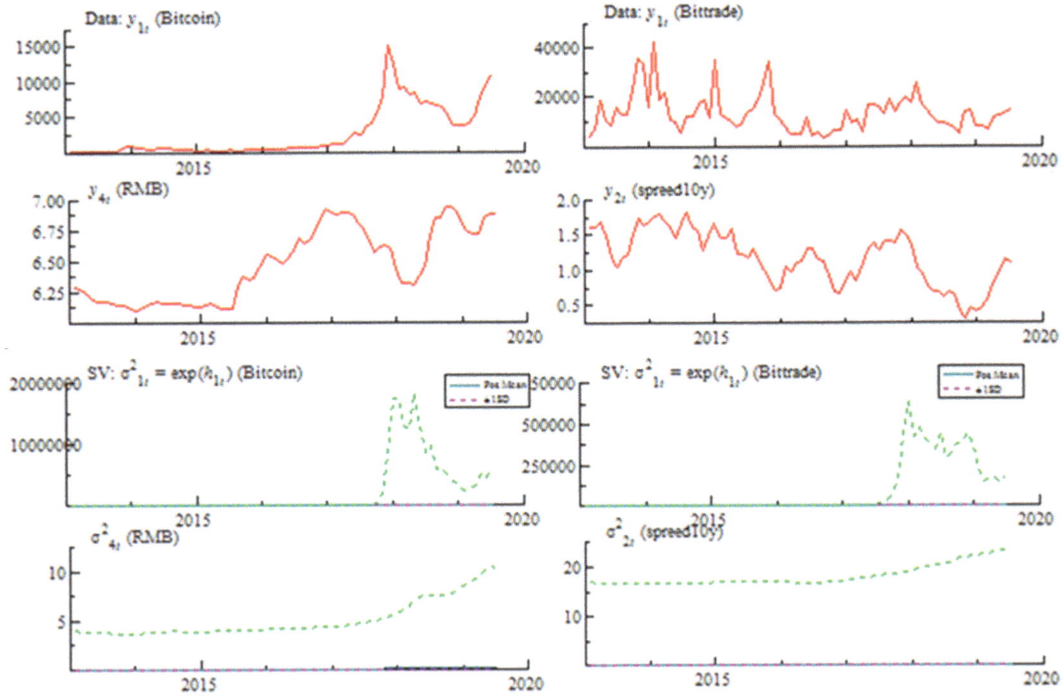

Fig. 4.4 MCMC simulation results of selected volatilities over time

volume followed a similar pattern but maintained a longer period of high volatility after the peak.

4.5.2 Impulse Response Functions

Note that responses of an impulse vary over the analysis time (periods after the shock), and TVP-VAR models can generate different impulse response functions (IRFs) over historical time. This chapter presents the IRFs in two ways: (i) selected IRFs at a specific analysis time over the complete historical time; and (ii) complete IRFs at specific points in historical time over the complete analysis time.

Figure 4.5 shows the time-varying responses of the Bitcoin price to various shocks. We select three analysis times of the IRFs (1, 3, and 5 periods after the shocks). The magnitude (absolute value) of the responses diminishes over analysis time for all three shocks. There are two clear features of the IRFs. First, the interest rate spread imposes a positive effect on Bitcoin price, while exchange rate inflicts a negative effect. Second, over the sample period, the effects of interest rate spread on Bitcoin price have been weakened, especially between 2013 to 2015. This process coincided with the reform of Chinese exchange rate management. Other IRFs are maintained relatively stable.

The positive effect of interest rate spread on Bitcoin price suggests that Bitcoin has a feature of "de-dollarization." A higher spread ($\equiv$ US interest rate minus China interest rate) leads to two effects. First, as conventional wisdom of international finance suggests, an interest rate hike by the Fed leads to appreciation of dollar-denominated assets because they become more appealing to yield-seeking investors. Second, the Bitcoin price tends to rise according to the IRF. Therefore, Bitcoin and dollar-denominated assets behave similarly (as competing investments). Similarly, the negative effect of exchange rate on Bitcoin price implies that Bitcoin has a feature of "de-renminbization" as well. A higher exchange rate ($\equiv$ price of 1 USD in terms of CNY) leads to two effects. On the one hand, a higher exchange rate of USD/CNY means a depreciation of CNY or renminbi (the alternative name of CNY). On the other

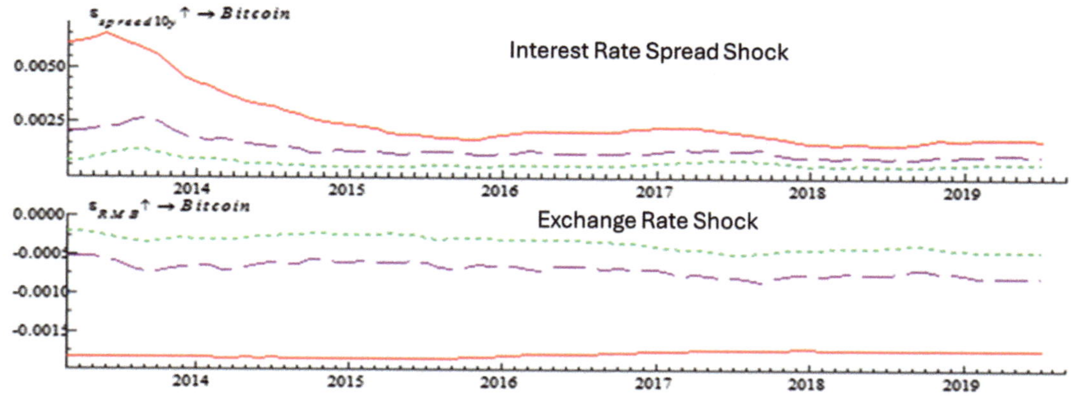

Fig. 4.5 IRFs of Bitcoin price over the complete historical time

hand, a higher exchange rate leads to a lower Bitcoin price according to the IRF. So, Bitcoin and renminbi-denominated assets behave similarly (as competing investments). Thus, Bitcoin exerts a challenge to both fiat currencies, which we refer to "de-fiatization."

Figure 4.6 shows the IRFs of Bitcoin trading volume. Again, the deviation from the steady state diminishes over time after the shock. There are two other features shown in the IRFs. First, both effects are positive on Bitcoin trading volume. Second, the magnitude of IRFs maintains stable over the sample period, but the interest rate spread has a greater effect than exchange rate. The effects on the Bitcoin volume reinforce the conclusion of de-fiatization feature of cryptocurrencies.

A positive effect of US-China interest rate spread on Bitcoin volume suggests that a greater divergence in monetary policy promotes trading activities in the crypto market. When monetary policies in the two largest economies run in opposite directions (e.g., the interest rate hike by the Fed), it raises the uncertainties in the financial market because it is not stable outside the "comfort zone." In this case, Bitcoin, as a decentralized currency, gains greater value, which has an effect of de-dollarization. Similarly, a positive effect of USD/CNY exchange rate on Bitcoin volume suggests that a devaluation of renminbi renders the market attention to Bitcoin too. This is an effect of de-renminbization. Therefore, both fiat currencies lost to the cryptocurrency, reinforcing the conclusion of de-fiatization.

To paint a more complete dynamic path of IRFs, we select three meaningful points in historical time and show the effects over complete analysis time. The three points are:

- Time 1 (T1): 2013M12. This time is featured by a low level of Bitcoin trading volume and a high level of interest rate spread caused by a monetary expansion in the US including quantitative easing.
- Time 2 (T2): 2018M2. This time is featured by high volatilities of Bitcoin price and a medium level of interest rate spread caused by monetary tightening in the US and the monetary independence movement in China. This period is within the "comfort zone" and is right before the start of the US-China trade war in 2018.
- Time 3 (T3): 2019M5. This time is featured by a surging level of Bitcoin price and a "comfort zone" level of US-China monetary policy difference. But this is a period of recovery and convergence. Bitcoin price rebounded from a big dip and the US-China policy deviations have re-converged to the "comfort zone."

As shown in Fig. 4.7, the positive effects of interest rate spread on Bitcoin price decrease from T1 to T2 but is not significantly different between T2 and T3. This is in line with the feature shown in the previous time-varying IRFs, which suggest a cutting point around 2016. The peak of the response is one period after the shock and the

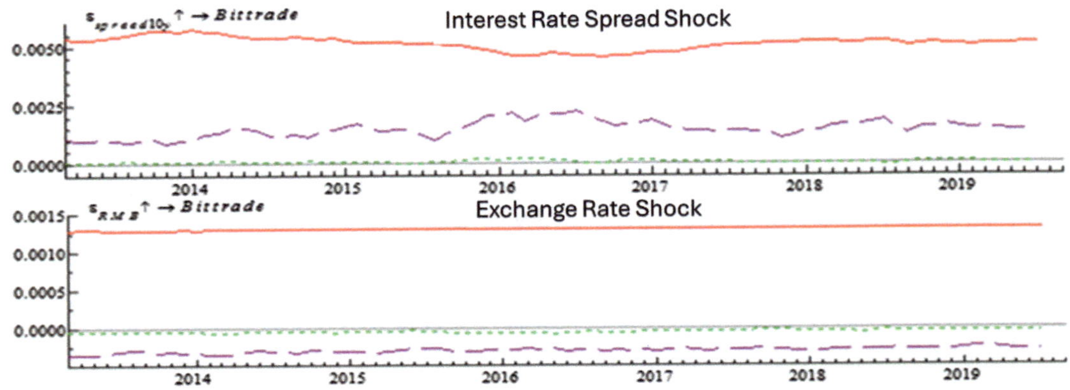

Fig. 4.6 IRFs of Bitcoin volume over the complete historical time

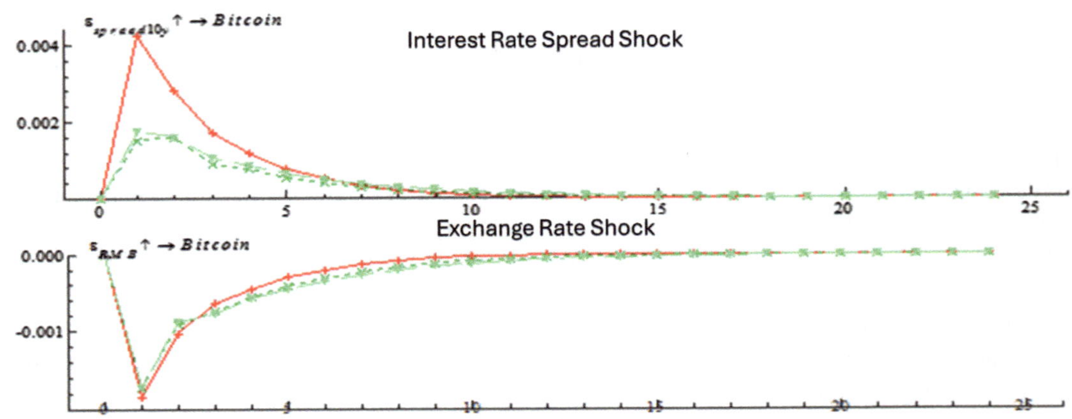

Fig. 4.7 IRFs of Bitcoin price over the complete analysis time

half-life effect is about three periods. In contrast, the negative effects of the exchange rate on the Bitcoin price do not change much over the sample period, again consistent with the earlier findings. The timing of peak effect and half-life of exchange rate shocks rhymes with that of interest rate spread shocks.

Figure 4.8 plots the IRFs of Bitcoin volume at the three historical points in time (T1, T2, T3). The timing of peak effects is the same for interest rate spread and exchange rate (one period after the shock). It is also shown that both effects are stable over the sample period and both IRFs are oscillatory. Oscillation occurs because Bitcoin has more speculative movements in the market, so overshooting behavior of prices and volume is a common phenomenon.

4.6 Conclusion

By introducing cryptocurrency into a two-country open-economy model, this study deduces the functional relationship among interest rate spread, exchange rate, and cryptocurrency transactions. The empirical analysis employs the Bayesian TVP-VAR model to capture the time variation of coefficients and volatilities. The key finding is that Bitcoin has an effect of de-fiatization. When there is a higher divergence in monetary policy between the US and China, Bitcoin attracts greater attention with a higher price, posing a competing force against USD. When there are greater fluctuations in the exchange rate of USD/CNY, investors are

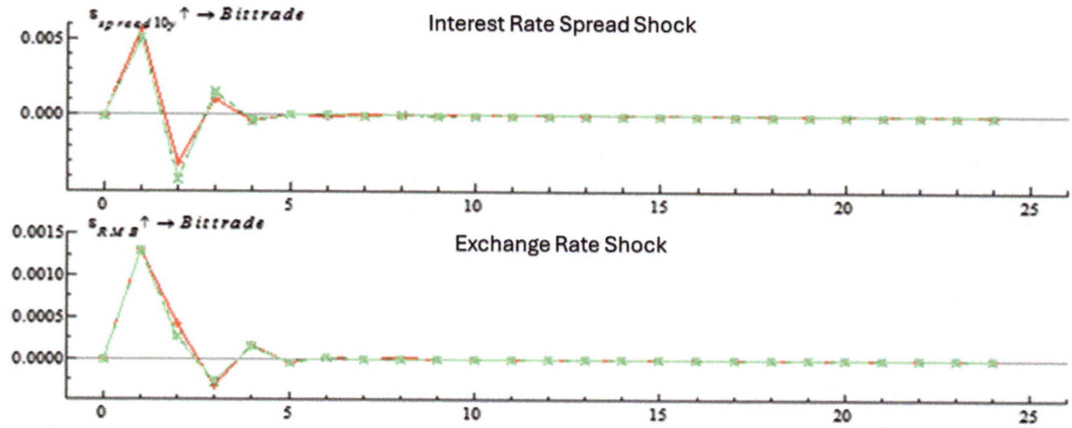

Fig. 4.8 IRFs of Bitcoin volume over the complete analysis time

diverted from CNY to Bitcoin. The fiat currencies of the two largest economies are losers while Bitcoin gains. Therefore, cryptocurrency not only decentralizes the role of commercial banks as a medium of payment but also decentralizes the role of central banks as a monetary policymaker.

However, in the empirical analysis, we find that Bitcoin price has excessive volatility which suggests that it is prone to artificial manipulation of "whale traders." In many cases, the trading volume shrinks after a surge in price, which is a common indicator of manipulation in traditional centralized trading platforms. As a result, a decentralized currency is still subject to centralized attacks which limit the potential of cryptocurrencies in the international payment system. As the crypto market plunged in 2022M5 (due to the event of Terra Luna), the market entered the "crypto winter." There is still a long way for cryptocurrencies to play an influential role in parallel with fiat currencies. Based on the findings, we draw three policy implications.

First, blockchain technology is a promising solution to trust, which is not necessarily limited to cryptocurrency. Commercial banks and central banks can benefit from adopting blockchain to improve efficiency and trust in financial services as well. For example, Nasdaq announced that it would start issuing, cataloguing, and managing transactions of their privately issued shares through blockchain technology in 2015. The first blockchain-based digital fiat currency, Digital Yuan, was issued by China's central bank in 2021. IBM recently developed blockchain-based solutions to transform the process of proof in traditional insurance such as healthcare, vehicle, and catastrophe (Zhou & Zhang, 2025). In summary, decentralized and traditional currencies and finance compete with each other, inspire each other, and co-evolve with each other.

Second, the biggest challenge to policymakers is to develop timely regulations to keep up with the development in cryptocurrency. The high volatility of cryptocurrency and its spillover effects create uncertainties to financial stability. As a multi-trillion market, it is hard to ignore cryptoassets and their effects on the financial system, the monetary system, and the economic system. Let alone the social and legal problems it may cause such as cybersecurity, privacy, and money laundering. This is not a country specific challenge though. As we have seen in the impulse responses, the USD also faces the same (maybe even bigger) challenge from cryptocurrency. Given that cryptocurrency is borderless and authority-less, it calls for international collaborations in regulatory effort.

Third, the de-fiatization effect of cryptocurrency not only decentralizes the old economic order but also decentralizes the old political order. The international monetary system has not changed much since 1973 when the Bretton Woods System collapsed. The rise of cryptocurrency since 2008 seems to start a possibility of a revolutionary era but the full potential is yet to be revealed. After all, the traditional US-led global financial system is still the dominating institution. Regional development (e.g., EU, RCEP) has already shaken the role of USD in trade. Global ambitions such as Bitcoin and Ethereum weaken the dominance of USD in the international financial market even more. Recent geopolitical conflicts between Russia and the West also promote the role of cryptocurrencies in the international payment system to surpass financial sanctions (Zhou & Guo, 2025). Along with this trend, other fiat currencies are facing greater opportunities if they can grasp the market gaps ripped open by cryptocurrencies.

References

Barrdear, J., & Kumhof, M. (2022). The macroeconomics of central bank digital currencies. *Journal of Economic Dynamics and Control, 142*, Article 104148.

Bjerg, O. (2016). How is Bitcoin Money? *Theory, Culture & Society, 33*(1), 53–72.

Dyhrberg, A. H. (2016). Bitcoin, gold and the dollar – A GARCH volatility analysis. *Finance Research Letters, 16*, 85–92.

Georgiadis, G. (2015). Examining asymmetries in the transmission of monetary policy in the euro area: Evidence from a mixed cross-section global VAR model. *European Economic Review, 75*, 195–215.

Glaser, F., Zimmermann, K., Haferkorn, M., Weber, M. C., & Siering, M. (2014). Bitcoin – asset or currency? Revealing users' hidden intentions. *EFL Quarterly: An E-Finance Lab Publication, 2014*(3), 4–5.

Guo, D., & Zhou, P. (2021). The rise of a new anchor currency in RCEP? A tale of three currencies. *Economic Modelling, 104*, Article 105647.

Guo, D., & Zhou, P. (2023). The evolution of financial market infrastructure: From digitalization to Tokenization. *International Journal of Innovation and Entrepreneurship, 2*(1), 2.

Kristoufek, L. (2015). What are the main drivers of the Bitcoin price? Evidence from wavelet coherence analysis. *PLoS ONE, 10*(4), Article e0123923.

Miranda-Agrippino, S., & Rey, H. (2022). The Global Financial Cycle. In G. Gopinath, E. Helpman & K. Rogoff (Eds.), *Handbook of international economics* (pp. 1–43). Elsevier.

Nakajima, J. (2011). Time-varying parameter VAR model with stochastic volatility: An overview of methodology and empirical applications. *Monetary and Economic Studies*, 107–142.

Nakamoto, S. (2008). Bitcoin: A peer-to-peer electronic cash system. *Decentralized Business Review*, 21260.

Pesaran, M. H., Til, S., & Weiner, S. M. (2004). Modeling regional interdependencies using a global error-correcting macroeconometric model. *Journal of Business & Economic Statistics, 22*(2), 129–162.

Primiceri, G. E. (2005). Time varying structural vector autoregressions and monetary policy. *The Review of Economic Studies, 72*(3), 821–852.

Raskin, M., & Yermack, D. (2018). Digital currencies, decentralized ledgers and the future of central banking. In P. Conti-Brown & R. Lastra (Eds.), *Research handbook on central banking* (pp. 474–486). Edward Elgar Publishing.

Slawotsky, J. (2020). US financial hegemony: The Digital Yuan and Risks of Dollar De-Weaponization. *Fordham International Law Journal, 44*(1), 39–100.

Wei, H., Tu, Y., & Zhou, P. (2023). Technical barriers to trade and export performance: Comparing exiting and staying firms. *Economic Modelling, 126*, Article 106439.

Yin, W., Wu, F., Zhou, P., & Kirkulak-Uludag, B. (2025). Exploring resilience in the cryptocurrency market: Risk transmission and network robustness. *International Review of Financial Analysis, 106*, Article 104546.

Zhang, B., & Zhou, P. (2021). Financial development and economic growth in a microfounded small open economy model. *The North American Journal of Economics and Finance, 58*, Article 101544.

Zhou, P., & Guo, D. (2025). Sanctions, Co-Sanctions, and Counter-Sanctions: A multilateral, evolutionary game among three global powers. *Defence and Peace Economics, 36*(1), 60–85.

Zhou, P., & Zhang, Y. (2025). Major conundrums and possible solutions in DeFi Insurance. *International Journal of Finance and Economics*. https://doi.org/10.1002/ijfe.3154

5 Trade Sanctions and Financial Sanctions

Abstract

Financial sanctions have replaced trade sanctions as the main economic weapon in contemporary political conflicts. Focusing on the US-Russia confrontation since 2014, we contrast financial with trade sanctions, trace their macro-financial transmission, and assess Russia's responses. A synthetic control counterfactual shows that sanctions lowered Russia's per capita output, while a TVP-VAR links the shock to successive waves: an immediate hit to expectations, a sharp ruble fall, capital flight, and later contraction of the sovereign-bond market that raised borrowing costs. Russia tried to blunt these blows by trimming USD reserves, building domestic payment and settlement platforms, and encouraging ruble invoicing. These steps softened—but did not reverse—the drag; growth remains subdued and financial vulnerabilities linger. The evidence suggests three lessons for countries exposed to similar pressure: diversify reserve currencies, foster deep local capital markets and payment networks, and run regular stress tests to prepare for sudden funding shocks. For sanctioning coalitions, the study warns that aggressive financial measures can spill over to the wider system and provoke costly retaliation. Ultimately, lasting security is more likely to arise from negotiated accommodation than from escalating economic coercion.

Keywords

Trade sanction · Financial sanction

Classification

SDG16 · SDG17

5.1 Introduction

The most frequently utilized tool in traditional economic warfare is trade sanctions, which aim to impede trade between the sanctioned party and other countries through methods such as trade blockades. The goal is to cause economic pressure and harm to the sanctionee's trade interests. However, academic research and historical analysis indicate that traditional trade sanctions have been largely ineffective (Peksen, 2019). As a result, economic warfare has shifted toward the use of "smart sanctions" which are more targeted and efficient (Drezner, 2011). Smart sanctions add a substantial cost of shielding (Ahn & Ludema, 2020). Financial sanctions, in particular, have emerged as a prominent form of smart sanctions in the competition between major powers. Countries like Russia, Iran, North Korea, Venezuela, and Syria have been financially sanctioned by the US and EU since 2010.

Compared with trade sanctions, financial sanctions differ in nature, objective, impact, scope, and legality. First, trade sanctions involve restrictions

D. Guo and P. Zhou, *Beating Financial Swords into Developmental Plowshares*, Sustainable Development Goals Series, https://doi.org/10.1007/978-981-95-5152-1_5

on trade and commerce between the sanctioning country and the target country. This can take the form of trade embargoes, quotas, or tariffs. Financial sanctions, on the other hand, involve the use of economic tools, such as freezing assets, banning financial transactions, or restricting access to financial markets. Second, the main objective of trade sanctions is to restrict the target country's access to international trade and commerce, which can lead to economic hardship and political pressure. The objective of financial sanctions is to restrict the target country's access to the global financial system, which can also lead to economic hardship and political pressure. Third, trade sanctions have a direct impact on the target country's economy and can lead to reduced trade and investment, inflation, and economic hardship. Financial sanctions have an indirect impact and can lead to reduced access to credit and investment, inflation, and economic hardship. Fourth, trade sanctions are often applied to specific sectors or industries, such as arms trade, oil, or luxury goods. Financial sanctions can be more broadly applied to target financial institutions, specific individuals or entities, or even entire countries. Finally, trade sanctions are subject to international trade laws and may require authorization from international organizations such as the WTO. Financial sanctions are often implemented unilaterally by individual countries or groups of countries without the need for international legal authorization.

There has been a vast literature on the effects of sanctions, but research on sanctions rarely considers the perspective of the sanctionee. Sanctions and anti-sanctions are strategically interdependent. In this chapter, we first provide a narrative summary of the historical evolution of the US-Russia case. Then, we use macro-level and micro-level evidence to identify the transmission mechanisms of sanctions and anti-sanctions. Drawing on the empirical findings, we evaluate the time-varying effectiveness of smart sanctions and propose countermeasures that a sanctioned country could adopt.

5.2 History

Economic wars have been a part of human history for centuries, but nature and scope have evolved over time. During the age of mercantilism (sixteenth–eighteenth centuries), European powers engaged in economic wars to establish monopolies over overseas colonies and trade routes. The goal was to accumulate as much wealth as possible by exporting more goods than importing, and by limiting the ability of other countries to compete. Entering the nineteenth century, many countries adopted protectionist policies to protect their domestic industries from foreign competition. Economic wars during this period were characterized by tariffs, quotas, and other trade barriers that made it difficult for other countries to export goods. In the late nineteenth and early twentieth centuries, economic wars took on a new dimension with the rise of imperialism. European powers competed for control over territories and resources, leading to the exploitation of colonies for their raw materials and labor. The late twentieth century saw the rise of globalization, which led to increased economic interdependence between countries. Economic wars during this period have focused on issues such as intellectual property rights, currency manipulation, and unfair trade practices. In recent years, economic wars have become more complex and multi-dimensional. Countries have used a variety of tools such as sanctions, cyberattacks, and diplomatic pressure to advance their economic interests. Additionally, the emergence of new economic powers such as China and India have challenged the dominance of traditional powers like the US and Europe.

Economic sanctions are a tool used by countries to exert pressure on other countries, organizations, or individuals by restricting their access to trade, finance, or other economic resources. Economic sanctions have been used throughout history, from the ancient Greeks who imposed trade embargoes on certain city-states to the Roman Empire that used trade restrictions as a means of political control. In the nineteenth century, European powers imposed economic blockades on each other during times of war. The League of Nations, established after WW1, created a framework for international cooperation and sanctions. Economic sanctions were used to punish countries that violated international law or committed acts of aggression, such as the sanctions imposed on Italy after its invasion of Ethiopia in 1935. During the Cold War, economic sanctions were used as a tool of containment against the Soviet Union and its allies. The US and its allies imposed economic sanctions on the Soviet Union, Cuba, and other communist countries, while the Soviet Union and its allies imposed sanctions on the US and its allies. In the post-Cold War era, economic sanctions were used in response to a wide range of issues, from human rights violations to nuclear proliferation. The US and its allies have imposed sanctions on countries such as Iran and North Korea, while Russia has used economic sanctions against countries such as Ukraine and Turkey. Economic sanctions have become increasingly sophisticated in the modern era. They can be targeted at specific individuals or entities, rather than entire countries. They can also be imposed by non-state actors, such as international organizations, and can include measures such as asset freezes and travel bans. In recent years, economic sanctions have become a more prominent tool of foreign policy, with countries using them to achieve a wide range of objectives. Nevertheless, they can also have unintended consequences, such as harming the civilian population of target countries and damaging the global economy.

Specifically, financial sanctions are a type of economic sanction that targets an individual, organization, or country's financial system, often by freezing assets or restricting financial transactions. The use of financial sanctions can be traced back to ancient times, where leaders would impose embargoes on trade and financial transactions with rival cities or nations. In the Middle Ages, monarchs often imposed taxes or levies on foreign traders to restrict their access to local markets. During WW1, countries imposed financial sanctions on each other, including asset freezes and trade embargoes. The US, for example, prohibited all financial transactions with Germany in 1917. During WW2, the US and its allies imposed financial sanctions on Japan, including an embargo on oil exports, which ultimately led to Japan's attack on Pearl Harbor. The Allies also froze the assets of Nazi leaders and their collaborators after the war. During the Cold War, the US and its allies imposed financial sanctions on the Soviet Union and its allies. These sanctions included freezing assets, restricting access to capital markets, and banning technology transfers. In the post-Cold War era, financial sanctions became a more prominent tool of foreign policy. The US and its allies have imposed financial sanctions on countries such as Iran, North Korea, and Russia for a variety of reasons, including terrorism, nuclear proliferation, and human rights violations. In the modern era, financial sanctions have become more sophisticated and targeted. They can be imposed on specific individuals or entities, rather than entire countries, and can include measures such as restricting access to correspondent banking, prohibiting certain types of financial transactions, and freezing assets. Overall, financial sanctions have become an increasingly important tool of foreign policy, and their use has evolved over time to become more targeted and sophisticated.

Due to the unique role of the US in the international monetary and financial system, it can impose asymmetric financial sanctions, such as blocking Swift access for some Russian banks. However, Russia lacks similar countermeasures to impose against the US. As a result, financial sanctions have become an increasingly popular foreign policy for the US. To summarize, there are mainly five forms of financial sanctions.

i. Asset freezes: This involves freezing the assets of individuals or entities, such as bank accounts, investments, and property. This can prevent them from accessing their funds and can limit their ability to conduct financial transactions.
ii. Transaction restrictions: This involves limiting or prohibiting certain financial transactions, such as wire transfers, currency exchanges, and trade finance. This can

prevent individuals or entities from engaging in specific types of business activities.

iii. Correspondent banking restrictions: This involves restricting access to correspondent banking relationships, which are necessary for banks to conduct international transactions. This can limit a country's ability to access the global financial system and can make it more difficult to conduct international trade.

iv. Sectoral sanctions: This involves targeting specific sectors of a country's economy, such as the energy or financial sectors, with sanctions. This can restrict access to financing and technology and can limit a country's ability to develop these sectors.

v. Export/import restrictions: This involves restricting or prohibiting the import or export of certain goods, such as weapons or technology, to or from a country. This can limit a country's ability to trade and can impact its economy.

The competition between the sanctions and anti-sanctions of major powers in the case of Russia is seen as one of the most representative examples of the use of financial sanctions and anti-sanctions in the modern era. In March 2014, following the annexation of Crimea by Russia, the US and EU imposed the first round of sanctions against Russian officials and individuals close to the Russian president, Vladimir Putin. Subsequently, several rounds of sanctions were imposed, targeting Russia's economy, energy sector, financial institutions, and defense industry. The sanctions have had a significant impact on Russia's economy, contributing to the decline in its GDP and causing inflation and economic hardship. In response, Russia has implemented its own countermeasures, including import bans on certain Western goods and restrictions on the activities of Western companies in Russia. Since the outbreak of the Ukraine war in 2022, various economic sanctions have been used in conjunction with military support by the West. The actions and reactions of the sanctioner (US/EU) and the sanctionee (Russia) continue to this day. A timeline of the sanctions against Russia is summarized in Fig. 5.1.

The financial sanctions to Russia have two features: extensive coverage and currency localization. On the one hand, the scope of financial sanctions has been extended to wider individuals, entities, industries, and countries. Initially, the US sanctions only directly applied to the Russian economy—US citizens are prohibited from engaging in sanction-related transactions with Russian companies. In the next stage, secondary sanctions are introduced to penalize non-US individuals, entities, or countries that engage in business or other transactions with Russia. These sanctions are intended to deter foreign actors from doing business with the target country or entity by cutting off their access to the US financial system and market. In the case of Russia, examples of secondary sanctions include CAATSA (Countering America's Adversaries Through Sanctions Act) Section 231, Section 242, and Executive Order 13,883. These provisions authorize the US government to impose sanctions on individuals or entities that engage in significant transactions with Russia's defense and intelligence sectors. They have been used to impose sanctions on entities in countries such as China, India, and Turkey that have purchased Russian military equipment.

On the other hand, currency localization restricts the use of foreign currencies, particularly USD, in transactions and financing activities involving Russian companies or individuals that are subject to sanctions. For example, the US financial sanctions against Russia's treasury bonds took effect on June 14, 2021. After that time, US companies were barred from buying Russian government bonds (denominated in rubles), but Russian government bonds can be traded in the secondary market (the "government bond restriction sanction"). This is a typical smart sanction, which belongs to the fourth category of financial sanctions measures in the US ("ban the global financial institutions from doing business with the targeted parties").

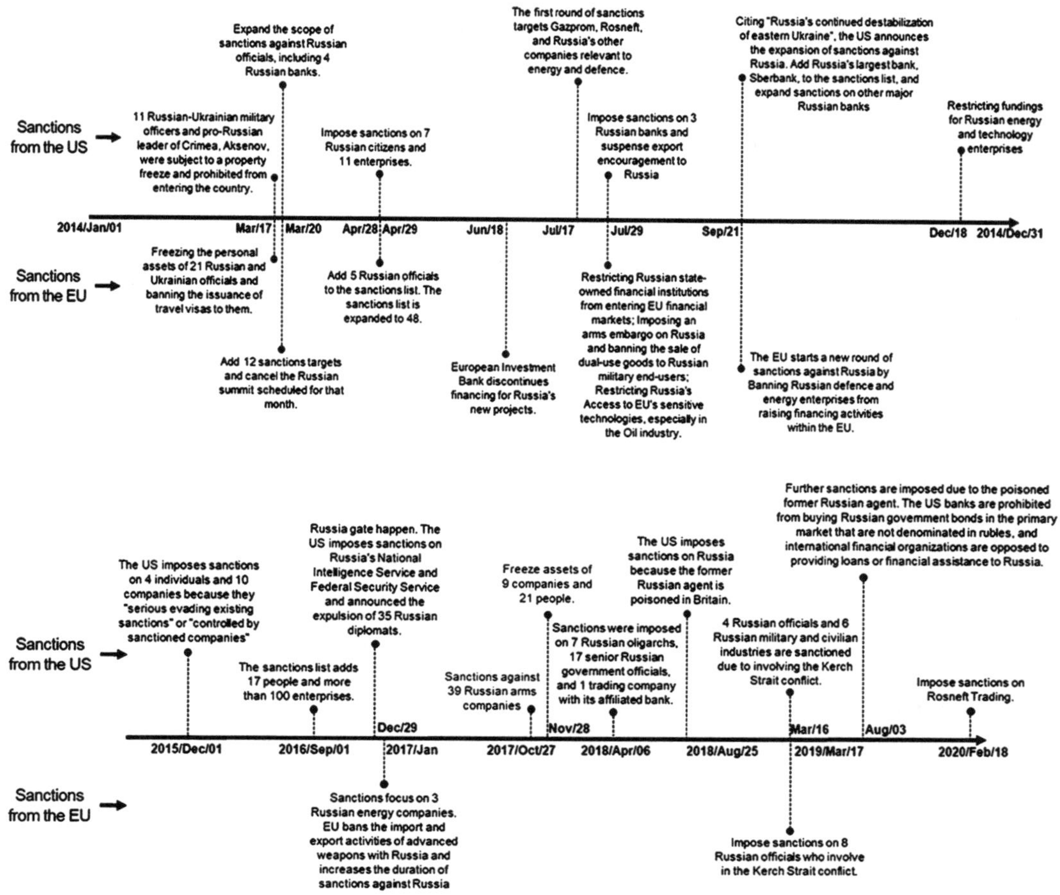

Fig. 5.1 Timeline of financial sanctions to Russia (2014–2020)

5.3 Empirical Analysis

The sanctions to Russia have lasted for about a decade by now, the intensity and extensity have been changing constantly. It provides a good dataset for evaluating the effect of sanctions on the economy. The aim of the paper is to quantitatively evaluate the time-varying effect of sanctions taking into account both sanctions and anti-sanctions. The empirics are featured with a mixed-method approach. First, we quantify the impact of financial sanctions on GDP per capita using the synthetic control method proposed by Abadie and Gardeazabal (2003). Second, we analyze the impact of sanctions on financial stability using the TVP-VAR model considering strategic dependencies between sanctions and anti-sanctions. Finally, based on macro and micro evidence, we discuss possible countermeasures from the sanctionee's perspective.

5.3.1 The Synthetic Control Method

Following Abadie and Gardeazabal (2003), we select Slovakia, Cyprus, Lithuania, Serbia, Saudi Arabia, and other seven Eastern European countries to build a "synthetic Russia" and then set economic development indicators to compare the "synthetic Russia" that is not sanctioned with the "real Russia" that is sanctioned.

In Fig. 5.2, we use the difference in GDP per capita between the "real Russia" and the "synthetic Russia" to measure the effect of financial sanctions. Before 2014, the difference was close to

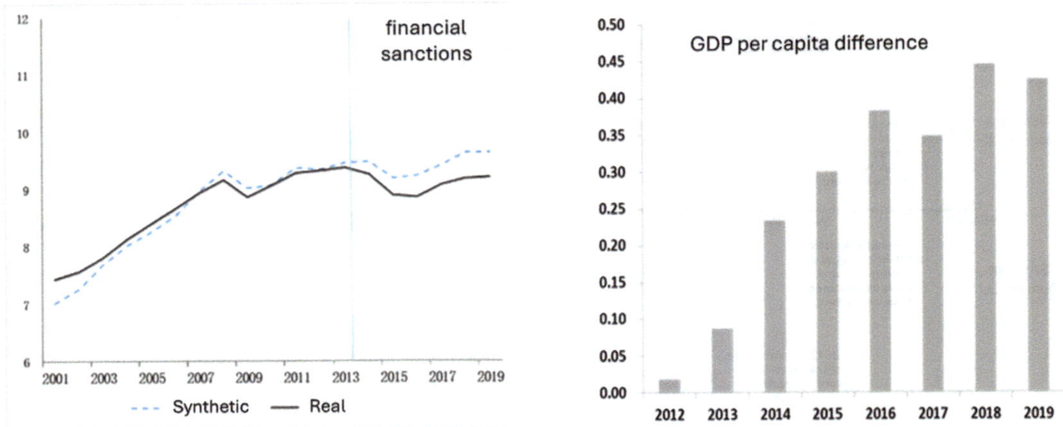

Fig. 5.2 GDP differences between the "synthetic Russia" and the "real Russia"

0. After the Ukraine crisis in 2014, the difference became negative, implying the negative impact of financial sanctions on the Russian economy. The cumulative effect of financial sanctions shows an increasing trend.

Despite the adverse effects on the Russian economy, sanctions also stimulated Russian patriotism. As a result, sanctions not only failed to change Russia's position on the Crimea issue, but also helped Putin's government consolidate public opinion support rates. In response to the US sanctions, Russia has implemented a series of anti-sanction measures. The first measure is to provide government support to sanctioned institutions, such as introducing foreign currency repurchase agreements to provide foreign currency financing for its financial institutions. The second measure is to reduce the proportion of USD-denominated assets in international reserves, such as selling US treasury bonds and increasing the use of local currencies in international trade. The third measure is to develop a Russia-led international payment system, such as establishing a Russian national payment card system and attempting to create a Swift-like financial information transmission system.

The effectiveness of the anti-sanctions can be measured by the changing speed of sanctions' effect or the difference in differences. We use the change of log difference of GDP per capita between the "synthetic Russia" and the "real Russia" to reflect the change in sanction effects. As shown in Fig. 5.3, the difference has an increasing trend at the beginning of the sanction (2014–2015). After 2015, the change significantly decreased, with a trend of convergence to zero. It shows that Russia's anti-sanctions achieve good results as countermeasures. The weakening sanction effect is partly due to the opinion discrepancies between the US and the EU as well as among EU members regarding whether and how to impose sanctions on Russia.

5.3.2 The TVP-VAR Model

There are both macro and micro strategic objectives in financial sanctions: the former aims to restrict the financial facilities of sanctioned countries by "blocking" their financing ability in both local and foreign currencies. The macro-objective is to dismantle the financial system and induce financial turmoil in the targeted countries (such as capital flight, market collapse, etc.), ultimately destabilizing their economic system and affecting people's livelihoods. Existing research in this area primarily focuses on the quantitative analysis of macro-objectives but lacks consideration of micro-objectives.

We assess financial stability by monitoring changes in national debt, exchange rates, and inflation indices. We designate the term interest rate as

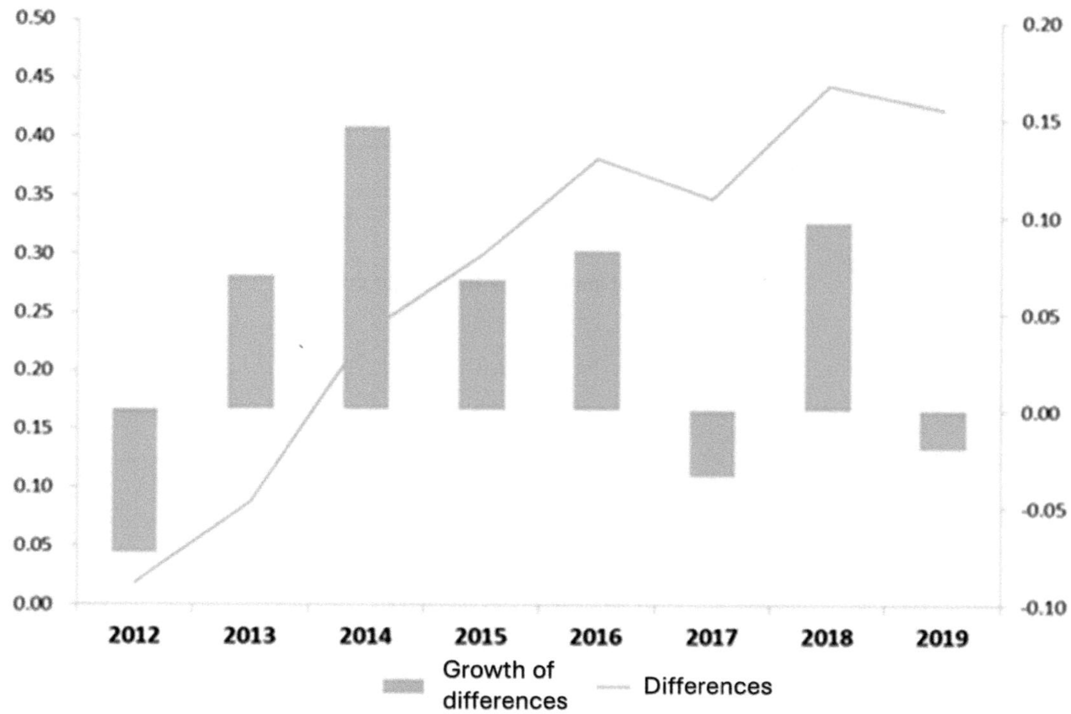

Fig. 5.3 Change of log difference of GDP per capita

the national debt index, assuming that financial sanctions disrupt financial markets, thereby influencing changes in the shape of the national debt benchmark curve. Additionally, considering the timing of multiple rounds of sanctions imposed by the US and Europe, we create a dummy variable for financial sanctions as the exogenous shock.

In Fig. 5.4, we select the concentrated sanctions period in 2014, the period of relative easing of sanctions in 2015, and the period of strengthened sanctions in 2018 as representative shock events. The impact of financial sanctions on the value of the ruble is significantly stronger than that on national debt and CPI indicators. This result can be attributed to two reasons: first, financial sanctions have a notable effect on price-based micro-indicators, reflecting the high efficiency of their "precision strike" capability; second, price-based indicators are greatly influenced by market expectations.

Consequently, financial sanctions have the potential to destabilize financial markets by influencing market expectations. In cases where countermeasures against sanctions are ineffective, the excessive panic induced by financial sanctions can lead to greater turmoil than initially anticipated by the market. This phenomenon is known as the "leverage effect" of financial sanctions, wherein irrational market sentiment exacerbates the impact of financial sanctions, amplifying market panic and resulting in leverage within financial markets.

The time-varying changes in exchange rates and government bonds exhibit opposite trends. Exchange rate changes peaked in the early stages of sanctions in 2014, followed by a significant continuous weakening of growth rates from 2014 to 2015. Subsequently, there was a continuous decrease until reaching a nadir in 2016. This phenomenon can be explained by the following reasons.

First, according to the theory of market expectations, the initial stage of financial sanctions (prior to 2015) prompted investors to panic-sell, particularly leading to the withdrawal of cross-border funds. Notably, the reaction speed of cross-border funds exceeded that of the foreign exchange market. Furthermore, as Russia adopted anti-sanction measures, the market gradually

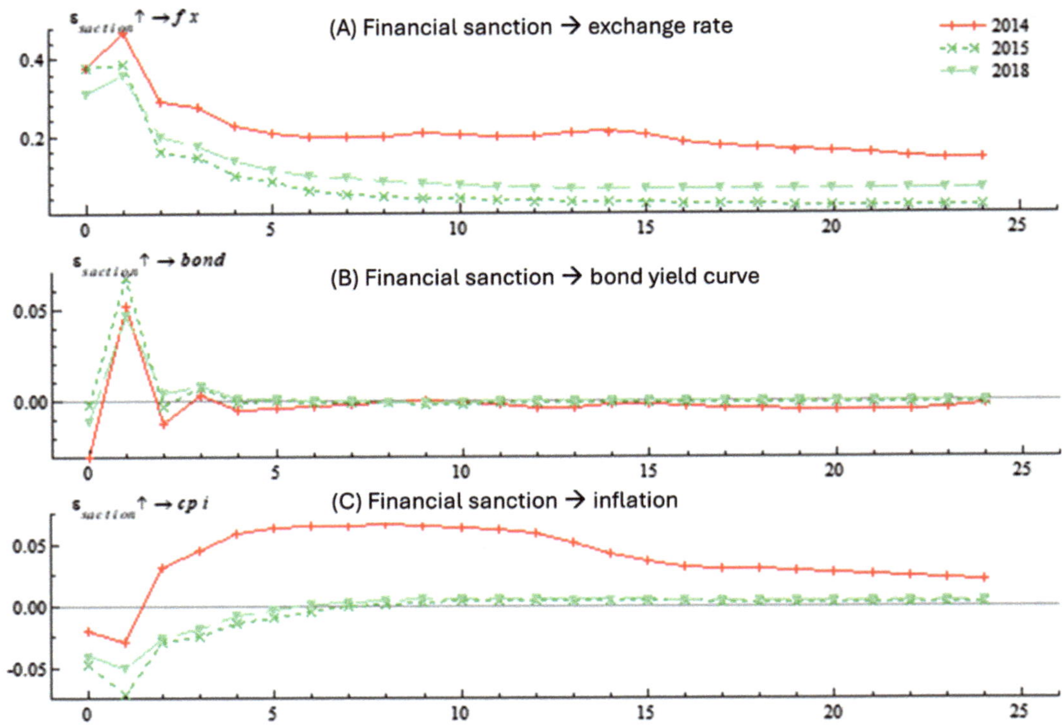

Fig. 5.4 Time-varying impulse response functions

shifted from excessive panic to rationality, thereby slowing down the adverse effects of sanctions.

Second, during the period of 2015–2016, the strengthening of financial sanctions primarily impacted the Russian bond market itself. The Russian bond market, characterized by its limited size and a significant proportion of treasury bonds, experienced a notable decline in issuance following sanctions imposed by the US and EU. Consequently, changes in short-term issuance and reductions in bond size heightened investor price sensitivity. For instance, decreased issuance of new bonds made it easier for existing bonds to reflect impulsive impacts.

Third, the impact of sanctions on the Russian bond market steadily diminished from 2016 until the early stages of the COVID-19 pandemic. As depicted in Fig. 5.5, after the financial sanctions in 2014, the issuance of Russian treasury bonds sharply declined. Although issuance rebounded in 2015, it remained below pre-sanction levels. This decline in Russian treasury bond issuance during 2014–2016 alleviated the impact of withdrawn cross-border funds. Moreover, issuance significantly increased and surpassed pre-sanction levels in 2017, indicating the effectiveness of Russia's anti-sanction measures. Specifically, Russia bolstered both economic and trade usage of the ruble's sovereign currency, thereby converting restricted international money financing into domestic market financing. Consequently, investment institutions absorbed sharp increases in issuance, showcasing the resilience of the Russian bond market to the crisis.

Based on the impacts of US financial sanctions on the Russian bond market, we identify the following key characteristics of modern financial sanctions. Financial sanctions have emerged as new tools to replace the "hot and cold war" dynamics among major powers' conflicts. Given the US's hegemony in the current international monetary system, it possesses a significant asymmetric advantage, facilitating the implementation of such "smart sanctions." US financial sanctions employ various approaches, often adopting a combination strategy that can inflict multi-channel simultaneous impacts and damage on targeted

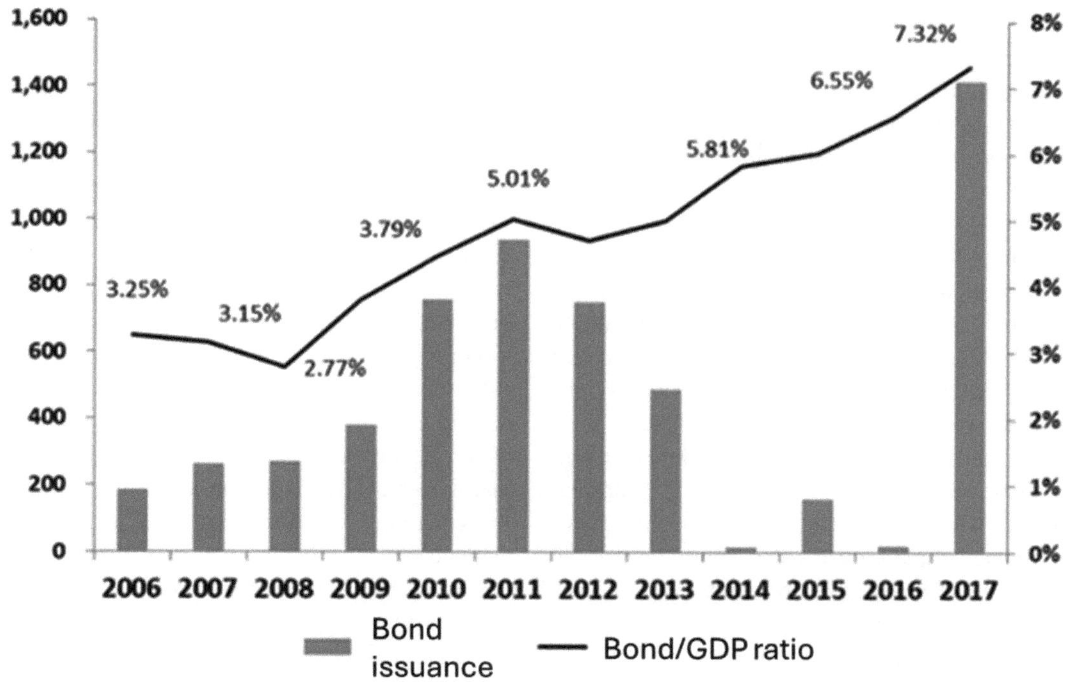

Fig. 5.5 Impacts of financial sanctions on Russian bond market

countries. In the context of globalization, financial sanctions are likely to become the new normal "war pattern" preceding localized conflicts.

There is a trend of financial sanctions expanding in scope and encompassing local currencies. Since 2014, US financial sanctions against Russia have escalated from level one to level two, extending jurisdiction to third countries. Consequently, the core element of financial sanctions no longer solely revolves around international currencies like the US dollar. Instead, they aim to block Russia's external financing and launch a "precise attack" on its treasury bonds, directly impacting Russia's sovereign money market.

Finally, modern financial sanctions exert both macro and micro impacts on the market. Macro assessments reveal the cumulative negative effects of financial sanctions, yet effective anti-sanctions measures can mitigate their impact. Financial sanctions exert long-term inhibitory effects on the economic growth of targeted countries, as evidenced by Russia's sluggish growth rates or even negative growth. Effective anti-sanctions measures can slow down the deterioration of the economy. At the micro level, financial sanctions follow a price-based path of financial stability destruction, triggering panic that amplifies their impact. These sanctions threaten the livelihoods of sanctioned countries through market price transmission mechanisms, inducing market turmoil before achieving the macro goal of economic entity destruction. Using Russia as an example, the irrational expansion of market sentiment exacerbates the impact of financial sanctions, resulting in a risk and loss expansion effect akin to financial leverage.

5.4 Conclusion

The case of US financial sanctions on Russia highlights the dual nature of modern financial sanctions, which entail both micro and macro risks for the sanctioned country. In response, anti-sanction approaches serve as both self-protection measures and deterrence strategies. These approaches not only facilitate rational decision-making in major power conflicts but also contribute to achieving a peace-promoting effect through optimal game equilibrium. In the following, we draw some policy implications from the sanctionee's perspective. It is relevant to countries like China, Iran, and Cuba.

- Strengthen Diversification. Sanctionees should diversify their holdings in treasury bonds to reduce reliance on any single source of financing. This diversification can enhance resilience against potential financial sanctions and mitigate the impact of market panic.
- Enhance Domestic Market Development. Developing a robust domestic market for treasury bonds can provide alternative sources of financing and reduce vulnerability to external shocks. This entails improving market infrastructure, enhancing regulatory frameworks, and promoting investor confidence.
- Enhance Risk Management. Implementing effective risk management practices can help identify and mitigate potential risks associated with financial sanctions and market volatility. This includes developing contingency plans, conducting stress tests, and enhancing surveillance mechanisms.
- Strengthen International Cooperation. Countries like China should actively engage in international cooperation and dialogue to address challenges related to financial sanctions and promote stability in the global financial system. This includes participating in multilateral forums and initiatives aimed at enhancing financial resilience and mitigating systemic risks.

However, the most advantageous strategy for both parties involved, whether as sanctioners or sanctionees, is to abstain from deploying sanctions altogether. While sanctions may be perceived as a tool for exerting pressure or achieving specific objectives, their implementation often leads to unintended consequences and exacerbates tensions between nations (Zhou & Guo, 2025). For sanctioners, refraining from sanctions avoids potential retaliation, economic disruptions, and unintended humanitarian consequences. Instead of resorting to punitive measures, seeking diplomatic solutions and engaging in constructive dialogue can foster trust and collaboration, ultimately contributing to long-term stability and mutual prosperity. Similarly, for sanctionees, avoiding sanctions preserves economic stability, protects national sovereignty, and promotes sustainable development. Rather than being subjected to punitive measures that disrupt economic activities and impede growth, sanctionees can focus on implementing reforms, strengthening institutions, and fostering domestic resilience.

Ultimately, both parties stand to benefit from pursuing diplomatic solutions, engaging in dialogue, and upholding principles of mutual respect and cooperation. By prioritizing diplomacy over coercion, nations can build trust, resolve disputes, and work toward shared goals, fostering a more peaceful and prosperous global community.

References

Abadie, A., & Gardeazabal, J. (2003). The Economic costs of conflict: A case study of the Basque Country. *American Economic Review, 93*(1), 113–132.

Ahn, D. P., & Ludema, R. D. (2020). The sword and the shield: The economics of targeted sanctions. *European Economic Review, 130*, Article 103587.

Drezner, D. W. (2011). Sanctions sometimes smart: Targeted sanctions in theory and practice. *International Studies Review, 13*(1), 96–108.

Peksen, D. (2019). Autocracies and economic sanctions: The divergent impact of authoritarian regime type on sanctions success. *Defence and Peace Economics, 30*(3), 253–268.

Zhou, P., & Guo, D. (2025). Sanctions, co-sanctions, and counter-sanctions: A multilateral, evolutionary game among three global powers. *Defence and Peace Economics, 36*(1), 60–85.

6 Co-Sanctions and Counter-Sanctions

Abstract

Since 2014, successive sanctions and counter-sanctions have defined the Russia-US-EU relationship, intensifying after the 2022 invasion of Ukraine. This chapter asks how strategic interdependence among these three actors shapes sanction effectiveness. An evolutionary game-theory framework models Russia (sanctionee), the US (lead sanctioner), and the EU (co-sanctioner), capturing shifting alliances, coordination frictions, and adaptive behavior. Simulations reveal a feedback loop: strong US measures trigger robust Russian retaliation, while internal distributional costs press the EU toward milder positions, fragmenting the coalition. The EU thus becomes the structural "weak link," especially when energy trade and domestic politics raise its adjustment costs. Persistent Russian counter-sanctions barely deter Washington but amplify stress on Europe, eroding the combined coercive power. Policy lessons follow. Effective sanctions require clearly aligned US-EU strategies that reflect each side's political and economic limits. Reducing Russia's capacity to retaliate—through diversified energy sources or financial insulation—can prolong pressure. Yet broad sectoral sanctions inflict collateral harm on civilians. Policymakers should weigh these trade-offs and pursue cooperative dispute-resolution channels to minimize long-term economic and diplomatic damage.

Keywords

Co-sanction · Counter-sanction · Strategic interdependence

Classification

SDG16 · SDG17

6.1 Introduction

Since the end of the Cold War, few issues in international affairs have proved as stubborn as the conflict between Russia and the Western powers. In response to the 2014 annexation of Crimea, the US, the EU, and several allies introduced sanctions targeting specific Russian officials, businesses, and, eventually, entire sectors (Besedeš et al., 2021). Those penalties, initially confined to travel bans and asset freezes, soon evolved into wide-ranging commercial and—most importantly—financial restrictions. When Russia invaded Ukraine in February 2022, the existing measures were tightened yet again, but their overall effectiveness remains contested (Peksen, 2019).

- **Stage 1 (2014 M3)**—Travel bans and asset freezes directed at individuals involved in the Crimea operation, led by the US and copied by the EU, prompted only symbolic Russian counters (Peksen & Jeong, 2022).

D. Guo and P. Zhou, *Beating Financial Swords into Developmental Plowshares*,
Sustainable Development Goals Series, https://doi.org/10.1007/978-981-95-5152-1_6

- **Stage 2 (2014 M7–2018 M2)**—After flight MH-17 was shot down, restrictions broadened from arms and energy to banking and capital markets. The EU, now more active than Washington, simultaneously faced Russian limits on agricultural imports (Simola, 2014).
- **Stage 3 (2018 M3–2022 M1)**—The Salisbury poisoning triggered another escalation. US measures threatened Russia's access to SWIFT, yet Moscow's response was muted, partly because falling oil prices and COVID-19 had weakened its finances. Germany's interest in Nord Stream 2 underlined diverging European preferences.
- **Stage 4 (since 2022 M2)**—Following the full-scale invasion of Ukraine, the West barred Russian oil, froze reserves, and expelled key banks from SWIFT. Unable to match such financial pressure, Russia relied on military action instead.

Sanctions have thus moved from narrow, symbolic measures to comprehensive financial warfare. Stage 2 alone reduced Russia's growth by about 0.2% and exports by 7.4% (Crozet & Hinz, 2020). Yet the pattern of alternating US–EU initiative hints at "strategic substitutability": as one sender intensifies pressure, the other often hesitates (Joshi & Mahmud, 2020). Institutional constraints inside the EU and the uneven cost of sanctions across member states complicate a unified stance (Weber & Schneider, 2020).

Scepticism about coercive success is not new. Analyses covering more than 100 historical cases found major objectives met only one-third of the time (Hufbauer et al., 1990). Severe sanctions can even entrench the targeted regime by fuelling nationalism (Kaempfer & Lowenberg, 1988). Nevertheless, earlier studies largely examined dyads in which the sender was overwhelmingly stronger (e.g., the US vs. Cuba or North Korea). Russia, by contrast, is a nuclear power with considerable economic weight (Hufbauer & Jung, 2020).

Most theoretical work also treats sanctions as a bilateral game. Although recent network models allow for outside actors (Joshi & Mahmud, 2020), the interaction between a principal sender and a "co-sanctioner" is rarely modelled explicitly. In the present case, European interests cannot be reduced to a simple extension of US policy. Moreover, sanctions unfold over many years, yet static frameworks cannot capture shifting incentives. To address dynamics, we borrow from evolutionary game theory, previously applied to deterrence (Cressman, 1995) and public-goods problems (Gürerk et al., 2006).

To better understand how sanctioners and sanctionee interact and how strategies change over time, this chapter aims to address the following research question: *How does strategic interdependence shape the success or failure of sanctions when three actors—the US (leading sender), the EU (co-sender), and Russia (target)—confront each other over an extended horizon?*

There are three contributions of this chapter to the sanction literature. First, we develop a trilateral evolutionary game that embeds both multilateral interaction and time-varying strategies in a single framework. Second, the model endogenizes "sanction technology": the probability that a measure will bite depends on costly choices between acting alone or in concert. Third, numerical simulations reproduce stylized facts such as alternating US-EU leadership and Russia's shift from economic to military responses.

6.2 Methodology

Research on economic sanctions has long borrowed from bargaining theory. Early formal models portray sanctions as a coercive-diplomacy tool intended to reshape the target's cost–benefit calculus rather than to restrict its immediate capabilities (Eaton & Engers, 1992, 1999; Garoupa & Gata, 2002). These frameworks emerge from the literature on militarized bargaining (Powell, 1996; Schelling, 1966) and the recent discussion of "hybrid threats" (Balcaen et al., 2022). Yet sanctions and armed conflict differ in crucial respects, so importing war models wholesale can mislead policy analysis (Felbermayr et al., 2021). Three limitations of the traditional approach motivate a new framework.

1. **Time horizon**. Sanctions often persist for years or decades, as illustrated by the measures against Russia, Cuba, or North Korea. The sequential game proposed by Eaton and Engers (1992) allows an infinite horizon, but its equilibrium does not evolve once set, leaving long-run strategic drift unexplained.
2. **Uncertainty**. Over an indeterminate future, both the intensity of sanctions and the effectiveness of counters are uncertain. Most models simply treat these probabilities as fixed parameters (Drezner, 1998; Eaton & Engers, 1999; Krustev & Morgan, 2011), sidestepping technology choice and learning dynamics.
3. **Multilaterality**. The EU speaks with many voices, and its interests do not always coincide with those of the US. Russia has repeatedly exploited those divisions (e.g., via Nord Stream 2). Domestic bargaining therefore spills into interstate behavior (McLean & Whang, 2014), and "smart" sanctions try to exploit such heterogeneity (Ahn & Ludema, 2020; Drezner, 2011). Nonetheless, most formal work still models only a sender–target pair.

To address these gaps, the chapter adopts **Evolutionary Game Theory (EGT)**. EGT combines insights from evolutionary biology, nonlinear dynamics, and game theory (Cressman, 1995). Mixed strategies become population shares (Smith, 1982), and the core solution concept is the **Evolutionarily Stable Strategy (ESS)** (Smith & Price, 1973). An ESS is always a Nash equilibrium, whereas some Nash equilibria fail to be evolutionarily stable (Hofbauer et al., 1979; Taylor & Jonker, 1978).

EGT relaxes the hyper-rationality and common-knowledge assumptions that underpin classical games, allowing agents to learn and adapt through repeated interaction (Sandholm, 2010). Empirical evidence suggests that real decision-makers rarely solve a once-and-for-all equilibrium (Sugden, 2021).

Traditional games also confront two well-known obstacles: (i) some contests lack a pure-strategy Nash equilibrium, and (ii) others feature multiple equilibria without an obvious selection rule. EGT sidesteps both by interpreting mixed strategies as evolving shares and by letting natural selection refine the equilibrium set (Samuelson, 1997).

Leveraging these strengths, the chapter develops a **trilateral evolutionary game** linking the leading sender (US), the co-sender (EU), and the target (Russia). In its baseline version, the model treats sanction strength as exogenous; a subsequent extension endogenizes those probabilities through a simple "sanction technology," clarifying when unilateral or coordinated action is likely to prevail.

6.3 The Sanction Game

Imagine a three-way chessboard where each piece can change shape over time. On one side sits the US, able to move powerful economic pieces at will. Across from it stands the EU—a coalition that shares the same board but must first consult its many members before shifting its own pieces. Opposite them is Russia, the target, whose goal is to keep exporting, financing, and projecting power while avoiding checkmate.

6.3.1 Opening Moves

Signaling Intention. *Washington often moves first*, announcing restrictions that block Russian officials from traveling or accessing dollar funding. The move is designed less to cause instant pain than to *test reactions* and create moral pressure.

Coalition Calculation. The EU then decides whether to echo, soften, or ignore the American thrust. Because EU states differ in energy reliance and commercial exposure, *forging a common stance takes time*. When the Union finally advances, it may broaden the front—say, by limiting access to euro capital markets—but the delay gives Russia breathing room.

Counter-Moves. Russia rarely answers symmetrically; it cannot match dollar or euro dominance. Instead, it redirects exports to non-Western buyers, subsidizes affected firms, or, if stakes are existential, *resorts to military force* to shift the conversation off the economic board entirely.

6.3.2 Mid-Game Dynamics

Learning by Doing. Each round teaches something. If partial bans on bonds barely slow Russian borrowing, Washington and Brussels tighten the screws next time. Conversely, if a harsh step backfires—raising gas prices in Europe—unity frays, and future moves become cautious.

Alternating Leadership. Because domestic costs differ, leadership oscillates. When US sanctions hurt European banks more than American ones, Brussels hesitates. At other moments, the EU's geographic proximity and public outrage push it ahead of Washington.

Technology of Pressure. Sanctions are more than legal texts; they rely on payment networks, compliance software, and global insurers. Over time, both senders upgrade their technology—for instance, by denying access to SWIFT or forcing credit-card companies to exit. Russia counters by building alternatives, but scale disadvantages remain.

6.3.3 Endgame Scenarios

Concession and De-escalation. If combined pressure drains reserves, curtails investment, and saps domestic support, Russia may offer limited policy changes—withdrawal from a region, prisoner exchanges, or negotiated ceasefires. Sanctions then pause or partially lift, though "snap-back" clauses linger.

Stalemate. The more common outcome is strategic plateau. Sanctions bite, yet Russia adapts enough to survive. Costs rise for all sides, but none sees a better alternative. The game continues at lower intensity while each player waits for political turnover or exogenous shocks.

Escalation Beyond Economics. If either camp believes the economic board cannot deliver victory, it shifts to other arenas—cyberattacks, disinformation, or open conflict—escalating risks for everyone.

This tri-actor contest illustrates how finance has become a weapon system comparable to conventional arms. It also shows the limits of that power: success rests on coordination, credibility, and staying power, not just on who controls the largest capital pool. Understanding the narrative arc—signal, coalition, counter, adapt—helps policymakers craft measures that protect their own economies while nudging targets toward constructive change rather than indefinite resistance.

6.3.4 Strategic Dependence

To clarify the logic behind the three propositions, this part looks at **strategic dependence** among the US (sanctioner), the EU (co-sanctioner), and Russia (sanctionee). Two broad patterns occur. When the players' preferred actions move in the same direction, we speak of **strategic complementarity**—the textbook Prisoner's Dilemma is a well-known illustration. By contrast, if one side's harder line makes the other side soften, their choices exhibit **strategic substitutability**.

These relationships can be summarized with an *impulse–response* matrix (Table 6.1). An *impulse* is any outside change in payoffs, costs, or sanction strength that hits one actor; the *response* is how another actor's preferred strategy shifts. Because the origin of the shock matters, the same pair of players may display complementarity in one direction and substitutability in the other.

6.3.5 Extension: Sanction Technologies

Until this point the model has treated the "bite" of a sanction—the chance that it actually changes Russia's behavior—as something fixed. In reality, Washington must first build the tool kit before it can use it. That prior investment, which we call sanction technology, is an additional choice

Table 6.1 Strategic dependence among the three players in the evolutionary game

		Response		
		Sanctioner	Co-Sanctioner	Sanctionee
Impulse	**Sanctioner**	–	Substitutability	Substitutability
	Co-Sanctioner	Substitutability	–	Substitutability
	Sanctionee	Complementarity	Complementarity	–

the US faces alongside the familiar question of whether to push sanctions hard or keep them limited. Earlier debates framed the issue as a simple contest between unilateral measures (Kaempfer & Lowenberg, 2002) and multilateral campaigns (Haass, 1997). More recent work shows that either path can win, depending on circumstances (Early & Spice, 2015; Weber & Schneider, 2020).

Our framework therefore lets the US pick among three technological packages, each of which produces a different level of sanction strength (Zhou & Guo, 2025).

- Basic sole-sanctions (the "weak" package): Traditional, narrowly defined restrictions—blacklists, licensing hurdles, and travel bans—that Washington can assemble on its own. Because these tools are well known and relatively cheap to organize, they require only modest up-front spending. Their effectiveness, however, tops out at a moderate success rate, setting the baseline for later comparisons.
- Expanded sole-sanctions (a "strong" unilateral package): A deeper, home-grown arsenal: cutting Russian banks off from dollar clearing, limiting access to US capital markets, and tightening export controls on advanced technology. The US now channels a larger share of its own political and administrative resources into the job. Those extra resources raise the probability that the measures will hurt, but only after subtracting higher fixed costs—new regulations, staffing, and compliance systems. Because all effort comes from Washington, the final punch reflects purely domestic capacity.
- Expanded co-sanctions (a "strong" multilateral package): A coordinated campaign with close allies—the EU, the UK, Canada, Japan, and others—so that each partner focuses on what it does best. For example, the US uses its sway over global finance, while the EU leverages its trade and energy links. Joint action promises bigger gains because parallel systems (SWIFT access, euro- and pound-denominated finance, insurance, maritime services) are closed at once. Yet coordination is never free. Negotiations, carve-outs, and domestic politics inside the coalition eat up time and may dilute the final outcome; we capture that risk as a loss factor that scales down potential effectiveness.

Before any sanctions are announced, US policymakers compare the expected payoff from the two strong packages. Expanded co-sanctions dominate when three conditions line up:

- fixed development costs are low enough to keep the price of cooperation manageable;
- the productivity edge from allied participation outweighs the inevitable coordination loss; and
- foreign partners can commit to sustained enforcement.

If those conditions fail—say, because diplomatic wrangling drags on or because domestic agencies already possess highly efficient unilateral tools—the US will stick with an expanded sole-sanction strategy.

6.4 Simulation

We calibrate the model to demonstrate dynamics of the trilateral evolutionary game. The numerical experiment treats one "day" in the model as one period and releases the three players onto an evolutionary track. Figure 6.1 traces their paths under the baseline calibration. Russia's choice hardens almost immediately: within about

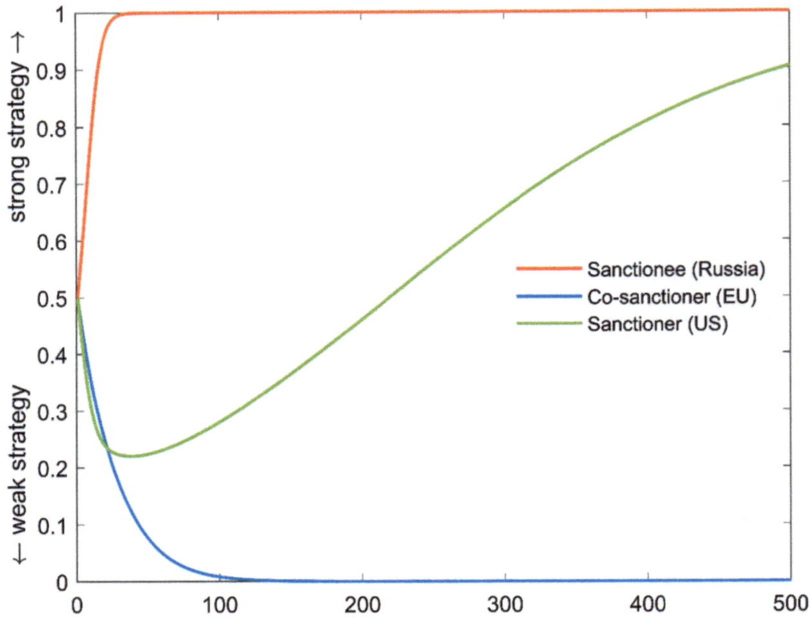

Fig. 6.1 Evolutionary paths of the baseline model

a month its strategy locks into permanent, forceful counter-sanctions. The EU's journey is slower and more hesitant. It starts in step with Washington but, as costs accumulate and internal divisions widen, it drifts toward lighter, largely symbolic measures; only after roughly six months does that softer stance stabilize. The US follows a different rhythm. It begins with modest restrictions, then, sensing that Russia will not yield and that European resolve is fading, gradually ramps up pressure. The turnaround occurs a little over a month into the simulation, yet full commitment to a comprehensive embargo is not complete until three simulated years have passed. These contrasting speeds capture the real-world impression that Moscow reacts fastest, Brussels wavers, and Washington escalates in slow motion.

The same model was rerun many times with alternative assumptions. When the EU's prospective gain from a successful embargo becomes larger, Brussels leans in more firmly at the outset, which lets Washington hang back for a while. When that gain shrinks, the opposite happens: the US shoulders the burden and the EU retreats sooner. Making counter-sanctions more expensive for Russia prolongs Moscow's decision time and, in turn, lessens US zeal; making them cheaper does the reverse.

Raising Europe's own cost of coordination weakens its appetite for joint action and obliges the US to move forward alone, a pattern that mirrors the uneasy division of labor observed during debates over energy bans. Lowering Washington's fixed cost of administering financial blacklists triggers earlier American escalation; raising it makes a lasting, tough embargo unlikely.

Across all of these variations the same qualitative rule emerges: whenever one side's move becomes easier or more rewarding, the other players either slow down or stiffen their stance, confirming the model's themes of strategic complementarity and substitutability.

6.5 Conclusion

This chapter put forward a three-actor evolutionary framework that links sanctions, co-sanctions, and counter-sanctions among the US, the EU, and Russia. The model successfully reproduces three stylized regularities. First, whether strategies move together or in opposite directions hinges on where an external shock originates: a shock on the senders typically yields strategic substitutability, whereas one on the target brings about complementarity. Second, the US and EU rarely march in lockstep. Because costs and domestic politics differ, their pressures substitute for one another—Washington's stance weakens before later firming up, while Brussels begins relatively forcefully but steadily settles into a softer line. Third, joint campaigns are not automatically superior. When technology or coordination costs are unfavorable, a well-designed unilateral program can dominate a multilateral one. Beyond matching these qualitative patterns, the simulated adjustment speeds mirror the observed timing of past sanction rounds, lending quantitative credibility to the framework.

The numerical exercises point to three broad policy lessons. First, the target's preferred response is remarkably resilient. Across a wide range of scenarios Russia gravitates to a forceful counter-sanctions posture and stays there. Altering that path requires raising the cost of retaliation—tightening import channels for critical goods, for example—rather than merely layering on additional financial penalties (Dong & Li, 2018).

Second, the EU's commitment is naturally fragile. Because benefits and burdens are unevenly spread across member states, its willingness to sustain tough measures fluctuates. A stronger push from Washington often reduces Brussels's appetite for risk, making Europe the most likely fracture point that Moscow can exploit (Bělín & Hanousek, 2021).

Third, a hard-line strategy is usually stable for the leading sender unless sanction costs spiral. Greater Russian resistance tends to stiffen the US position, yet vigorous EU action can let Washington ease off temporarily—an example of strategic free-riding. Whether the US opts for co-sanctions or stands alone depends on a simple cost–benefit calculus: where the fixed expense of coordination is low and partners add genuine leverage, cooperation pays; otherwise, an expanded unilateral toolkit remains rational (Ahn & Ludema, 2020; Drezner, 2011).

Taken together, these insights illuminate the post-Cold-War reality that major powers often fight with balance sheets rather than battle tanks. Commercial embargoes strike narrow sectors, whereas financial sanctions aim at the circulatory system of an economy. That reach, however, cuts both ways. Broad measures can hurt ordinary households in Russia and the EU, generate humanitarian concerns, and erode confidence in the sanctioning currencies themselves. Sanctions are therefore a triple-edged sword: every side bleeds, though not equally. They should be weighed against alternative instruments of conflict resolution, lest economic warfare become a self-inflicted wound. As the ancient maxim reminds us, "the finest victory is won without fighting." A strategy that relies solely on financial force invites escalation; a strategy that combines calibrated pressure with credible diplomacy offers a clearer path to sustainable peace.

References

Ahn, D. P., & Ludema, R. D. (2020). The sword and the shield: The economics of targeted sanctions. *European Economic Review, 130*, Article 103587.

Balcaen, P., Du, B. C., & Buts, C. (2022). A game-theoretic analysis of hybrid threats. *Defence and Peace Economics, 33*(1), 26–41.

Bělín, M., & Hanousek, J. (2021). Which sanctions matter? Analysis of the EU/Russian sanctions of 2014. *Journal of Comparative Economics, 49*(1), 244–257.

Besedeš, T., Goldbach, S., & Nitsch, V. (2021). Cheap talk? Financial sanctions and non-financial firms. *European Economic Review, 134*, Article 103688.

Cressman, R. (1995). Evolutionary game theory with two groups of individuals. *Games and Economic Behavior, 11*(2), 237–253.

Crozet, M., & Hinz, J. (2020). Friendly fire: The trade impact of the Russia sanctions and counter-sanctions. *Economic Policy, 35*(101), 97–146.

Dong, Y., & Li, C. (2018). Economic sanction games among the US, the EU and Russia: Payoffs and potential effects. *Economic Modelling, 73*, 117–128.

Drezner, D. W. (2011). Sanctions sometimes smart: Targeted sanctions in theory and practice. *International Studies Review, 13*(1), 96–108.

Early, B. R., & Spice, R. (2015). Economic sanctions, international institutions, and sanctions busters: When does institutionalized cooperation help sanctioning efforts?1. *Foreign Policy Analysis, 11*(3), 339–360.

Eaton, J., & Engers, M. (1992). Sanctions. *Journal of Political Economy, 100*(5), 899–928.
Eaton, J., & Engers, M. (1999). Sanctions: Some simple analytics. *American Economic Review, 89*(2), 409–414.
Felbermayr, G., Morgan, T. C., Syropoulos, C., & Yotov, Y. V. (2021). Understanding economic sanctions: Interdisciplinary perspectives on theory and evidence. *European Economic Review, 135*, Article 103720.
Garoupa, N. R., & Gata, J. E. (2002). A theory of international conflict management and sanctioning. *Public Choice, 110*(1), 41–65.
Gürerk, Ö., Irlenbusch, B., & Rockenbach, B. (2006). The competitive advantage of sanctioning institutions. *Science, 312*(5770), 108–111.
Haass, R. (1997). Sanctioning madness. *Foreign Affairs, 76*, 74–85.
Hofbauer, J., Schuster, P., & Sigmund, K. (1979). A note on evolutionary stable strategies and game dynamics. *Journal of Theoretical Biology, 81*(3), 609–612.
Hufbauer, G. C., & Jung, E. (2020). What's new in economic sanctions? *European Economic Review, 130*, Article 103572.
Hufbauer, G. C., Schott, J. J., & Elliott, K. A. (1990). *Economic sanctions reconsidered: History and current policy*. Peterson Institute.
Joshi, S., & Mahmud, A. S. (2020). Sanctions in networks. *European Economic Review, 130*, Article 103606.
Kaempfer, W. H., & Lowenberg, A. D. (1988). The theory of international economic sanctions: A public choice approach. *The American Economic Review, 78*(4), 786–793.
Kaempfer, W. H., & Lowenberg, A. D. (2002). Unilateral versus multilateral international sanctions: A public choice perspective. *International Studies Quarterly, 43*(1), 37–58.
Krustev, V. L., & Morgan, T. C. (2011). Ending economic coercion: Domestic politics and international bargaining. *Conflict Management and Peace Science, 28*(4), 351–376.
McLean, E. V., & Whang, T. (2014). Designing foreign policy: Voters, special interest groups, and economic sanctions. *Journal of Peace Research, 51*(5), 589–602.
Peksen, D. (2019). Autocracies and economic sanctions: The divergent impact of authoritarian regime type on sanctions success. *Defence and Peace Economics, 30*(3), 253–268.
Peksen, D., & Jeong, J. M. (2022). Coercive diplomacy and economic sanctions reciprocity: Explaining targets' counter-sanctions. *Defence and Peace Economics, 33*(8), 895–911.
Powell, R. (1996). Bargaining in the shadow of power. *Games and Economic Behavior, 15*(2), 255–289.
Samuelson, L. (1997). *Evolutionary games and equilibrium selection*. MIT Press.
Sandholm, W. (2010). *Population games and evolutionary dynamics*. MIT Press.
Schelling, T. (1966). *Arms and influence.*, New Haven, CT: Yale University Press.
Simola, H. (2014). *Russia's restrictions on food imports*. BOFIT Policy Brief.
Smith, J. M. (1982). *Evolution and the theory of games*. Cambridge University Press.
Smith, J. M., & Price, G. R. (1973). The logic of animal conflict. *Nature, 246*(5427), 15–18.
Sugden, R. (2021). Hume's experimental psychology and the idea of erroneous preferences. *Journal of Economic Behavior & Organization, 183*, 836–848.
Taylor, P. D., & Jonker, L. B. (1978). Evolutionary stable strategies and game dynamics. *Mathematical Biosciences, 40*(1), 145–156.
Weber, P. M., & Schneider, G. (2020). How many hands to make sanctions work? Comparing EU and US sanctioning efforts. *European Economic Review, 130*, Article 103595.
Zhou, P., & Guo, D. (2025). Sanctions, co-sanctions, and counter-sanctions: A multilateral, evolutionary game among three global powers. *Defence and Peace Economics, 36*(1), 60–85.

7 Tail Risks and Green Bonds

Abstract

Green bonds marry environmental finance and risk management. This chapter asks whether they protect investors against tail events. Using daily data on US and Chinese green bond indices from 2016–2024 and copula models that track time-varying extreme co-movements with government bonds, equities, commodities, and foreign exchange, we test hedging capacity before and after COVID-19. Results show green bonds preserve value when conventional assets sag. Their correlations with stocks and commodities remain weakly positive and time-limited; during the 2020–2021 pandemic phase, the link even turned negative in the US, offsetting exchange rate stress. In China, green bonds gained hedging power against bond and forex risk as domestic markets tightened. Across both economies value-at-risk and expected shortfall metrics fall by up to one-third when green bonds are added to balanced portfolios. Policy takeaways follow. Credible green bond taxonomies and disclosure rules can widen the investor base, lower funding costs for climate projects, and enhance systemic resilience. China could anchor market depth by courting offshore institutional holders, while global standard-setting would boost transparency and align safe-haven demand with sustainable development.

Keywords

Green bonds · Tail risks · Hedging

Classification

SDG7 · SDG12 · SDG13

7.1 Introduction

The environment provides natural resources for and imposes limits on economic growth. Therefore, sustainable growth must be environmentally friendly growth. In the face of intensifying environmental concerns, there is a thriving trend in both developed countries (Sarkodie et al., 2021) and emerging economies (Song & Zhou, 2021) to achieve carbon–neutral growth by green energy-based innovations. Nevertheless, technological progress is not the only driver of sustainable growth. The finance-growth nexus (Beck et al., 2014; King & Levine, 1993; Zhang & Zhou, 2021) implies that green finance is needed to boost green growth (Yu et al., 2021). As a popular financing tool and investment vehicle, green bonds have gained increasing attention in global financial markets (Taghizadeh-Hesary et al., 2021; Zhou et al., 2025). According to World Bank and OECD, green bonds are defined as "fixed-income securities to exclusively develop eco-friendly and sustainable projects like renewable energy industries." The earliest green bonds were issued by

D. Guo and P. Zhou, *Beating Financial Swords into Developmental Plowshares*, Sustainable Development Goals Series, https://doi.org/10.1007/978-981-95-5152-1_7

the European Investment Bank in 2007 (Banga, 2019). Since 2008, the World Bank has issued over USD 13 billion equivalent in green bonds in 20 currencies (World Bank, 2021). In recent years, emerging economies like China have been actively in green bond issuance and management. In 2016, China issued more than one-third of the global green bond issuance (USD 81 billion), ranking the first in the world. A burgeoning green bond market provides financial capital for sustainable growth as well as alternative investment opportunities for investors.

In addition to its sustainability feature, green bonds also have a safe-heaven feature against tail risks (Jin et al., 2020; Yi et al., 2021). Specifically, during the COVID-19 pandemic, the global financial markets underwent sharp downturns and volatile fluctuations (Uddin et al., 2021). Based on historical experience, financial crises due to epidemics are expected to be deeper but short-lived compared to the global financial crisis of 2009. For example, the Chinese stock market even grew by 20% during SARS in 2003. However, the crisis following the COVID-19 pandemic seems to be much prolonged compared to past experience. In the early stages of the outbreak in 2020, 30% of the worldwide stock market value evaporated within weeks, and that loss is yet to recover in mid-2021. Investors are forced to look for safe-heaven investment opportunities and hedging tools to diversify tail risks caused by rare disasters.

The pandemic causes abnormal fluctuations in financial markets and leads to the failure of conventional hedging techniques. Campbell et al. (2002) find that benefits of diversification across asset classes substantially drop if the market experiences high volatility. This is because the distributional dependence among assets varies substantially in different quantiles. The tail dependence in rare disasters can be significantly different from mean dependence in normal times. For example, both cryptocurrencies and gold fail to provide safe-haven hedge against pandemic crisis (Kristoufek, 2020). Luckily, green bonds seem to provide a promising solution to this trouble. Evidence suggests that clean energy assets, especially green bonds, are great hedging tools in the US (Kuang, 2021; Reboredo & Ugolini, 2020). Han and Li (2022) find no risk spillovers between green bonds and stocks, suggesting that green bonds have outstanding diversification benefits for stock investors in China.

This chapter is inspired by earlier studies in various countries but before the COVID-19 pandemic. The existing literature either focus on the safe-heaven feature of green bonds in developed economies like the US and the EU (e.g., Abakah et al., 2021; Reboredo et al., 2020) or on non-hedging features of green bonds in China (e.g., Yi et al., 2021). We aim to provide updated evidence for the hedging capability of green bonds against rare disasters (or tail risks) using a comparative study of a representative developed economy (US) and emerging economy (China), before and after the pandemic. This research contributes to the empirical understanding of the role of green bonds in both US and China as a safe-heaven asset against tail risks. Evidence supports the idea that green bonds have great potential to hedge against tail risks for traditional assets. We find that the financial markets in the two countries converge in many ways. The hedging effect of green bonds became slightly weaker for most assets after the pandemic but stronger for the forex market. We first provide a brief review of green finance literature.

7.2 Literature

As its name suggests, green bonds have two defining features. One is "green" and the other is "bond." Thus, the literature on green bonds is rolled out along these two dimensions. The green/sustainability literature highlights the effects on corporate social responsibility (Zhou & Cui, 2019) and corporate performance (Alonso-Conde & Rojo-Suárez, 2020). A consensus in this strand of green literature is that the sustainability nature of green bonds reaps the so-called "environmental benefit dividends" in line with the long-run direction of economic development and technological progress. This is effectively a micro-finance perspective into the long-run, fundamental factors of financial performance of green bonds. The bond/finance literature, on the other hand, accentuates the green bond risk premium. Many empirical studies find that green bonds enjoy higher yields, lower variance, and greater liquidity (Bachelet et al., 2019). Moreover, it is also found that green bonds have an asymmetric volatility feature—more responsive to positive shocks than negative shocks (Park et al., 2020). Therefore, it is argued that green bonds, or clean energy assets in general, can be a safe-haven tool to hedge against various risks (Kuang, 2021; Xia et al., 2019). This is more a macro-finance perspective into the short-run, cyclical factors of financial properties of green bonds.

Empirical studies usually employ multivariate time-serious models to capture the dynamic features of green bond markets. For example, Naeem et al. (2021) apply rolling window wavelet techniques to examine the time-varying features of correlation between green bonds and other assets. Park et al. (2020) adopt DCC-GARCH model to study the volatility spillovers between equity and green bond markets using US data. Reboredo (2018) applies Copula models to study the tail dependence features and diversification benefits of green bonds. Reboredo and Ugolini (2020) use a structural VAR with heteroskedasticity to study interdependence between green bond and other financial assets. In the recent empirical literature (listed in Table 7.1), there are four trending approaches to studying co-movements between green bonds and other financial assets.

The first one is quantile-based approach, such as cross-quantilogram (Han et al., 2016; Naeem et al., 2021) and quantile autoregressive distributed lag (He et al., 2021). The advantage of quantile-based approach is that it can help identify the signs of the relationship not only at the mean but also at the tails of the complete distribution when the markets experience extreme decreases or increases. It can deal with the so-called "asymmetric tail dependence," i.e., cases where two returns exhibit greater correlation during market downturns than market upturns (Ang & Chen, 2002; Erb et al., 1994; Patton, 2006). However, these models cannot accommodate complicated dynamics among assets such as volatility clustering.

To capture interdependence and volatility clustering at the same time, multivariate GARCH models (Engle, 2002) is an obvious choice. So, it becomes the second trending approach in green bond literature (Gao et al., 2021; Jin et al., 2020; Maghyereh et al., 2019). But GARCH-type models (e.g., CCC or DCC) are restrictive due to the linear specification among assets and the Gaussian assumption of the joint distribution (Wang et al., 2011).

To overcome these limitations, copula method (the third approach) is developed to relax the Gaussian restrictions while maintaining the rich interdependence feature. The Copula method is influential in finance research for its flexibility in distributional assumptions, making it appropriate for explaining joint tail risks. Another advantage of copula method is its two-step procedure of estimating marginal and joint distributions. Therefore, it soon gains its popularity in green bond literature (Gong et al., 2019; Reboredo, 2018). Early copula methods assume constant parameters (e.g., Patton, 2004), but extensions like generalized autoregressive score solve this issue by introducing a dynamic copula (Patton, 2006).

Like other approaches, copula methods also have limitations. It focuses on the dependence of the variance–covariance matrix, leaving little to say on the dependence of the means. This is where a multivariate GARCH (MGARCH) model can be complementary. Note that ordinary MGARCH models are unable to capture the time-varying feature of interdependence. In this regard, the time-varying parameter vector autoregressive (TVP-VAR) approach is appealing if the focus is on the evolution of the relationship between assets (Antonakakis et al., 2020). Compared with the copula method which can also capture time variation but only in the copula, TVP-VAR can capture time-varying features in both mean and variance–covariance matrices following a Bayesian interpretation (Pham & Nguyen, 2022). The drawback of TVP-VAR is that it cannot accommodate the fat-tail feature of returns documented in financial markets (Barro, 2006; Rietz, 1988). This is a critical limitation for our purpose because the focus of this chapter is on tail risks and tail dependence.

Table 7.1 List of key literature

Literature	Period	Country	Method	Assets
Naeem et al. (2021)	2008–2019	US	cross-quantilogram	GBs, oil, gold, commodities
Park et al. (2020)	2010–2020	US	DCC-GARCH	GBs, stock
Reboredo (2018)	2014–2017	US	copula	GBs, bond, oil
Reboredo et al. (2020)	2014–2018	US, EU	wavelet	GBs, bond, stock, oil
Reboredo and Ugolini (2020)	2014–2019	US	SVAR	GBs, bond, stock, oil, forex
Maghyereh et al. (2019)	2001–2018	US	wavelet	GBs, oil, stock
Jin et al. (2020)	2008–2018	US	DCC-GARCH	GBs, stock, oil, commodities
Gao et al. (2021)	2015–2020	China	DCC-GARCH	GBs, stock, bond, forex
Yi et al. (2021)	2019–2020	China	event study method	GBs

To summarize, all four prevailing empirical approaches have their advantages and limitations. Table 7.2 compares the key features of the four approaches in the recent green bond literature. It is arguable that the copula method is preferred to quantile-based method in terms of time variation modeling, and superior to TVP-VAR and multivariate GARCH in terms of tail dependence modeling. Therefore, this chapter is going to adopt the copula approach, with the quantile-based approach to provide a complementary measure of the dependence among assets.

7.3 Model

Returns of any assets, including green bonds, corporate bonds, stocks, oil index, and dollar index, can be modeled in the following general form. The subscript g denotes green bonds, i denotes any other asset, and t is time. To be general, we allow both mean and volatility to change over time.

$$r_{gt} = \mu_{gt} + \xi_{gt}, \text{ where } \xi_{gt} \equiv \sigma_{gt}\varepsilon_{gt} \tag{7.1A}$$

$$r_{it} = \mu_{it} + \xi_{it}, \text{ where } \xi_{it} \equiv \sigma_{it}\varepsilon_{it} \tag{7.2B}$$

The mean component ($\mu_{\blacksquare}t$) of any asset ($\blacksquare = g, i$) can be modeled as an ARMA (p, q) process. To write the model in an elegant form, econometricians usually use polynomials of lag operator L, such as $\boldsymbol{\phi}(L; p) = \phi_1 L + \cdots + \phi_p L^p$ and $\boldsymbol{\psi}(L; q) = \psi_1 L + \cdots + \psi_p L^p$, to express the ARMA model:

$$\mu_{\blacksquare}t = \boldsymbol{\phi}(L; p)\mu_{\blacksquare_t} + \boldsymbol{\psi}(L; q)\xi_{\blacksquare_t} \tag{7.3}$$

Similarly, the volatility component ($\sigma^2_{\blacksquare_t}$) of the model is assumed to exhibit a threshold generalized autoregressive conditional heteroskedasticity (TGARCH). The polynomials $\boldsymbol{\alpha}(L; m)$, $\boldsymbol{\beta}(L; n)$, and $\boldsymbol{\gamma}(L; s)$ are defined in a similar way for the GARCH (m), ARCH (n), and TARCH (s) terms.

$$\sigma^2_{\blacksquare_t} = \alpha_0 + \boldsymbol{\alpha}(L; m)\sigma^2_{\blacksquare_t} + \boldsymbol{\beta}(L; n)\xi^2_{\blacksquare_t} + \boldsymbol{\gamma}(L; s)\xi^2_{\blacksquare_t}\Big|_{\xi_{\blacksquare_t}<0} \tag{7.4}$$

Nothing is new up to this point. Equations [7.1]A, [7.2]B, [7.3] and [7.4] are time-series models widely applied in finance literature since 1980s. To extend this simple model, as we summarized in the literature review above, there are four directions. If the focus is on the tail dependence between ϵ s, then we arrive at the quantile-based approach. If we are more interested in the mean dependence, then we have MGARCH. If the research embarks on the temporal variation of the dependence, then TVP-VAR is a good choice. If one wants to capture all features to a certain degree, then the copula approach is the optimal choice. So, we will adopt the copula approach as the baseline in this chapter.

In the copula approach, joint distributions between ϵ_{gt} and ϵ_{it} are obtained in two steps in the light of Sklar's theorem. The theorem

Table 7.2 Comparison of trending empirical approaches in green bond literature

Type	Mean Dependence	Tail Dependence	Fat Tail	Time-Varying
Quantile-Based	Yes	Yes	Yes	No
MGARCH	Yes	No	No	No
TVP-VAR	Yes	No	No	Yes
Copula	No	Yes	Yes	Yes

states that every multivariate cumulative distribution function (CDF) $F(\bullet)$ of a set of jointly distributed random variables (say, ϵ_{gt} and ϵ_{it}) can be expressed in terms of the marginal CDFs ($F_g(\epsilon_{gt})$ and $F_i(\epsilon_{it})$) and a copula function ($C(\bullet)$) to link the marginals:

$$F(\epsilon_{gt}, \epsilon_{it}) = C(F_g(\epsilon_{gt}), F_i(\epsilon_{it}))$$

Copulas provide a more complete description of dependence between two or more random variables than linear correlation coefficient (Patton, 2006). Thus, the copula approach deals with the interdependence between random variables via ϵ s rather than via μ s as opposed to MGARCH and TVP-VAR. Distributional dependence is therefore the core of the copula approach.

In the first step of the copula approach, marginal CDFs ($F_g(\epsilon_{gt})$ and $F_i(\epsilon_{it})$) can be separately estimated. This feature grants great flexibility in practice—the underlying marginals can have different distributions and/or different parameters, without having to conform with the restrictions if a multivariate distribution is directly applied to model the dependence of assets. In the green bond literature, it is well established that a Student's t distribution (with a fat tail) tends to be the most appropriate marginal distribution (Reboredo, 2018), so we are going to use t distributions for the marginals.

Turning to the second step of specifying copula models, we largely follow the classical approach developed by Patton (2006). The tail dependence of the lower and upper ends of marginal CDFs can be formulated as:

$$\begin{aligned}\tau_L &= \lim_{x\to 0} \Pr(F_g(\epsilon_{gt}) \le x | F_i(\epsilon_{it}) \le x)\\ &= \lim_{x\to 0} \frac{C(x,x)}{x}\end{aligned}$$

$$\begin{aligned}\tau_U &= \lim_{x\to 1} \Pr(F_g(\epsilon_{gt}) \ge x | F_i(\epsilon_{it}) \ge x)\\ &= \lim_{x\to 1} \frac{1-2x+C(x,x)}{1-x}\end{aligned}$$

The two tail dependence measures τ_L and τ_U describe the probability that both assets are in their lower or upper joint tails, i.e., during extreme events like the financial crisis and the COVID-19 pandemic. There are many different copulas with different features of tail dependence. We discuss the most popular and relevant ones here.

- **Gaussian/Normal copula**. It does not allow for tail dependence of the underlying marginal distributions, so both tail dependence measures τ_L and τ_U are equal to zero. Dependence is simply measured by Pearson's correlation coefficient $-1 \le \rho \le 1$.
- **Student's t copula**. It has a fat tail, so tail dependence is possible. The symmetry of the t distribution implies an equal lower and upper tail dependence $\tau_L = \tau_U$ which depends on the two copula parameters, the correlation coefficient ρ and the degree of freedom ν.
- **Clayton copula**. It is an asymmetric distribution with greater lower tail dependence $\tau_L > 0$ than upper tail dependence $\tau_U = 0$. There is only one parameter of the Clayton copula $\vartheta \ge 1$, where $\vartheta = 1$ means independence.
- **Rotated Clayton copula**. It is the reverse of the Clayton copula, so it allows for positive upper dependence $\tau_U > 0$ but zero lower dependence $\tau_L = 0$. In practice, one can simply transform the data to swap the tails before estimation.
- **SJC copula**. It allows for asymmetric tail dependence $\tau_L \ne \tau_U$ and the two measures can be estimated directly.

In addition to the copulas described above, Gumbel copula is also popular, but it is close to Clayton copula. They, together with their rotated counterparts, are called the Archimedean copulas (Creal et al., 2011).

To capture time variation of copulas, an autoregressive conditional density in the spirit of Hansen (1994) is usually used. The advantage of this method, relative to alternatives, regime switching method for example, is that it is more efficient and parsimonious in parameterization. Assume the time-varying parameters in copulas ($\theta_t \equiv \rho_t|\tau_{Lt}|\tau_{Ut}$) are summarized by an ARMA-type process (Patton, 2006).

$$\theta_t = \Lambda\left(a + b\theta_{t-1} + c\frac{1}{K}\sum_{k=1}^{K} H(\epsilon_{g,t-k}, \epsilon_{i,t-k})\right) \tag{7.5}$$

In Equation [7.5], $\Lambda(\bullet)$ is a logistic transformation to keep measures of tail dependence within defined domains. $H(\bullet)$ is product of normal quantile functions for normal copula, product of t quantile functions for t copula, absolute difference function for Clayton, Gumbel, and SJC copulas. According to Patton (2006), the length of lags $K = 10$ is chosen, which corresponds to 2 working weeks for daily data.

7.4 Results

Following the convention of the green bond literature, we select bond market, stock market, energy market, and forex market to study the dependence of green bond market. We will compare our results of a developed economy (US) with an emerging economy (China) which plays a significant role in green bond issuance.

7.4.1 Data Description

For the US, we use the daily data of Barclays MSCI green bond index (USGB) from Aug/2014 to Aug/2021. There are, of course, many alternative indices for green bonds, such as S&P Dow Jones green bond index, Solactive green bond index, and Bank of America Merrill Lynch green bond index. According to Reboredo (2018), different green bond indices share very similar patterns, so the choice of index does not matter much in our empirical results. The bond market is proxied by the 10-year US government bonds (USB). For the stock market in the US, we use Dow Jones index (USS). The forex market fluctuations are measured by the US dollar index (USF). As an important commodity related to green bonds, West Texas Intermediate (USO) crude oil index is used to measure changes of energy price in the US. It is preferred to Oil Brent Crude because the latter covers markets beyond the US.

For China, there are about ten representative green bond indices to choose from 2014M7 to 2021M8. We use the essential green bond index (CNGB) which meets the strictest criteria of green bonds in China and most countries in the world. The bond market in China is represented by the 10-year Chinese government bond index (CNB). The stock market in China is proxied by the Shanghai Security Exchange composite index (CNS). Fluctuations of the forex market are measured by returns of USD/CNY exchange rate (CNF). China does not have a well-established domestic oil price index due to its net importing position as a price-taker in the international oil market. We use Brent oil price as a proxy of the international oil price that the Chinese market faces (CNO).

Table 7.3 reports descriptive statistics for daily returns of the abovementioned financial assets. The means of daily returns of all assets are close to zero and stationary according to ADF and KPSS tests, and they all have abnormal fat tails (kurtosis greater than 3 and JB tests are significant). Green bonds in both countries tend to be negatively correlated with fixed income markets and other assets, especially in China. The descriptive statistics in Table 7.3 focuses on univariate properties of each asset. To visualize the dependence between assets, we plot scatter plots of selected assets against green bonds. Figure 7.1 shows the nonparametric joint distributions of assets in the US, while Fig. 7.2 shows the counterparts in China. To facilitate comparisons over time, we use different colors to indicate pre-COVID and COVID samples. We can see some salient features from between-assets, cross-country, and overtime comparisons. First, there is a clear negative dependence between green bonds and the dollar index in the US, but the most salient negative dependence in China lies in the bond markets. It implies a different hedging role for green bonds in the two markets. Second, the distribution of green bonds in China tends to be more concentrated around its mean than those in the US, but green bonds in both countries enjoy lower uncertainty than other assets. In other words, the between-assets difference is smaller than the cross-country difference. Third, tail risks of most assets become more significant after the COVID-19 pandemic, since the distributions become thicker in tails and flatter in peaks. One outstanding example is the oil price, which dropped to negative for the first time in history on 20th April 2020 due to the pandemic and the oil price war between Russia and Saudi Arabia. In contrast, green bonds do not have obvious changes in terms of tail risks. Therefore, green bonds have great potential to be a safe-heaven asset resilient to rare disasters.

To descriptively measure tail risks and tail dependence, the empirical literature develops metrics like Value at Risk (VaR), Conditional VaR (CoVaR), and Delta CoVaR (ΔCoVaR). Intuitively, VaR measures the loss of holding an asset if rare disasters with a specific probability (e.g., 5%) occur. In our case, it simply ranks historical (daily) returns of each asset and identifies the return at the specific percentile. More generally, CoVaR is developed to estimate possible loss under any conditions (Girardi & Ergün, 2013). The condition can simply be the downward risks below VaR of the asset per se or when other assets fall below their VaRs. Therefore, CoVaR provides a simple measure of tail dependence and risk spillover. Furthermore, ΔCoVaR represents the difference between the CoVaR of one asset (e.g., green bonds) under the distressed state of the other asset (e.g., stocks during the pandemic) and the CoVaR of the asset under the benchmark state (within 95% confidence intervals). The difference is usually divided by the benchmark CoVaR to show the marginal risk contribution of one asset vis-à-vis the overall risk of another asset (Shahzad et al., 2018).

As shown in Table 7.4, all the assets in the US experienced significant lower VaRs during COVID-19 compared to pre-COVID periods, apart from green bonds (USGB) and forex (USF). The difference in China seems less significant, especially for green bonds (CNGB) and forex (CNF) as well. It suggests that in both countries green bonds and forex markets share an immune feature to COVID-19 related fluctuations.

In addition, the tail dependence between green bonds and other assets are qualitatively described by CoVaRs and quantitatively measured by ΔCoVaRs. It is obvious that the VaRs of green bonds in both countries have positive VaRs when other assets are in stressed states with only one exception (USS) during COVID-19. It suggests that green bonds have a great potential to hedge against tail risks for most assets. Magnitude-wise, the hedging effect of green bonds (as quantified by ΔCoVaRs) drops in the US over the pandemic but rises in China. These observations will be formally tested by the copula approach.

7.4.2 Marginal Distributions

Estimation results of the marginal distributions are presented in Table 7.5. The lag lengths are chosen according to AIC and BIC information criteria from the following ranges: $p, q \in \{0,1,2,3,4,5\}$, $m, n, s \in \{0,1,2\}$.

The mean equations of different assets have different lag lengths or different lengths of memory. Specifically, West Texas Intermediate (USO) crude oil index has no dynamic terms at all in the mean component. Turning to the volatility equations, all returns have significant GARCH and ARCH terms, indicating conditional heteroskedasticity or volatility clustering features. The leverage effects are also found for assets in both countries, which suggests that negative shocks tend to generate greater volatility.

To allow for thick tails, we assume Student's t distribution for marginal distributions. The estimated degrees of freedom confirm this hypothesis—a lower degree of freedom means a thicker

Table 7.3 Descriptive statistics for daily returns of financial assets in US and China

US	USGB	USB	USS	USF	USO	China	CNGB	CNB	CNS	CNF	CNO
Obs	1830	1830	1830	1830	1830	Obs	1799	1799	1799	1799	1799
Mean	0.0001	0.0001	0.0005	0.0001	–0.0018	Mean	0.0002	–0.0002	0.0004	0.0000	0.0002
Max	0.0222	0.4074	0.0938	0.0235	0.3766	Max	0.0097	0.0367	0.0576	0.0186	0.2102
Min	–0.0299	–0.2703	–0.1198	–0.0207	–3.0597	Min	–0.0089	–0.0568	–0.0849	–0.0099	–0.2440
SD	0.0036	0.0322	0.0111	0.0035	0.0834	SD	0.0010	0.0082	0.0140	0.0021	0.0261
Skew	–0.7719	1.4912	–0.6993	0.2503	–28.76	Skew	–0.0898	–0.2741	–0.9888	0.5941	–0.2613
Kurtosis	10.63	36.82	23.80	8.89	1.0E + 03	Kurtosis	19.98	6.73	9.86	10.72	16.4785
JB	4.6E + 03	8.8E + 04	3.3E + 04	2.7E + 03	7.9E + 07	JB	2.2E + 04	1.1E + 03	3.8E + 03	4.6E + 03	1.4E + 04
ADF	–39.64	–43.50	–52.52	–45.85	–31.76	ADF	–26.38	–36.68	–40.44	–38.76	–41.88
KPSS	0.0524	0.0511	0.0192	0.0792	0.0638	KPSS	0.4125	0.1245	0.1316	0.1168	0.0726
Corr	USGB	USB	USS	USF	USO	Corr	CNGB	CNB	CNS	CNF	CNO
USGB	1					CNGB	1				
USB	–0.3792	1				CNB	–0.5265	1			
USS	–0.0078	0.3905	1			CNS	–0.0368	0.1294			
USF	–0.593	–0.0249	–0.2223	1		CNF	–0.0119	0.0395	–0.0433	1	
USO	0.0178	0.1074	0.1633	–0.0876	1	CNO	–0.0387	0.0299	–0.0016	0.0087	1

Note The null hypothesis of the JB test is that the data come from a normal distribution. The null hypothesis of the ADF test and the KPSS test is that the data have a unit root. All hypotheses are rejected at 5% significance levels

tail. A t distribution converges to normal distribution if the degree of freedom is higher than 20. In our case, all estimated degrees of freedom are lower than 8, showing significant thick-tail features. Relatively speaking, green bonds in China tend to have lower degrees of freedom or greater tail risks.

7.4.3 Copula Functions

Based on the residuals of the marginal distribution models, we then estimate copulas between green bonds and each asset. Table 7.6 presents the estimation results of constant copula models with popular specifications.

For time-invariant models, we estimate normal, student's t, Clayton, rotated Clayton, and SJC copula distributions to show robustness and to facilitate model selection. We report both correlation coefficients ρ s as well as tail dependence measures τ s. Normal distribution has no tail dependence ($\tau_L = \tau_U = 0$), Student's t assumes symmetric tail dependence, which are positive for all assets ($\tau_L = \tau_U > 0$). This result implies that when there is a negative *rare* shock in some asset, it is likely that green bonds also undergo a negative *rare* shock. Be aware that tail dependence is not to be confused with correlation coefficient, which is a measure of linear dependence. In fact, most estimated ρ s are negative ($\rho < 0$)—in normal times, if there is a negative shock to some asset, it is likely to have a positive shock to green bonds. In other words, the hedging effect of green bonds can differ between normal times and crisis times. Clayton copula assumes lower tail dependence ($\tau_L \neq 0$) but no upper tail dependence ($\tau_U = 0$), while rotated Clayton assumes the reverse, but none of them are significant. The SJC copula assumes asymmetric tail dependence, but the estimates are very small despite being significant. Using AIC as the model selection criterion, Student's t copulas stand out as the most efficient assumption for most assets apart from CNF and CNO in which normal distribution is preferred.

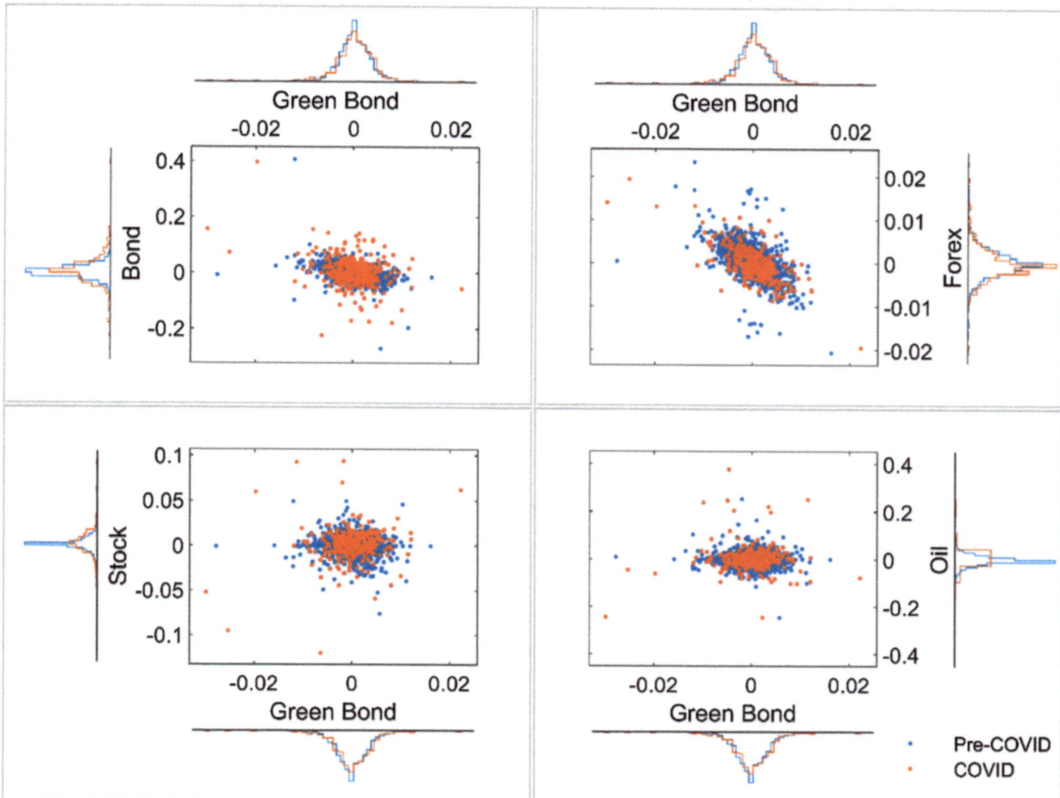

Fig. 7.1 Scatter histograms of assets versus green bonds in US

To visualize the estimated copulas, we use 3D mesh plots (Fig. 7.3) to compare assets and countries. Starting with green bonds and "brown" bonds, the copulas of US and China are almost identical. Both copulas show tail dependence at lower and upper quantiles. Moving to green bonds and stocks, the two countries again share very similar shapes only with thicker tails (larger degrees of freedom). Next, the US dollar index still maintains a similar copula to bonds and stocks, while the copula for Chinese exchange rate is almost flat (with a degree of freedom close to 100), which means it is basically a normal copula. Turning to oil indices, the US and China share a similar shape, but China has a flatter copula due to its weak position in the international oil market.

If time variation of copula functions is allowed, then correlation coefficient (ρ_t) and tail dependence (τ_{Lt}, τ_{Ut}) can change over time t. This dynamic feature is modeled following Reboredo (2018). Given that Student's t copula is the optimal choice, we focus on Student's t time-varying copulas, with normal time-varying copulas for CNF. We present the estimation results of time-varying copulas in Table 7.7. It is shown that time variation coefficients (a, b, c) are mostly significant.

To demonstrate time-varying features, correlation coefficients between green bonds and these assets are plotted in Fig. 7.4. The fluctuations during the COVID-19 pandemic become erratic. It is worth mentioning that, unlike the US, the correlation between green bonds and the forex market in China (i.e., USD/CNY currency pair, denoted as CNF) is stable throughout the sample period. Other asset markets in the US and China largely converge, especially in bond markets where the correlations are consistently negative for both countries.

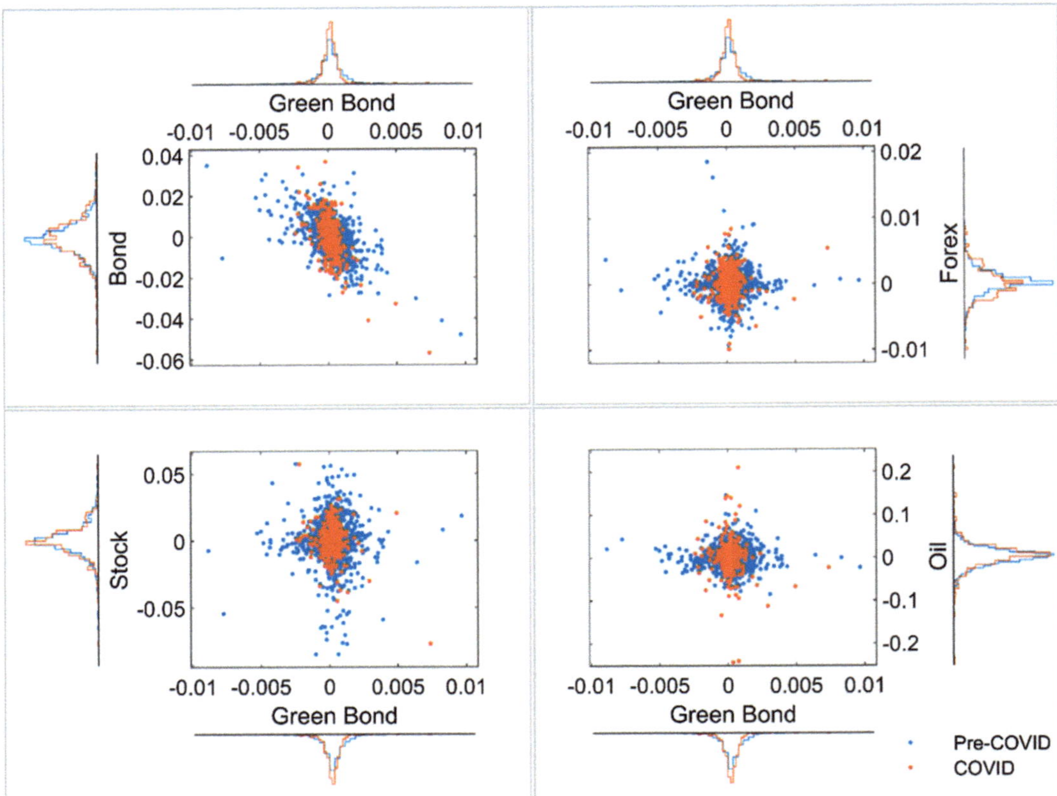

Fig. 7.2 Scatter histograms of assets versus green bonds in China

Table 7.4 VaR, CoVaR, and ΔCoVaR of financial assets in US and China

	VaR at 5%		CoVaR at 5%		ΔCoVaR	
	Pre-COVID	COVID	Pre-COVID	COVID	Pre-COVID	COVID
USGB	–0.52%	–0.60%	–0.77%	–1.11%		
USB	-3.34%	–6.44%	0.28%	0.18%	19.631	5.879
USS	–1.45%	–2.19%	0.12%	–0.28%	33.808	–9.302
USF	–0.49%	–0.53%	0.47%	0.60%	109.112	26.948
USO	–3.87%	–6.02%	0.04%	0.02%	5.259	0.555
CNGB	–0.13%	–0.08%	–0.26%	–0.15%		
CNB	–1.28%	–1.50%	0.17%	0.13%	6.630	7.888
CNS	–2.09%	–1.86%	0.03%	0.08%	0.431	5.824
CNF	–0.33%	–0.35%	0.02%	0.03%	0.002	0.901
CNO	–3.67%	–4.75%	0.04%	0.05%	1.046	2.121

Note The VaR columns are VaRs of different assets of the two countries at 5% percentiles. The CoVaR columns are the difference between the return of green bonds and the returns of other assets under stress conditions (defined as 5% percentiles). The USGB and CNGB rows are green bond VaRs conditional on green bond markets per se. Other rows are green bond VaRs conditional on other assets. The ΔCoVaR columns are ratios of return differences under stressed and normal states over the normal return

Table 7.5 Estimation results of marginal distributions

Mean	USGB	USB	USS	USF	USO	CNGB	CNB	CNS	CNF	CNO
AR(1)ϕ_1	–0.1239	0.0792	0.1208***	0.0448***		1.0151***		0.4015***	0.9069***	0.6866***
AR(2)ϕ_2	0.6235***	–0.0353	0.0206***	0.0426		0.3813***		–0.3046***		–0.68**
AR(3)ϕ_3	0.314*	–0.2377**		0.0414***		0.2819***		0.5373***		0.5724**
AR(4)ϕ_4	–0.7067***	0.7674***		0.042***		–0.9868***		–0.8682***		0.3638
AR(5)ϕ_5				0.0378***		0.3083***		–0.0438*		0.0385
MA(1)ψ_1	0.1585	–0.101	0.1212***	0.0416***		–0.5975***	0.1635***	–0.3928***	–0.8776***	–0.7225***
MA(2)ψ_2	–0.6175***	0.0651		0.0427*		–0.5934***	–0.0588**	0.3308***		0.7002**
MA(3)ψ_3	–0.3575**	0.2063*		0.0409***		–0.5511***		–0.5403***		–0.5835**
MA(4)ψ_4	0.6766***	–0.7853***		0.0412***		0.7368***		0.8548***		–0.3631
MA(5)ψ_5				0.0352***		0.0052				
Variance	USGB	USB	USS	USF	USO	CNGB	CNB	CNS	CNF	CNO
Constant α_0	0	0**	0***	0	0***	0	0*	0**	0	0***
GARCH(1)α_1	0.9276**	0.4314*	0.0186***	0.043	0.0279***	0.5118***	0.8866***	0.9032***	0	0.887***
GARCH(2)α_2	0	0.4653**		0.0418***					0.6611***	
ARCH(1)β_1	0.0796***	0.0491***	0.0144	0.015***	0.0437**	0.4287***	0.1017***	0	0.171***	0.0421**
ARCH(2)β_2				0.0151**				0.0942**	0.121**	
Leverage(1)γ_1	–0.0536**	0.1044***	0.0505***	0.0219	0.0778***	0.119	–0.0079	0.0457	0.0709	0.1123***
Leverage(2)γ_2				0.0212*				–0.0406	0.023	
DoF ν	5.0915***	7.6199***	0.3058***	0.3939***	0.1904***	2.5852***	5.2495***	3.8525***	3.8343***	4.981***
No. of Obs	1830	1830	1830	1830	1830	1799	1799	1799	1799	1799
AIC	–15,746.1	–8731.85	–12,785	–15,977.9	–8795.99	–21,313.2	–12,596.4	–11,231.2	–17,789.7	–8821.59
BIC	–15,668.9	–8654.68	–12,740.9	–15,878.7	–8768.43	–21,230.8	–12,558	–11,143.3	–17,734.7	–8744.66

Note Significance level, 1% ***, 5% **, 10% *

Table 7.6 Estimation results of time-invariant copulas

		USB	USS	USF	USO	CNB	CNS	CNF	CNO
Normal	ρ	–0.400***	–0.054**	–0.597***	–0.01	–0.478***	–0.046*	–0.02	–0.004
	$\tau_L = \tau_U$	0	0	0	0	0	0	0	0
	AIC	–318.07	–3.374	–805.21	1.812	–466.4	–1.82	1.248	1.965
Student's t	ρ	–0.427***	–0.063**	–0.612***	–0.005	–0.457***	–0.050**	–0.02	–0.001
	DoF ν	4.423***	7.036***	4.041***	8.619***	4.375***	8.816***	99.99***	28.28***
	$\tau_L = \tau_U$	0.0144	0.0166	0.0059	0.0124	0.0126	0.0093	0	0
	AIC	–416.34	–36.7	–913.11	–19.51	–533.5	–19.864	3.539	2.103
Clayton	ρ	0.0001	0.0001	0.0001	0.0134	0.0001	0.0001	0.0001	0.0001
	τ_L	0	0	0	0	0	0	0	0
	AIC	2.099	2.001	2.166	1.639	2.132	2.014	2.01	2.007
Rotated	ρ	0.0001	0.0001	0.0001	0.0082	0.0001	0.0043	0.0001	0.0182
Clayton	τ_U	0	0	0	0	0	0	0	0
	AIC	2.096	2.007	2.16	1.875	2.128	1.962	2.005	1.438
SJC	τ_U	0	0***	0	0**	0	0***	0***	0
	τ_L	0	0***	0	0	0	0***	0***	0***
	AIC	49.982	8.261	74.253	4.551	59.776	8.082	8.798	5.983

Note Significance level, 1% ***, 5% **, 10% *

Inclusion of time variation features imposes overparameterization costs, but the improved goodness of fit justifies a more sophisticated model according to the AIC information criterion. Comparing the AICs between Tables 7.6 and 7.7, most time-varying models are superior to time-invariant models apart from USB and CNS. The benefit of employing a time-varying model increases as the sample includes more pandemic observations. In fact, in an earlier run when only 2020 data are included, constant parameter models are favored. This finding suggests that modeling choice can depend on data availability. Policymakers and decision-makers in the financial market should frequently update their models on new data arrival.

7.4.4 Robustness

As shown in the previous section, estimated copulas display significant tail dependence. To provide a robustness check, we adopt two quantile-based measures to quantify the dependence of joint distributions between these assets and green bonds. The first measure is the quantile dependence, which calculates correlation coefficient within different quantiles (Patton, 2006). The second measure is the exceedance correlation developed by Ang & Chen (2001). A correlation at a given exceedance level is defined as the correlation between a pair of random variables when both rise or drop of more than a given number of standard deviations away from the means. It is a more flexible measure allowing for different degrees of dependence at different quantiles. The two measures provide a nonparametric alternative to copulas to describe the distributional dependence of chosen asset pairs. The advantage of the quantile-based approach, as discussed in the literature review, is that it can capture dependence in the entire joint distribution, not limited to the tails or means only. Also, it is nonparametric, so it is free from specification bias.

Figure 7.5 illustrates the two measures for the US and China. According to the quantile dependence (the upper two panels), the dollar index (forex) has the weakest tail dependence with green bonds in the US, followed by bonds, stocks, and

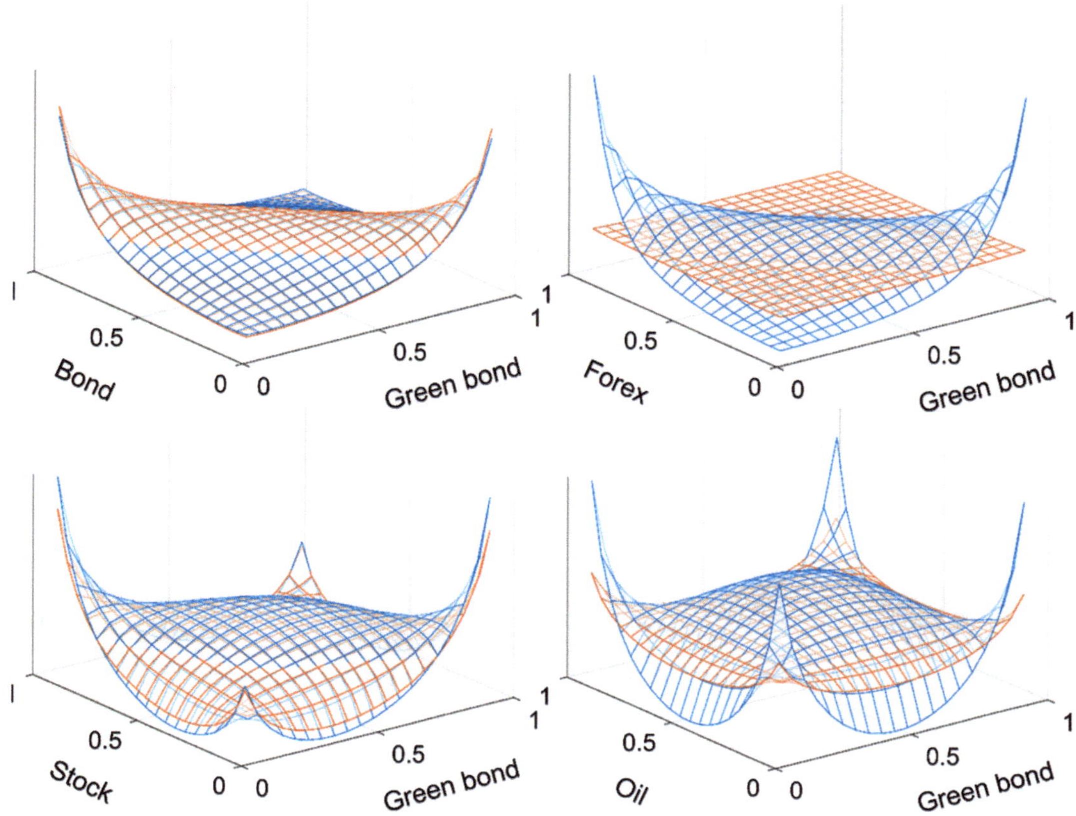

Fig. 7.3 Copula distributions with green bond in US and China. Notes: Blue mesh surfaces are copulas in the US, and red ones are copulas in China. The copulas are assumed to follow Student's t distributions

Table 7.7 Estimation results of time-varying copulas

		USB	USS	USF	USO	CNB	CNS	CNF	CNO
Normal	ρ	0.835***	–0.149	0.979***	0.684***	–0.98***	0.6717*	0.638	0.675
	a	–0.989***	–0.011	–0.236***	0.0017	–0.989***	–0.178*	–0.076	–0.031
	b	0.0319	0.051***	–0.079***	0.400***	–0.136***	0.077	0.3804**	–0.51***
	c	–0.388***	1.638***	2.013***	–1.996***	0.3321***	–1.93***	–1.97***	–0.675
	AIC	–313.09	–4.5049	–808.96	–6.5371	–471.92	2.148	2.398	–1.967
Student's t	ρ	0.357	–0.156	0.967	0.660	–0.98***	–0.599	0.018	0.654
	ν	4.484***	7.096***	3.964***	9.489***	4.468***	8.566***	99.81***	31.12***
	a	–1.906***	–0.012	–3.108***	0.004	–1.200**	–0.150	–0.078	–0.02
	b	0.031	0.047***	–0.091	0.274***	–0.05	0.139	0.3533***	–0.48***
	c	–2.411***	1.728***	–2.570***	–1.996***	–0.285***	–1.30***	–2.007***	–0.664***
	AIC	–412.46	–41.11	–914.79	–24.04	–535.37	–15.5094	4.2018	–1.5362

Note Significance level, 1% ***, 5% **, 10% *

oil. In China, by contrast, it is the bond market that has the weakest tail dependence. In terms of the exceedance correlation (the lower two panels), tail dependence is asymmetrical for all assets in both countries. For example, in the US, the lower tail dependence of forex market and green bond

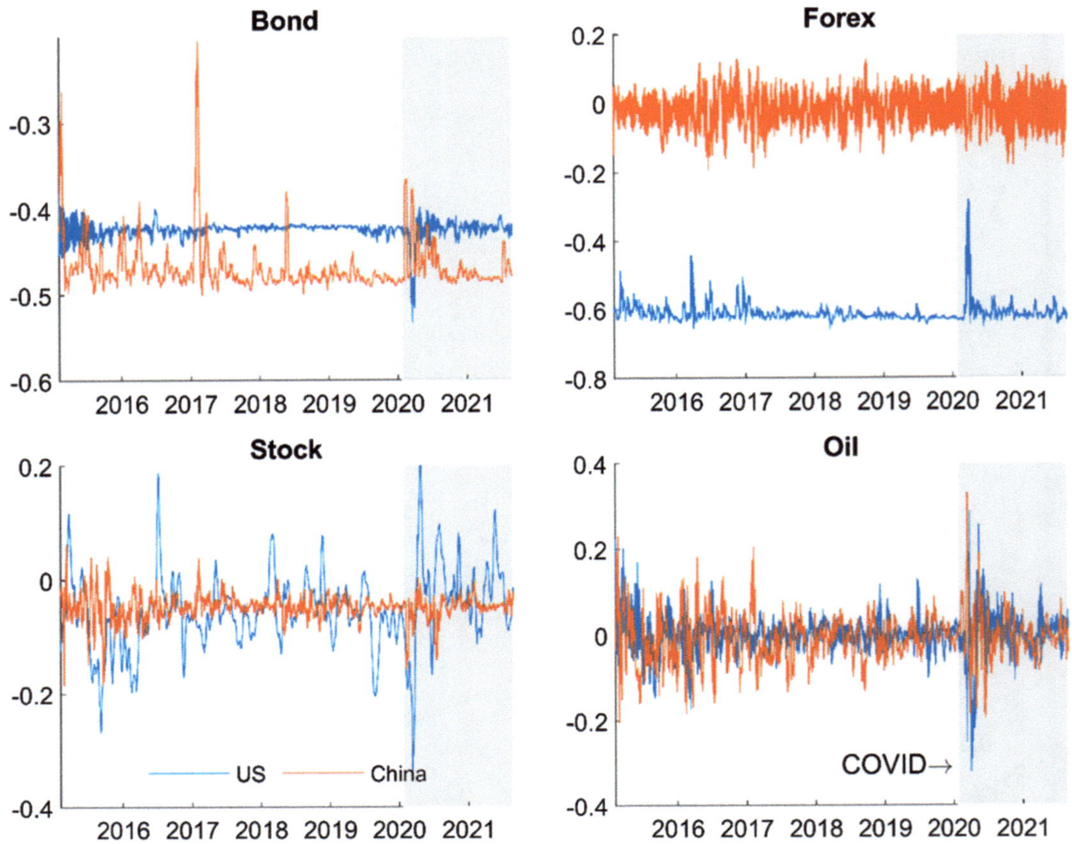

Fig. 7.4 Time Variation of correlations with green bond in US and China. Notes: Blue lines are correlations of the US (left axes), and red ones are correlations of China (right axes). The shaded areas indicate the COVID-19 pandemic (according to the WHO announcement)

market is 0.6, but the upper tail dependence is negative. This suggests that if there is a rare, bad shock, both markets tend to get hit, but if there is a rare, good shock, only one market is likely to receive it. This asymmetry is also observed in Chinese markets.

Compared with the estimation results in Table 7.6, tail dependence estimated in the copula approach and the quantile-based approach shares qualitative consistency. For example, the nonparametric quantile dependence (the upper panels) is mostly symmetric at tails in line with the symmetric feature of Student's t copulas. Exceedance correlations, however, are more erratic because they are based on stepwise exceedance and subject to small sample bias toward tails. This is an important drawback of nonparametric approaches since it does not leave noise processes out of the analysis. In contrast, the copula approach controls dynamics in mean, so the results are more stable and reliable.

7.5 Discussion

The results show that the correlations between green bonds and other financial assets are significant, time-varying, and quantile-dependent. How can we make use of this information in investment practice? To evaluate the potential role of green bonds as safe-heaven assets to hedge against rare risks, it is common to calculate the optimal hedging weight (HW) and evaluate the hedging effectiveness (HE) of green bonds in a portfolio.

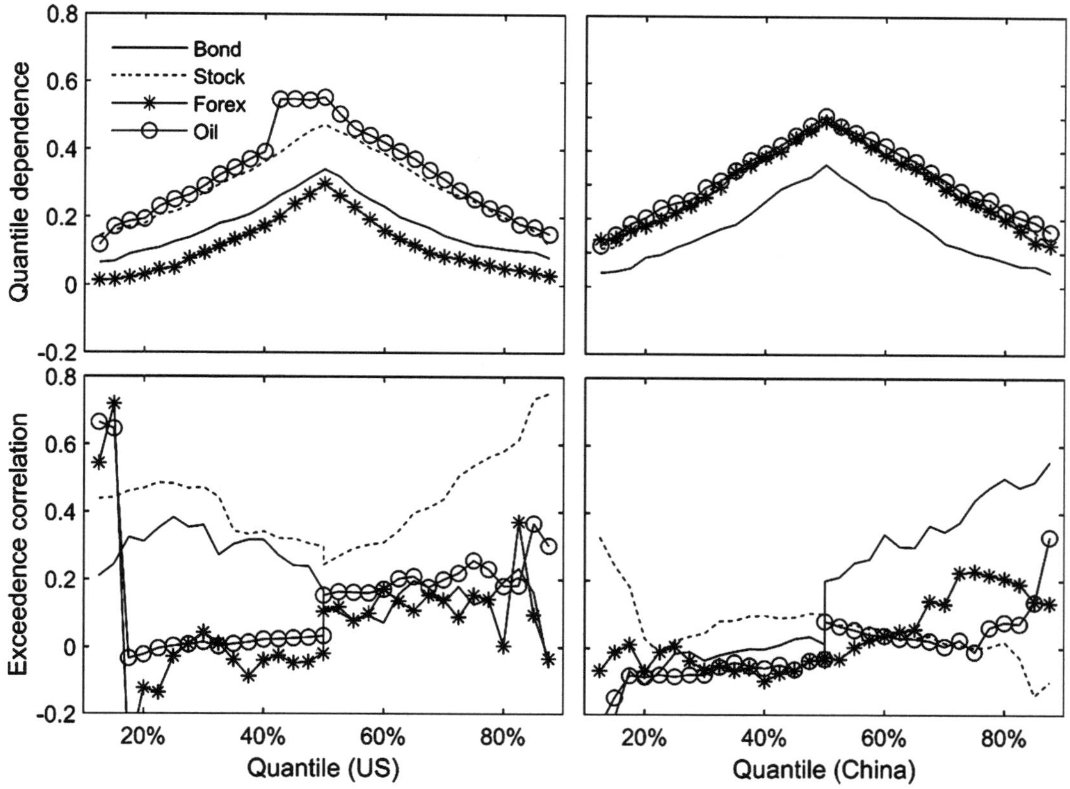

Fig. 7.5 Quantile dependence with green bond in US and China

We follow Jin et al (2020) and adopt the Theory of Minimum Variance Heading Ratio (Johnson, 1960). Assume a portfolio is composed of an asset and a green bond index. The return of the hedged portfolio, r_{ht}, and its variance, $V(r_{ht})$, depend on the HW of green bond index (w_{gt}):

$$r_{ht} = \left(1 - w_{gt}\right)r_{it} + w_{gt}r_{gt}$$

$$V(r_{ht}) = \left(1 - w_{gt}\right)^2 V(r_{it}) + w_{gt}^2 V\left(r_{gt}\right) + 2\left(1 - w_{gt}\right)w_{gt}Cov\left(r_{it}, r_{gt}\right)$$

To minimize the variance of the hedged portfolio, take partial derivative of $V(r_{ht})$ with respect to w_{gt} to obtain the optimal HW (w_{gt}^*):

$$\frac{\partial V(r_{ht})}{\partial w_{gt}} = 0 \rightarrow w_{gt}^* = \frac{V\left(r_{gt}\right) - Cov\left(r_{it}, r_{gt}\right)}{V(r_{it}) + V\left(r_{gt}\right) - 2Cov\left(r_{it}, r_{gt}\right)}$$

Note that if $w_{gt}^* > 0$, then the hedged portfolio contains a long position of green bonds. If $w_{gt}^* < 0$, then the portfolio is hedged by holding a short position of green bonds. Covariance and variance terms are conditional forecasts based on the estimated marginal distribution of TGARCH models.

Figure 7.6 presents the time-varying optimal HW w_{gt}^* for the selected financial assets of the two countries. In the cross-country dimension, it is surprising that the correlations between green bonds and other bonds in the US and China are closely tracking each other, both before and after the COVID-19 pandemic. It shows that the bond markets and green bond markets of the US and China are determined by similar factors such as monetary policy and green technological progress. In contrast, other markets such as stock and forex between the two markets significantly diverge (Guo & Zhou, 2021). In the over-time dimension, the COVID-19 pandemic seems to reduce the correlations between financial assets and green bonds. It implies that the hedging role of green bonds is reduced during rare tail risks. Other influential events like the US-China trade

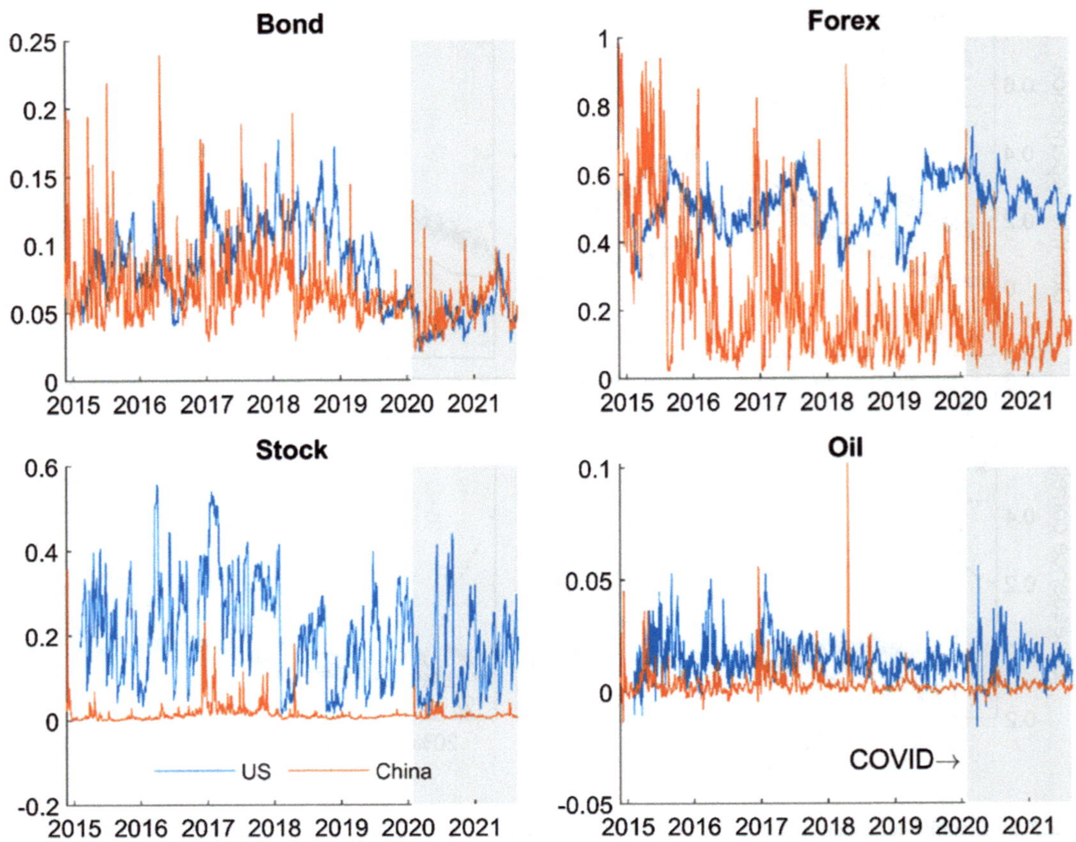

Fig. 7.6 Optimal hedging weights of green bonds in US and China. *Notes* Blue lines are correlations of the US, and red ones are correlations of China. The shaded areas indicate the COVID-19 pandemic (according to the WHO announcement).

war since 2018 and the oil price plunge in early 2020 may disturb the correlations temporarily but the influences are short-lived.

From equation [31], it is straightforward that the diversification benefit of a hedged portfolio depends on the correlation between the underlying assets and the variances of them. To better quantify the diversification benefit of green bonds, it is useful to have a metric to summarize the hedging effect. Ku et al. (2007) propose a measure termed hedging effectiveness (HE) based on risk reduction:

$$HE \equiv \frac{V(r_{it}) - V(r_{ht})}{V(r_{it})} \tag{7.6}$$

Table 7.8 compares the optimal HWs and HEs of green bonds in the US and China, before and after the COVID-19 pandemic. We can draw two important conclusions. On the one hand, the hedging effects of green bonds in China tend to be smaller than those in the US before the pandemic, but the gap becomes smaller or even reversed (e.g., bond market) since COVID-19. This indicates a fast development of green bonds in China relative to the US in recent years. In fact, China issued more than one-third of the global green bond issuance, ranking the first in the world. On the other hand, as a tail risk, the pandemic substantially reduced the hedging effects of green bonds with respect to bonds, stocks, and oil in both countries, but the hedging effects are still positive. It is worth pointing out that, despite being smaller, this is unfair to compare HEs before and after the pandemic. It is because the

Table 7.8 Hedging weights and hedging effectiveness (pre-COVID VS. COVID)

		US		China	
		Pre-COVID	COVID	Pre-COVID	COVID
Bond	HW	9.13%	4.65%	6.97%	5.23%
	HE	18.65%	9.45%	14.24%	10.65%
Stock	HW	21.23%	14.75%	1.62%	1.03%
	HE	34.88%	25.30%	3.16%	2.05%
Forex	HW	50.16%	52.58%	26.88%	13.87%
	HE	**71.55%**	**74.15%**	**6.02%**	**23.76%**
Oil	HW	1.49%	1.35%	0.35%	0.17%
	HE	2.95%	2.69%	0.71%	0.34%

Table notes HW = hedging weight, HE = hedging effectiveness.

HEs before the pandemic measure the hedging effect in normal times, while the HEs after the pandemic measure the hedging effect against tail risks. Specifically, the hedging effects in forex markets grow even stronger for both US and China since 2018, partly due to the exacerbating US-China trade war. Uncertainties in forex markets create greater hedging capacity for green bonds in both countries.

To summarize, optimal HWs during the pandemic slightly dropped because of positive tail dependence between green bonds and other assets. However, it does not mean the hedging effect of green bonds in extreme times is weak. It is weaker compared to normal times. In fact, recent literature finds similar results for alternative hedging assets like Brent oil (Kang et al., 2021), gold (Salisu et al., 2021), and other precious metals (Mensi et al., 2021).

7.6 Conclusion

Green bonds provide financial capital for sustainable growth and a safe-heaven investment vehicle against financial shocks. It is well documented in the literature that, in normal times, hedging effectiveness of green bonds is significant in both developed countries like the US and emerging economies like China. But evidence for the hedging effects during the COVID-19 pandemic is still scanty.

To choose the most reliable method to address this research question, we critically review and comprehensively compare four prevailing approaches in the green finance literature. The copula approach is adopted for its flexibility and reliability in capturing tail dependence between assets. It is found that the pandemic does reduce the hedging effectiveness of green bonds with bonds, stocks, and oil, but boosts the hedging effectiveness in forex markets. The behavior of green bonds in the US and China resembles each other, especially during the pandemic. There is a converging international green bond market in terms of both marginal distribution and copula function.

This chapter offers new evidence for the connectedness between conventional financial assets and green financial assets. It is important for portfolio management and risk diversification in both US and China, during both normal times and crisis times. Moreover, it also points some directions for policymakers. First, given the significant hedging effect of green bonds, governments should issue related regulations and industrial standards, which are recognized by international counterparts. International convergence of green bond standards can improve information disclosure and transparency, which can in turn strengthen the diversification function of green bonds for both developed and emerging economies. Second, resilience against rare disasters like climate risks and pandemic risks is the most important theme of the international community of our times, particularly after the COVID-19 pandemic. Major economies like the US, the EU, and China adopt a sustainability strategy and support investment in green assets. It is an inevitable trend of an expanding international green bond market. Nevertheless, as a safe-heaven asset, green bonds may be used by arbitragers and hot money in cross-border speculations. For emerging countries like China, it is advisable to develop offshore institutional investors to hold long-term positions of green bonds. It can reduce the short-term shocks to the stability of the green bonds market due to speculative activities in the forex market.

References

Abakah, E. J. A., Addo, E., Gil-Alana, L. A., & Tiwari, A. K. (2021). Re-examination of international bond market dependence: Evidence from a pair copula approach. *International Review of Financial Analysis, 74*, Article 101678.

Alonso-Conde, A.-B., & Rojo-Suárez, J. (2020). On the effect of green bonds on the profitability and credit quality of project financing. *Sustainability, 12*(16), 6695.

Ang, A., & Chen, J. (2002). Asymmetric correlations of equity portfolios. *Journal of Financial Economics, 63*(3), 443–494.

Antonakakis, N., Chatziantoniou, I., & Gabauer, D. (2020). Refined measures of dynamic connectedness based on time-varying parameter vector autoregressions. *Journal of Risk and Financial Management, 13*(4), 84.

Bachelet, M. J., Becchetti, L., & Manfredonia, S. (2019). The green bonds premium puzzle: The role of issuer characteristics and third-party verification. *Sustainability, 11*(4), 1098.

Banga, J. (2019). The green bond market: A potential source of climate finance for developing countries. *Journal of Sustainable Finance & Investment, 9*(1), 17–32.

Barro, R. J. (2006).Rare disasters and asset markets in the twentieth century. *The Quarterly Journal of Economics, 121*(3), 823–866.

Beck, R., Georgiadis, G., & Straub, R. (2014). The finance and growth nexus revisited. *Economics Letters, 124*(3), 382–385.

Campbell, R., Kees, K., & Kofman, P. (2002). Increased correlation in bear markets. *Financial Analysts Journal, 58*(1), 87–94.

Creal, D., Jan, K. S., & Lucas, A. (2011). A dynamic multivariate heavy-tailed model for time-varying volatilities and correlations. *Journal of Business & Economic Statistics, 29*(4), 552–563.

Engle, R. (2002). Dynamic conditional correlation. *Journal of Business & Economic Statistics, 20*(3), 339–350.

Erb, C. B., Harvey, C. R., & Viskanta, T. E. (1994). Forecasting international equity correlations. *Financial Analysts Journal, 50*(6), 32–45.

Gao, Y., Li, Y., & Wang, Y. (2021). Risk spillover and network connectedness analysis of China's green bond and financial markets: Evidence from financial events of 2015–2020. *The North American Journal of Economics and Finance, 57*, Article 101386.

Girardi, G., & Tolga Ergün, A. (2013). Systemic risk measurement: Multivariate GARCH estimation of CoVaR. *Journal of Banking & Finance, 37*(8), 3169–3180.

Gong, X.-L., Liu, X.-H., & Xiong, X. (2019). Measuring tail risk with GAS time varying copula, fat tailed GARCH model and hedging for crude oil futures. *Pacific-Basin Finance Journal, 55*, 95–109.

Guo, D., & Zhou, P. (2021). The rise of a new anchor currency in RCEP? A tale of three currencies. *Economic Modelling, 104*, Article 105647.

Han, H., Linton, O., Oka, T., & Whang, Y.-J. (2016). The cross-quantilogram: Measuring quantile dependence and testing directional predictability between time series. *Journal of Econometrics, 193*(1), 251–270.

Han, Y., & Li, J. (2022). Should investors include green bonds in their portfolios? Evidence for the USA and Europe. *International Review of Financial Analysis, 80*, Article 101998.

Hansen, B. E. (1994). Autoregressive conditional density estimation. *International Economic Review, 35*(3), 705–730.

He, X., Mishra, S., Aman, A., Shahbaz, M., Razzaq, A., & Sharif, A. (2021). The linkage between clean energy stocks and the fluctuations in oil price and financial stress in the US and Europe? Evidence from QARDL approach. *Resources Policy, 72*, Article 102021.

Jin, J., Han, L., Wu, L., & Zeng, H. (2020). The hedging effect of green bonds on carbon market risk. *International Review of Financial Analysis, 71*, Article 101509.

Johnson, L. L. (1960). The theory of hedging and speculation in commodity futures. *The Review of Economic Studies, 27*(3), 139–151.

Kang, S., Hernandez, J. A., Sadorsky, P., & McIver, R. (2021). Frequency spillovers, connectedness, and the hedging effectiveness of oil and gold for US sector ETFs. *Energy Economics, 99*, Article 105278.

King, R. G., & Levine, R. (1993). Finance and growth: Schumpeter might be right. *The Quarterly Journal of Economics, 108*(3), 717–737.

Kristoufek, L. (2020). Grandpa, grandpa, tell me the one about Bitcoin being a safe haven: New evidence from the COVID-19 pandemic. *Frontiers in Physics, 8*, 296.

Ku, Y.-H.H., Ho-Chyuan, C., & Chen, K.-H. (2007). On the application of the dynamic conditional correlation model in estimating optimal time-varying hedge ratios. *Applied Economics Letters, 14*(7), 503–509.

Kuang, W. (2021). Are clean energy assets a safe haven for international equity markets? *Journal of Cleaner Production, 302*, Article 127006.

Maghyereh, A. I., Awartani, B., & Abdoh, H. (2019). The co-movement between oil and clean energy stocks: A wavelet-based analysis of horizon associations. *Energy, 169*, 895–913.

Mensi, W., Nekhili, R., Vo, X. V., & Kang, S. H. (2021). Oil and precious metals: Volatility transmission, hedging, and safe haven analysis from the Asian crisis to the COVID-19 crisis. *Economic Analysis and Policy, 71*, 73–96.

Naeem, M. A., Nguyen, T. T. H., Nepal, R., Ngo, Q.-T., & Taghizadeh-Hesary, F. (2021). Asymmetric relationship between green bonds and commodities: Evidence from extreme quantile approach. *Finance Research Letters, 43*, Article 101983.

Park, D., Park, J., & Ryu, D. (2020). Volatility spillovers between equity and green bond markets. *Sustainability, 12*(9), 3722.

Patton, A. J. (2004). On the out-of-sample importance of skewness and asymmetric dependence for asset allocation. *Journal of Financial Econometrics, 2*(1), 130–168.

Patton, A. J. (2006). Modelling asymmetric exchange rate dependence. *International Economic Review, 47*(2), 527–556.

Pham, L., & Nguyen, C. P. (2022). How do stock, oil, and economic policy uncertainty influence the green bond market? *Finance Research Letters, 45*, Article 102128.

Reboredo, J. C. (2018). Green bond and financial markets: Co-movement, diversification and price spillover effects. *Energy Economics, 74*, 38–50.

Reboredo, J. C., & Ugolini, A. (2020). Price connectedness between green bond and financial markets. *Economic Modelling, 88*, 25–38.

Reboredo, J. C., Ugolini, A., & Aiube, F. A. L. (2020). Network connectedness of green bonds and asset classes. *Energy Economics, 86*, Article 104629.

Rietz, T. A. (1988). The equity risk premium a solution. *Journal of Monetary Economics, 22*(1), 117–131.

Salisu, A. A., Vo, X. V., & Lawal, A. (2021). Hedging oil price risk with gold during COVID-19 pandemic. *Resources Policy, 70*, Article 101897.

Sarkodie, S. A., Ajmi, A. N., Adedoyin, F. F., & Owusu, P. A. (2021). Econometrics of anthropogenic emissions, green energy-based innovations, and energy intensity across OECD countries. *Sustainability, 13*(8), 4118.

Shahzad, S. J. H., Arreola-Hernandez, J., Bekiros, S., Shahbaz, M., & Kayani, G. M. (2018). A systemic risk analysis of Islamic equity markets using vine copula and delta CoVaR modeling. *Journal of International Financial Markets, Institutions and Money, 56*, 104–127.

Song, L., & Zhou, X. (2021). Does the green industry policy reduce industrial pollution emissions?—Evidence from China's national eco-industrial park. *Sustainability, 13*(11), 6343.

Taghizadeh-Hesary, F., Yoshino, N., & Phoumin, H. (2021). Analyzing the characteristics of green bond markets to facilitate green finance in the post-COVID-19 world. *Sustainability, 13*(10), 5719.

Uddin, M., Chowdhury, A., Anderson, K., & Chaudhuri, K. (2021). The effect of COVID—19 pandemic on global stock market volatility: Can economic strength help to manage the uncertainty? *Journal of Business Research, 128*, 31–44.

Wang, K., Chen, Y.-H., & Huang, S.-W. (2011). The dynamic dependence between the Chinese market and other international stock markets: A time-varying copula approach. *International Review of Economics & Finance, 20*(4), 654–664.

World Bank. (2021). *IBRD funding program*. World Bank.

Xia, T., Ji, Q., Zhang, D., & Han, J. (2019). Asymmetric and extreme influence of energy price changes on renewable energy stock performance. *Journal of Cleaner Production, 241*, Article 118338.

Yi, X., Bai, C., Lyu, S., & Dai, L. (2021). The impacts of the COVID-19 pandemic on China's green bond market. *Finance Research Letters, 42*, Article 101948.

Yu, C.-H., Wu, X., Zhang, D., Chen, S., & Zhao, J. (2021). Demand for green finance: Resolving financing constraints on green innovation in China. *Energy Policy, 153*, Article 112255.

Zhang, B., & Zhou, P. (2021). Financial development and economic growth in a microfounded small open economy model. *The North American Journal of Economics and Finance, 58*, Article 101544.

Zhou, P., Jin, S., Mazouz, K., & Ding, W. (2025). Choices and effects of different green labels in the EU bond market. *Journal of Business Ethics, 200*, 207–229.

Zhou, X., & Cui, Y. (2019). Green bonds, corporate performance, and corporate social responsibility. *Sustainability, 11*(23), 6881.

Maritime Economy and Blue Bonds

8

Abstract

Blue finance channels capital toward ocean conservation and sustainable maritime industries. This chapter asks whether blue bonds and debt-for-blue swaps can simultaneously protect marine ecosystems and bolster the fiscal resilience of coastal states. Surveying recent issuances in the US, China, and other jurisdictions, we map design choices—use-of-proceeds covenants, impact reporting, and concessional pricing—that determine environmental credibility and investor appeal. Evidence shows that well-structured blue bonds mobilize resources for biodiversity protection, pollution abatement, and fisheries governance while lowering borrowing costs for heavily indebted nations. The Seychelles and Belize swaps converted sovereign liabilities into long-term funding for marine protected areas, illustrating a debt-relief channel absent from conventional green finance. Yet the market remains vulnerable to greenwashing (or "bluewashing"), uneven taxonomies, and lax verification dilute impact. Three policy lessons follow. First, harmonized global standards and third-party auditing are essential to ensure genuine progress of sustainability. Second, high-debt coastal economies should integrate blue instruments into their debt-management strategies to unlock concessional capital. Third, cross-sector collaboration—linking governments, development lenders, private investors, and local communities—maximizes ecological returns and generates shared economic benefits.

Keywords

Blue bonds · Maritime economy

Classification

SDG12 · SDG13 · SDG14

8.1 Introduction

Contemporary global affairs are linked to maritime dynamics, as highlighted by Dehio (1962) who characterized the international system as a maritime one. The significance of the marine domain stems from its role as a conduit connecting nations and harboring vast resources (Thompson, 2022). Beyond its economic and political relevance, the maritime realm has substantial strategic value. The United Nations' inclusion of the concept of a "Community of Common Destiny of Mankind" in its 2017 resolution underscores the recognition within the international community of the importance of seeking common ground amidst diversity (Zhang, 2018).

This chapter provides practical guidance for the design of maritime strategy and its associated blue finance instruments. It first situates the contemporary aspiration to build a "marine community" within its historical context and then traces the

D. Guo and P. Zhou, *Beating Financial Swords into Developmental Plowshares*,
Sustainable Development Goals Series, https://doi.org/10.1007/978-981-95-5152-1_8

development of blue finance in tandem with recent innovations in financial instruments. The analysis proceeds in four steps. We begin by mapping the rise of modern maritime powers and demonstrating why the formation of a marine community is now essential. Next, we examine changes in the international financial system to identify the most recent advances in blue finance, with particular attention to instruments such as blue bonds and blue aid; we assess both their distinctive characteristics and their current limitations. We then investigate how blue debt-for-nature swaps operate in different settings and propose ways to alleviate the debt burdens of developing countries. Finally, we bring these insights together to outline likely future directions for blue finance and to propose a strategic framework for policymakers.

This chapter contributes on multiple fronts. It enriches scholarly discourse by elucidating the latest trends in blue finance, thereby fostering the emergence of more practical literature in this field. Furthermore, it offers academic insights into addressing the debt crisis confronting developing nations, a topic that has received scant attention, particularly concerning the application of blue finance in international debt governance. In addition, it introduces China's blue finance framework, encompassing aspects such as blue bond issuance, market infrastructure development, the design of RMB-denominated blue financial products, and China's strategic posture in international debt governance.

8.2 History

The development of maritime powers has been shaped by shifts in military technology, global maritime dynamics, and evolving modes of peaceful competition, leading to a multi-tiered maritime strategic landscape. Understanding the rise and fall of maritime powers holds significant implications for shaping contemporary maritime power structures and guiding the development trajectories of maritime nations.

The progression of maritime powers can be delineated through distinct stages characterized by colonial expansion, commercial capital proliferation, and industrial capital ascendancy. Initially, in the era of colonial expansion, Portugal and Spain ascended amidst the burgeoning shipbuilding and maritime technology of the sixteenth century, laying the groundwork for a global maritime network facilitating international trade. Employing maritime military prowess, these powers expanded their colonial territories, leveraging advancements in shipping technology to assert dominance over international trade routes.

In the subsequent phase, the Netherlands emerged as a dominant maritime force, capitalizing on the exponential growth of commercial capital in the seventeenth century. Spearheading maritime technology and military advancements, the Netherlands solidified its position as a hegemonic power, shaping global trade networks and exerting considerable influence on international affairs.

The industrial revolution ushered in an era of global expansion for commercial and industrial capital, propelling the UK and the US to maritime supremacy. Britain's reign as the "empire on which the sun never sets" during the eighteenth and nineteenth centuries underscored its unparalleled control over sea lanes and maritime trade, effectively dictating global economic structures to reflect its interests. Subsequently, the US assumed maritime hegemony in the twentieth century following World War II, supplanting Britain as the preeminent maritime power. Despite the backdrop of economic globalization and the multi-polarization of the twenty-first-century world, the US maintains significant control over key maritime routes, perpetuating its influence across political, economic, military, cultural, and ideological domains.

Moreover, ancient China also boasted maritime prowess during the era of sail. Dating back to the sixth century BC, China possessed a well-organized naval apparatus, exemplified by naval forces in regions such as Wu, Yue, and Chu during the Spring and Autumn Period and the Warring States Period. Advancements in gunpowder and navigation technology propelled China's maritime capabilities to unprecedented heights during the Song and Yuan Dynasties, fostering international connectivity through maritime trade. Notably, Zheng He's voyages to the West during the Ming Dynasty showcased China's formidable navigation technology and military prowess. However, the subsequent sea-forbidden policies enforced by the Ming and Qing Dynasties curtailed China's maritime ambitions, stifling the development of international trade and squandering opportunities for maritime dominance.

Historical narratives offer invaluable insights into contemporary maritime dynamics, elucidating four key lessons:

- The concept of comprehensive maritime power transcends mere naval prowess, encompassing a spectrum of international influence across politics, economics, military affairs, culture, and technology. The innovation capacity of a nation's technical infrastructure emerges as a pivotal determinant of maritime ascendancy, evident in historical examples such as Portugal's dhows, the Netherlands' Mercator charts, Britain's battleships, and the US' naval aviation.
- The dilemma faced by land-sea countries underscores the geopolitical constraints on maritime power development. While maritime powers like the UK and the US enjoy geographical advantages conducive to maritime dominance, land-sea countries like France and Germany grapple with inherent geopolitical limitations impeding maritime expansion. The pursuit of simultaneous land and sea advantages often precipitates power balance dynamics, exacerbating conflicts and potentially ensnaring nations in the Thucydides trap.
- The notion of limited sea power highlights the complex factors hindering the maritime ambitions of land-sea countries. Russia's centuries-long endeavor to expand its maritime control exemplifies the perils of relentless pursuit of sea power, ultimately contributing to its eventual decline.
- History illustrates two modes of maritime power ascent: confrontational and peaceful. While some nations adopt confrontational approaches akin to Germany's challenge to British maritime hegemony, others, like the US, pursue a peaceful rise, integrating into the international system and navigating hegemonic disputes with strategic finesse.

8.3 Blue Finance and Blue Bonds

The advancement of comprehensive maritime power relies heavily on the maritime economy, which in turn hinges on the "blue finance." Today, blue finance has garnered significant attention both academically and internationally. It encompasses various transactional activities aimed at developing the maritime economy, such as resource transfers and risk allocations. Additionally, blue finance plays a crucial role in bolstering countries' maritime capabilities and realizing the concept of a marine community. This financial support is vital for implementing maritime economy strategies. Furthermore, blue finance embodies environmental sustainability in marine protection efforts, thus promoting the sustainable development of the blue economy.

Blue finance encompasses two main concepts. First, in the realm of maritime economy, blue finance, also known as marine finance, encompasses all financial activities geared toward developing the maritime economy. Second, in terms of environmental protection, blue finance represents an emerging and highly prioritized area within climate finance. The rise of blue finance can be attributed to the close connection between the marine environment and the future well-being of humanity. For instance, the International Finance Corporation (IFC) projects that the total value of the maritime economy will reach $3 trillion by 2030, doubling the amount from 2010 and potentially creating job opportunities for 40 million people. In this context, well-developed blue finance is essential for ensuring the sustainable growth of the maritime economy.

Despite its importance, blue finance is still in its early stages of development, with its framework undergoing continuous improvement. Initially, the 14th Sustainable Development Goal (SDG14) of the United Nations' "Transforming

Table 8.1 Criteria and guidelines for blue finance

Criteria	Guideline
Classification	The project should meet all the requirements of green bond principle, green credit principle, and sustainable development goals (SDG6 and SDG14).
Risk	The project cannot pose risks to other SGDs, including hunger eradication (SDG2), affordable clean energy (SDG7), climate action (SDG12), and responsible consumption and survival (SDG13).
ESG	The project needs to clarify its minimum guarantee of ESG criteria. For instance, following the internationally applicable sustainable development standards, IFC'S performance evaluation standards, or World Bank's environmental/health/safety guidelines, etc. in addition, blue finance also needs to be applied to the provisions of specific production standards above national standards.

Table 8.2 Concepts of blue economy and blue finance

Blue concepts	Explanation
Blue economy	It refers to the sustainable development and utilization of marine resources, aiming at promoting economic growth, improving living standards and social employment, and at the same time maintaining the health of marine ecosystem and water resources.
Blue finance	Investment activities for marine protection and water resources management through financing and refinancing.
Blue loan	Based on principles of green credit, it exclusively serves financing and refinancing activities in marine protection and water resources management.
Blue bond	A fixed income instrument based on principles of green credit, which proceeds is used in marine protection and water resources management.
Blue impact	Quantitative indicators in evaluating marine-related physical, chemical, and biological changes.

our World: The 2030 Agenda for Sustainable Development" highlights the key financing areas and objectives of blue finance, emphasizing marine protection and sustainable resource usage. Subsequently, various organizations, including the European Commission (EC) and the World Wide Fund for Nature (WWFN), have proposed principles and guidelines for sustainable blue economy financing. Notably, the IFC has recently issued "Guidelines for Blue Finance," which expands on previous frameworks by incorporating additional Sustainable SDGs and evaluation criteria. Furthermore, the development of the blue financial market necessitates the integration of public and private resources. The "Guidelines for Blue Finance" encourage and support private investors to participate in blue financial projects, highlighting the market's characteristics of both governmental oversight and private sector involvement (Table 8.1 and Table 8.2).

Specifically, blue bonds are debt instruments issued by international organizations, governments, or other entities to raise funds for marine-related projects, assets, or strategies. The first blue bond was issued by Seychelles with the assistance of the World Bank in 2018, following the model of green bonds issuance. Blue bonds share similarities with green bonds but allocate proceeds specifically to marine development projects.

To promote the development of the blue bond market, international organizations and capital market participants have actively advocated for the establishment of blue bond standards and market frameworks. For instance, in 2019, the World Conservation Union and the United Nations Global Compact issued guidelines for blue bond issuance. Blue bonds have evolved into various types, including supranational, sovereign, financial, and non-financial corporate blue bonds. Notably, China has issued blue bonds through financial institutions and related enterprises, contributing to the development of the blue finance market.

Despite its relatively recent emergence, blue bonds have gained momentum in the financial sector. However, to achieve its environmental and economic goals, China must expedite the establishment of blue bond regulations and foster the integration of blue finance with green finance initiatives.

In the World Bank's Blue Economy Program, PROBLUE, financial instruments in the form of economic assistance complement traditional credit and bond instruments (Tirumala & Tiwari, 2022). PROBLUE, an umbrella multi-donor trust fund, aims to enhance the investment impact of blue finance by attracting greater attention and funding. Since its inception following the Blue Economy Conference in Nairobi in 2018, PROBLUE has garnered significant pledges, with Norway being the earliest investment partner and several other maritime countries subsequently joining.

PROBLUE, aligned with the World Bank's objectives of eradicating global poverty and promoting sustainable development, focuses on four key themes: fisheries and aquaculture management, marine pollution mitigation, sustainable development of marine sectors, and comprehensive marine resource management. PROBLUE provides financial support to sovereign countries or specific regional institutions for marine economic projects that adhere to blue financial guidelines. Both parties negotiate and select projects that meet the fund's criteria, with the World Bank overseeing project submissions to PROBLUE.

8.4 Governance

As a new financial tool, blue bonds generate new challenges in governance. We discuss the debt dilemma of blue bonds and its potential solution by blue swaps.

8.4.1 Debt Dilemma

Developing countries are grappling with a pressing debt crisis exacerbated by various global challenges such as economic downturns, climate change, and the COVID-19 pandemic (Fischer & Storm, 2023). These factors have significantly hindered the development of the maritime economy, leading to a double dilemma of high debt and weak growth. Coastal developing nations, particularly reliant on marine industries, face heightened debt challenges due to their singular focus and overreliance on marine resources. Rapidly accumulating debt in these countries hampers swift economic recovery, reducing their solvency while burdening them with unsustainable debt levels. Consequently, both creditors and the global market express concerns about the potential for an international debt crisis.

Additionally, the global international debt governance system is undergoing reform and transformation. The establishment of the Paris Club in 1956 marked the inception of international debt governance. Crisis management efforts in developing countries during the 1980s prompted the transformation of the initial international debt governance framework, shaping the core concepts, mechanisms, and models of contemporary international debt governance. Despite loose coordination by entities such as the Paris Club and international financial institutions, the existing debt governance system faces constraints, particularly in addressing the complexities of debt crisis management compounded by the "blue" factor.

Addressing the blue debt dilemma can be achieved through Debt-for-Nature and Climate Swaps (DNCS), which involve Debt-for-Environment Swaps with additional considerations for nature conservation and climate issues. Sustainable development principles, including ESG considerations, have become integral to international debt financing. As of 2021, debt financing for sustainable development has surpassed US$3 trillion, with sovereign debt markets witnessing significant growth. Blue finance, as part of sustainable finance, can leverage DNCS in international debt governance related to the marine sector.

Debt-for-Environment Swaps (DES) originated during the Latin American debt crisis and represent the earliest operational model of environmental debt swaps. DES involves private entities, such as Conservation International, aiding sovereign debt relief while financing environmental conservation projects. Despite declining usage since the 1990s, DES transactions have involved over 30 countries, providing over one billion dollars for environmental protection projects. DES operates through two primary mechanisms: substitution effect and local currency financing. The substitution effect involves reducing a low-income country's international debt and redirecting expenditures toward environmental goals. Subsequently, the debtor country raises funds in its local currency to invest in environmental projects as stipulated in the debt swap agreement.

8.4.2 Blue Swap

In 2016, the creditor group of the Paris Club utilized debt swaps to alleviate Seychelles' international debt, earmarking funds for marine protection and climate restoration. Although this debt swap incorporated a "blue" factor, it did not align with the principles or standards of blue finance. However, in November 2021, the Nature Conservancy (TNC) introduced the first innovative blue swap, representing the largest sovereign debt restructuring for marine protection to date.

This Debt-for-Blue Swap (DBS) involved a financial transaction of $364 million for Belize's sovereign debt reduction, with $180 million allocated to marine protection efforts (Delpla & Von Weizsäcker, 2010). Belize committed to investing in marine conservation projects within 30% of its territorial waters, enhancing fisheries management, and establishing mechanisms for coastal blue carbon projects. The DBS framework mirrors that of blue finance, encompassing sustainable development principles, green financial standards, and ESG concepts. Its operational process aligns with DNCS, demonstrating its potential to address both debt and environmental challenges effectively (Fig. 8.1).

8.5 Conclusion

Recent years have witnessed active participation from international organizations and NGOs in constructing the Blue Economic Order and the Blue Financial System. Initiatives such as the EU's "Sustainable Blue Economy Finance Initiative" and IFC's "Guidelines for Blue Finance" have laid the groundwork for a comprehensive blue financial framework. This framework encompasses green, low-carbon, sustainable development, and ESG principles, with a focus on SDG6 and SDG14.

Blue bonds, as innovative financial tools for global ocean governance, hold significant potential. Despite their relatively recent emergence, blue bonds have evolved into various types, including supranational, sovereign, financial, and corporate blue bonds. Unlike green financial instruments, blue bonds offer a distinct focus that

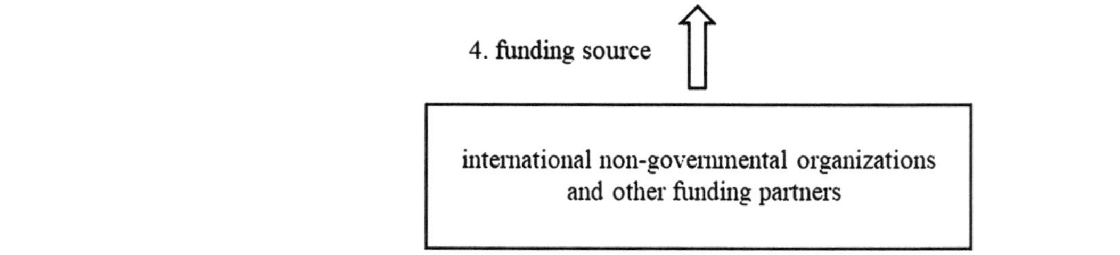

Fig. 8.1 Operation process of blue debt swap

can mitigate the risk of "green washing" and ensure genuine environmental impact.

To promote marine protection and foster a thriving blue economy, China has leveraged its "Marine Plan" from the 14th "Five-Year Plan." This initiative underscores China's commitment to global marine governance and the "community of marine destiny." Key actions include optimizing spatial layouts for maritime economy, accelerating modern marine industrial systems, enhancing innovation in marine science and technology, and safeguarding national maritime rights. As a country with both land economy and maritime economy, China faces unique geographic challenges, necessitating active engagement in international marine governance cooperation. China can contribute by shaping blue financial rules with its unique characteristics, bridging gaps in the rules system, and integrating these rules into global ocean governance cooperation efforts.

Blue bonds also offer a promising avenue for smaller countries to mobilize finance for sustainable ocean-related projects while promoting environmental conservation and economic development. These financial instruments can play a crucial role in addressing pressing challenges such as marine pollution, habitat degradation, and climate change impacts on coastal communities. By embracing blue finance frameworks and exploring blue bond opportunities, countries can align their financial systems with sustainable development goals and promote responsible investment in the blue economy. Strengthening regulatory frameworks and fostering international collaboration are essential steps to ensure the success of blue bond initiatives and maximize their impact on marine conservation and sustainable development. Additionally, prioritizing community engagement and monitoring and evaluating the impact of blue bond-funded projects are critical aspects of ensuring transparency, accountability, and inclusiveness in decision-making processes. By incorporating these policy implications, countries can harness the potential of blue bonds to drive positive change in marine ecosystems and coastal communities worldwide.

References

Dehio, L. (1962). *The precarious balance: Four centuries of the European power struggle*. Knopf.

Delpla, J., & Von Weizsäcker, J. (2010). The blue bond proposal. *Bruegel Policy Brief, 3*(6).

Fischer, A. M., & Storm, S. (2023). The return of debt crisis in developing countries: Shifting or maintaining dominant development paradigms? *Development and Change, 54*(5), 954–993.

Thompson, B. S. (2022). Blue bonds for marine conservation and a sustainable ocean economy: Status, trends, and insights from green bonds. *Marine Policy, 144*, 105219.

Zhang, D. (2018). The concept of 'Community of Common Destiny' in China's diplomacy: Meaning, motives and implications. *Asia & the Pacific Policy Studies, 5*(2), 196–207.

Sustainable Economy and Carbon Trade 9

Abstract

In the context of global climate action, carbon trading—originating with the Kyoto Protocol—frames greenhouse-gas reduction as an asset market. We analyze the European Union Emissions Trading System (EU ETS) as the world's benchmark and ask three questions: Do allowance prices behave like established commodities; do they move with oil and gold; and are they affected by US monetary policy? Daily data are examined with DCC-GARCH and time-varying parameter VAR models. Results show that allowance prices share volatility traits with oil and, to a lesser extent, gold, confirming the "energization" of carbon. Moreover, higher US interest rates and a stronger dollar dampen allowance prices, linking climate finance to central bank decisions. Strengthening markets through green finance incentives, hedging energy-transition risks, and incorporating carbon market stability into monetary deliberations can mobilize private capital while safeguarding macro-stability. Carbon trading therefore functions simultaneously as a disciplinary weapon against emissions and a developmental tool for a low-carbon economy.

Keywords

Carbon trade · Sustainable economy

Classification

SDG7 · SDG12 · SDG13

9.1 Introduction

Since the adoption of the Kyoto Protocol by the third Conference of the Parties of the UNFCCC in 1998, the carbon emissions trading system has gained traction, laying the groundwork for the carbon trading market. This market has matured over time, driven by factors such as policy oversight and market orientation. Today, a global network of fragmented carbon markets encompasses countries like the US, the EU, China, Japan, India, and Australia.

Carbon trading, popularized since the 1990s, involves trading rights for carbon emissions with the aim of incentivizing emissions reduction by converting environmental factors into tradable assets. It aligns with the notion of "financialization of climate policy," a concept emerging from economic globalization and the evolution of carbon emission markets.

Specifically, China's journey in developing its carbon trading market spans three stages: establishing clean development mechanisms (2005–2012), launching regional carbon emissions trading pilots (2013–present), and progressing toward a national carbon emissions trading market (2017–present). The recent launch of China's

D. Guo and P. Zhou, *Beating Financial Swords into Developmental Plowshares*,
Sustainable Development Goals Series, https://doi.org/10.1007/978-981-95-5152-1_9

national carbon emissions trading market on July 16, 2021, positions it to become the world's largest carbon finance market.

This study aims to offer quantitative insights into China's carbon trading market by addressing three key research questions:

- RQ1: Does the price of carbon trading exhibit similar features to major commodities?
- RQ2: Are fluctuations in carbon trading prices influenced by oil or gold prices?
- RQ3: Does the monetary policy of the Fed impact the carbon trading market?

To address these questions, we focus on the EU carbon market price due to its data availability. This study makes four primary contributions. First, it introduces a novel methodology for analyzing carbon finance, employing the DCC-GARCH and TVP-VAR frameworks to identify financial attributes and measure time-varying impacts. Second, it explores a new research avenue by examining the correlation between carbon finance and petroleum finance, expanding the energy characteristics of bulk commodities to the carbon finance domain. Third, it provides insights into the spillover effects of monetary policy on interest rates and exchange rates through time-varying methods. Finally, it introduces a new research direction on the financialization of climate policy, focusing on identifying characteristics and analyzing mechanisms such as "de-energization" (oil-dominated extrusion) and "decentralization" (weakening of US dollar hegemony), offering a reproducible quantitative methodology and fresh perspective for political economy research on "climate policy financialization."

9.2 Hypotheses

First, it is observed that the financial characteristics of carbon emission rights have become increasingly pronounced (Zhai et al., 2024). Carbon emission rights circulate in the carbon trading market as a distinct and valuable economic resource, possessing investment value and liquidity (Lo, 2013). While carbon emissions trading differs from commodity market trading targets in terms of the abstract and non-physical nature of emission rights, it shares many similarities with commodity trading in terms of market mode and investor structure. Thus, we can hypothesize that:

H1: The carbon trading market is gradually evolving into a new international commodity trading market akin to oil and gold.

Moreover, against the backdrop of financial market globalization, there exists a close relationship between the commodity market and the international crude oil market (Zhang & Wei, 2010). Fluctuations in international crude oil prices significantly impact the global commodity price trend due to oil's dual "commodity attributes" and "financial attributes" (Hu et al., 2021). The financialization of the crude oil market has substantial implications for other commodity prices, highlighting the energy-based characteristics of major commodities (Rizvi et al., 2022). For instance, the influence of international crude oil prices on agricultural product prices underscores the significant "energization" effect of agricultural commodities. Given the inherent conflicts between carbon trading and carbon emission reduction in the oil industry, we propose the following hypothesis:

H2: There is a reciprocal relationship between carbon trading and oil prices, and the phenomenon of "climate capitalism" is driving the evolution of financial market de-energization.

Lastly, we examine whether carbon trading exhibits dual attributes and spillover effects (Wang et al., 2024). Just as oil possesses dual attributes influenced by both market supply and demand and monetary policies, carbon trading may similarly exhibit both commodity and financial attributes (Zhao et al., 2023). Given the impact of the FRB's monetary policy on financial assets' pricing, it's crucial to consider the influence of different currencies and relevant monetary policies when studying carbon trading settled by Euros. Therefore, our final hypothesis focuses on the policy effect:

H3: Carbon trading has both commodity and financial attributes, so the Fed's monetary policy has spillover effects on the carbon financial market.

9.3 Method

Our study focuses on the price changes of major trading varieties in the European Energy Exchange, a key carbon financial market worldwide. We have chosen the settlement price of futures of the European Union Allowance (EUA), referred to as "carbon trading price," as our primary variable, denominated in €/ton of carbon dioxide equivalent. Our dataset encompasses daily EUA data from April 22, 2005, to September 7, 2021.

Additionally, we have selected two categories of impact variables related to the factors influencing carbon trading prices. The first category comprises energy commodity indices, including the West Texas Intermediate Light Crude Oil (WTI) index and the London spot gold price index (Gold). The WTI index is denoted in $/barrel, while the gold index is denoted in $/oz.

For the second category of impact variables, we have chosen indicators reflecting the spillover effects of the Fed's monetary policy, including the US bond index and the exchange rate index ($). Specifically, we have selected the 10-year US treasury yield to maturity as the US bond index and the generalized nominal dollar index as the exchange rate index.

In selecting monetary policy indicators, we considered two factors. First, based on empirical evidence, we determined that the 10-year US treasury bond interest rate exhibits better data characteristics for analyzing the interest rate transmission effects of the Federal Reserve's monetary policy. Second, we opted for the US dollar index (USDX) due to its broader representation, reflecting trade settlement between major countries and the US.

Before proceeding with empirical analysis, we compared the trends of carbon trading prices with those of impact variables. Figure 9.1 illustrates the trends of carbon trading price, gold price, US bond price, and USD index. It reveals that the carbon trading price exhibits similar characteristics to major commodities. Particularly, Panel (A) and (B) indicate strong trend relationships between carbon trading prices and oil/gold. Notably, basic metals and agricultural products also demonstrate strong correlations with oil and gold, reflecting the influence of the US dollar as the world currency and its impact on commodity pricing. Consequently, carbon trading is gradually aligning with major commodities.

Table 9.1 ADF test results

Variable (log difference)	ADF statistic
Carbon trading price	−10.8397
WTI oil price	−10.2669
Gold	−11.9865
Treasury bond price	−9.7153
USD index	−10.4033

Notes The 1% critical value to reject the null hypothesis (there is a unit root) is −3.4637

We propose two assumptions regarding the correlation between carbon trading prices and oil prices. First, carbon emission reduction exerts a significant crowding-out effect on the oil industry, affecting oil production costs and financial market allocations. Second, the energy characteristics of major commodities directly and indirectly influence carbon trading prices through emission reduction-related industrial channels and investment allocation channels of other commodities.

Figure 9.1 also illustrates periodic changes in the correlation between the Fed's monetary policy spillover index and carbon trading prices. Specifically, the correlation trend between the US debt index and carbon trading prices exhibits time-varying characteristics. Before the 2008 crisis, a certain positive correlation existed, which decoupled post-crisis, particularly during the adoption of unconventional monetary policies by the Fed. However, with the normalization of Fed's monetary policy post-2017, carbon trading prices and US debt interest rates showed an upward trend in tandem. Subsequently, amid escalating Sino-US trade friction and the

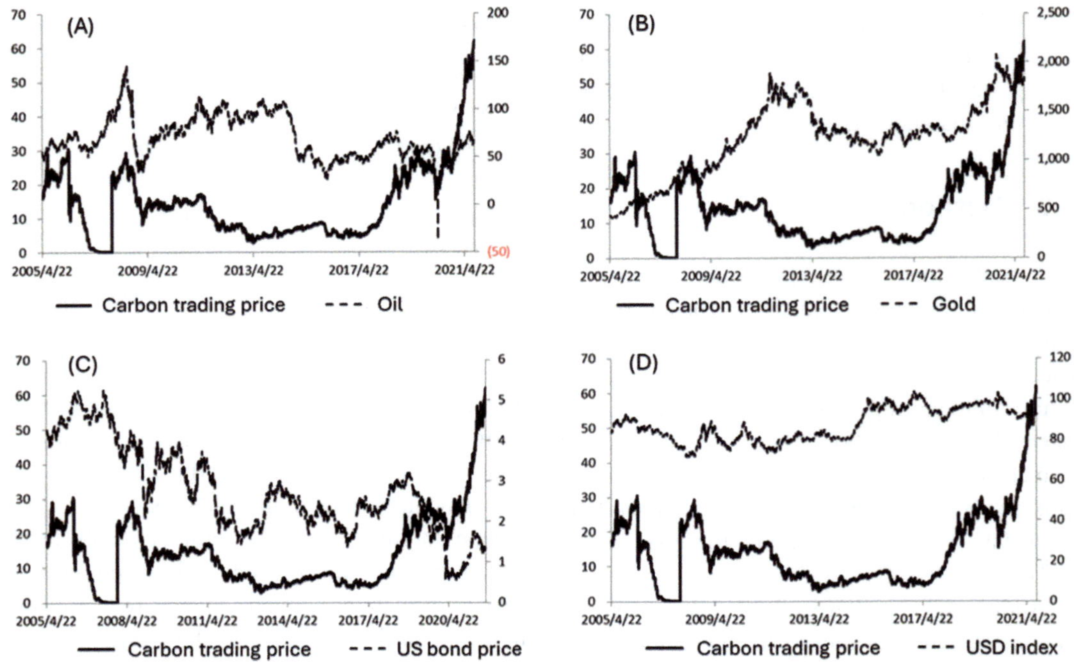

Fig. 9.1 Line charts of asset prices

Fed's deviation from normalization, both data sets entered a downward channel, albeit with correlated movements but with certain lag or lead periods. Following the COVID-19 epidemic, carbon neutrality has emerged as an international cooperation imperative and a strategic priority for all countries, resulting in rapid increases in carbon trading prices. Conversely, US debt interest rates displayed corresponding directional changes but exhibited new decoupling characteristics. To avoid spurious regressions due to non-stationarity, we take log differences of these variables. Augmented Dickey-Fuller (ADF) tests confirm that all variables are stationary at the 1% significance level.

In addition, we use 2018 as the time demarcation point based on carbon trading price changes, dividing the daily data into two sub-samples: sub-sample 1 and sub-sample 2. Specifically, sub-sample 1 exhibits characteristics similar to the entire sample, while sub-sample 2 displays heterogeneity. In sub-sample 2, carbon trading prices exhibit a skewed distribution to the left, indicating weakened risk characteristics compared to sub-sample 1. Additionally, sub-sample 2 highlights heightened leverage and risk characteristics for oil prices, US debt, and the US dollar, as evidenced by significantly higher kurtoses compared to sub-sample 1. Notably, gold prices demonstrate relatively stable characteristics throughout the sample period, with a sharp left-skewed distribution and low kurtosis.

Granger causality tests for the entire sample period suggest long-term correlations between carbon trading prices and the four selected variables at the 5% confidence level. However, carbon trading prices exhibit no significant Granger causality with commodity indices and monetary policy indices. Notably, gold prices display one-way Granger causality with oil prices and US debt. Similarly, conducting these tests on sub-samples reveals time-varying differences. Sub-sample 1 yields similar results to the entire sample, whereas sub-sample 2 exhibits heterogeneity. In sub-sample 2, carbon trading prices exhibit significant causal relationships with oil prices, with gold prices displaying one-way causality with carbon trading prices. Moreover, sub-sample 2 illustrates heterogeneous effects of monetary policy on interest rates and exchange rates. Specifically, the one-way causal relationship between the interest rate index and carbon trading prices suggests that the Fed's monetary policy can influence the carbon market through interest rate channels. Additionally, the one-way causal relationship between carbon trading prices and the exchange rate index suggests that carbon trading prices can influence the trend of the US dollar index through exchange rate channels.

9.4 Results

We focus on the spillover originating from the carbon financial market by the DCC-GARCH-TVP-VAR model. It involves two steps of analysis. In the first step, we utilize the multivariate DCC-GARCH model to examine the dynamic relationship between the energization of carbon finance and the spillover effect of monetary policy. This allows us to analyze how changes in carbon finance dynamics interact with fluctuations in monetary policy, providing insights into their interconnectedness over time. In the second step, we employ the GARCH model to identify significant indexes and then apply the TVP-VAR model to investigate the time-varying connectedness between the carbon financial market and related financial markets. This approach enables us to understand how the degree of interconnectedness between the carbon financial market and other financial markets evolves over different time periods, shedding light on the dynamics of risk transmission across these markets. Technical details of the TVP-VAR model can be found in Chap. 3.

9.4.1 DCC-GARCH

To determine the optimal lag length for the DCC-GARCH model, we compare different information criteria and choose the most preferred one (=2) as the lag length. The estimated DCC-GARCH model is reported in Table 9.2.

We separate the estimated parameters into two sets. Columns (1)–(5) are coefficients of the VAR system, describing the dynamics among carbon trading price and other asset prices. These dynamics parameters capture how these variables are linked with the past values of each other. Columns (6)–(8) are parameters of error terms, including variance, covariance, and correlation.

The dynamics parameters in Table 9.2 reveals that carbon trading prices are not significantly influenced by either oil price or USD index. However, carbon trading prices markedly affect major commodities. This suggests an emerging trend that commodities and carbon trading price become closely connected. Furthermore, carbon trading prices are positively correlated with gold prices, underscoring the shared hedging nature of gold and carbon quota. Additionally, the volatility parameters show a significant bi-directional GARCH effect between carbon trading prices and other asset prices. Therefore, the volatility of these variables are also closely connected. Specifically, a higher variance of carbon trading price can raise those of oil price, gold price, and USD index, showing evidence for cross-asset spillovers.

Figure 9.2 demonstrates the dynamic correlation coefficients (the defining feature of DCC models) between carbon trading price and other asset prices in the model. Panel (A) suggests that carbon trading price and oil price have positive correlation throughout the sample period, despite marked fluctuations. A similar pattern is found between carbon trading price and bond price in panel (C). In contrast, the correlations with the gold price (panel B) and USD index (panel C) are not significant or persistent.

9.4.2 TVP-VAR

Building on the findings of the DCC-GARCH model, we employ the TVP-VAR model to further characterize the time-varying features of the interdependence and dynamics of these assets. We apply the MCMC algorithm to estimate the TVP-VAR model in the Bayesian tradition.

Figure 9.3 shows that the self-correlation coefficients of the sample rapidly decay after an initial 100 iterations (top row). At the same time, the posterior mean of the parameters (middle row)

Table 9.2 DCC-GARCH model estimation results

	Dynamics Parameters					Volatility Parameters		
	(1)	(2)	(3)	(4)	(5)	(6)	(7)	(8)
C ➔ O	0.0008	−0.3059**	−0.0827	0.0108	0.2239**	0.0000	0.6674**	0.5574***
O ➔ C	0.0005*	−0.0072*	0.0083*	0.0108*	−0.0044	0.0000*	0.4874	0.4971***
C ➔ G	0.0323***	0.0608	−0.3596	−0.5755	−0.5280	0.0002	0.6399***	0.6990***
G ➔ C	0.0057**	0.0172***	−0.0068	0.2104***	−0.0552	0.0002	0.0897	0.7321***
C ➔ B	0.0009	−0.3173	−0.0490	0.1144	0.2730	0.0000	0.6785	0.5696***
B ➔ C	−0.0002	−0.0086**	0.0006	0.0964	−0.0328	0.0000	0.1509**	0.7184***
C ➔ U	0.0007	1.0034**	−0.0662	0.1640	−0.1817	0.0000	0.6306**	0.5619***
U ➔ C	0.0000	−0.0015	−0.0005	−0.0055	0.0394	0.0000	0.0824	0.8723***

Notes significance level, * 10%, ** 5%, *** 1%. C = carbon trading price, O = oil price, G = gold price, B = bond price, U = USD index

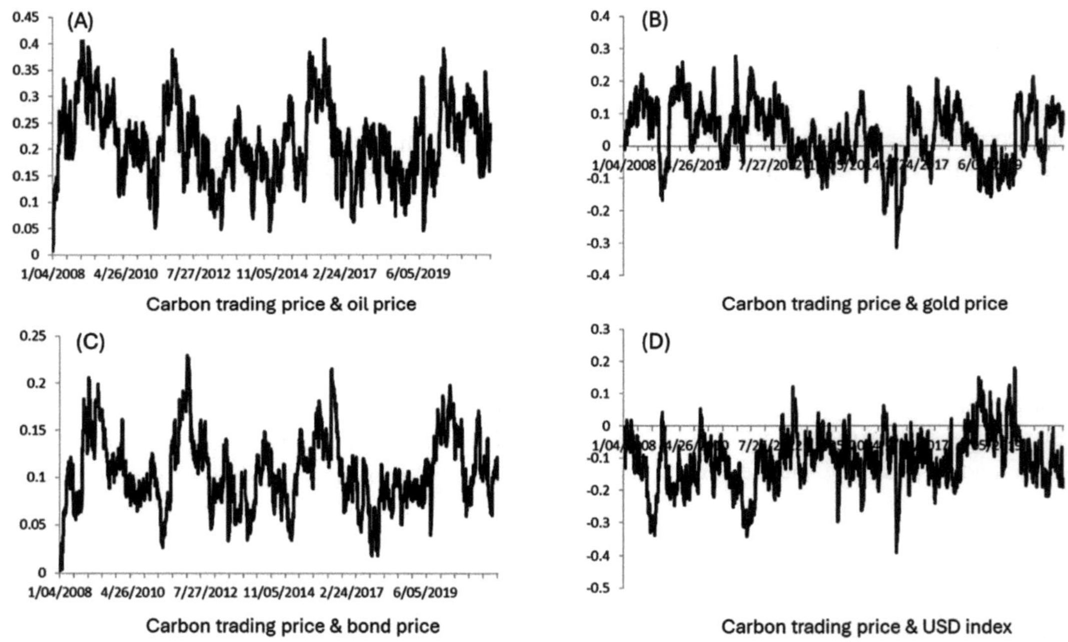

Fig. 9.2 Dynamic correlation coefficients

presents a white noise pattern, confirming the convergence in distribution. We show the posterior distributions of selected parameters in the bottom row. The estimated TVP-VAR model can generate time-varying impulse response functions (IRFs) due to the time-varying parameters. Here, we need to distinguish between analytical time and calendar time. IRFs at a point in calendar time describe how variables change over analytical time (number of periods after a hypothetical shock). In ordinary VAR models, IRFs are the same in different calendar times because parameters are all constant. In TVP-VAR, IRFs vary over both analytical time and calendar time.

To demonstrate, Fig. 9.4 plots the IRFs after 1, 3, and 5 periods (analytical time) of shocks over calendar time. The 1-period responses describe the knock-on effects of shocks, so the magnitudes are higher compared to 3-period and 5-period follow-up responses. The IRFs exhibit significant time-varying features in the knock-on effects, but very weak follow-up effects. Specifically, the

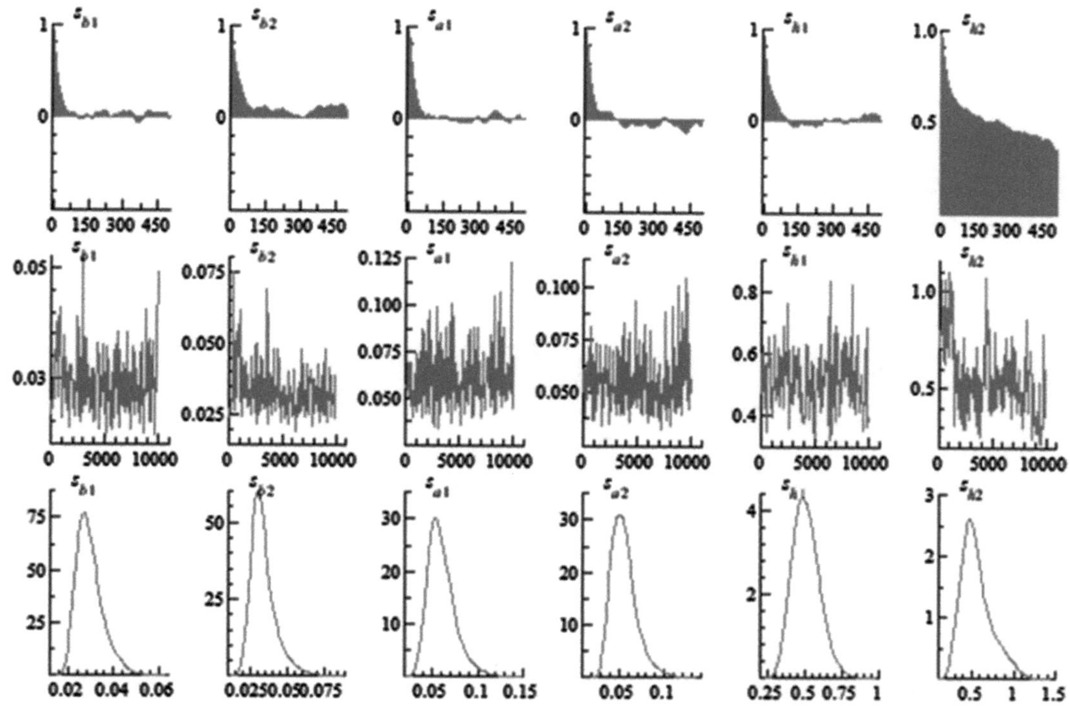

Fig. 9.3 Estimation results of the TVP-VAR model

effects of carbon trading price on oil price, bond price, and USD index grow stronger over time, while the reverse effects become weaker. This trend suggests that the carbon trading market has gained an increasingly important role in the mainstream asset markets. Thanks to its resilience to fluctuations in other asset markets, it has the potential to serve as a safe-haven asset.

9.5 Conclusion

The paper delineates the connectedness and evolution of the EU carbon trading market, highlighting the commodity and safe-haven features of carbon quota as an emerging financial asset. We observe the changing importance of the carbon market. Empirical evidence points to a discernible shift in the carbon trading price, reflecting the financial integration of climate policy. The pivotal year for this shift was 2018, aligning with a heightened global recognition of green finance. The year 2017 marked a reinvigoration of the green finance sector, correlating with climate change's ascent to a predominant global issue and the adoption of carbon peak and neutrality goals by key economies.

Carbon finance exhibits a pronounced disassociation from traditional energy metrics. While the interplay between carbon and oil prices is notably robust, the carbon market displays a unique independence from fluctuations of energy prices. Causality tests indicate a one-sided influence of carbon trading price on oil price—a stark contrast to the mutual impacts observed in conventional commodities. The influence of monetary policy (via treasury bond prices) on carbon finance is more significant. Using a combination of Granger causality tests, GARCH models, and impulse response analyses, we detect a bi-directional influence between carbon finance and monetary instruments like interest rates and exchange rates. This suggests an interaction within the predominant international monetary framework, where carbon finance experiences monetary policy influences. However, given the market's regional fragmentation, the Fed does not appear to be the principal driver of the carbon market at this stage.

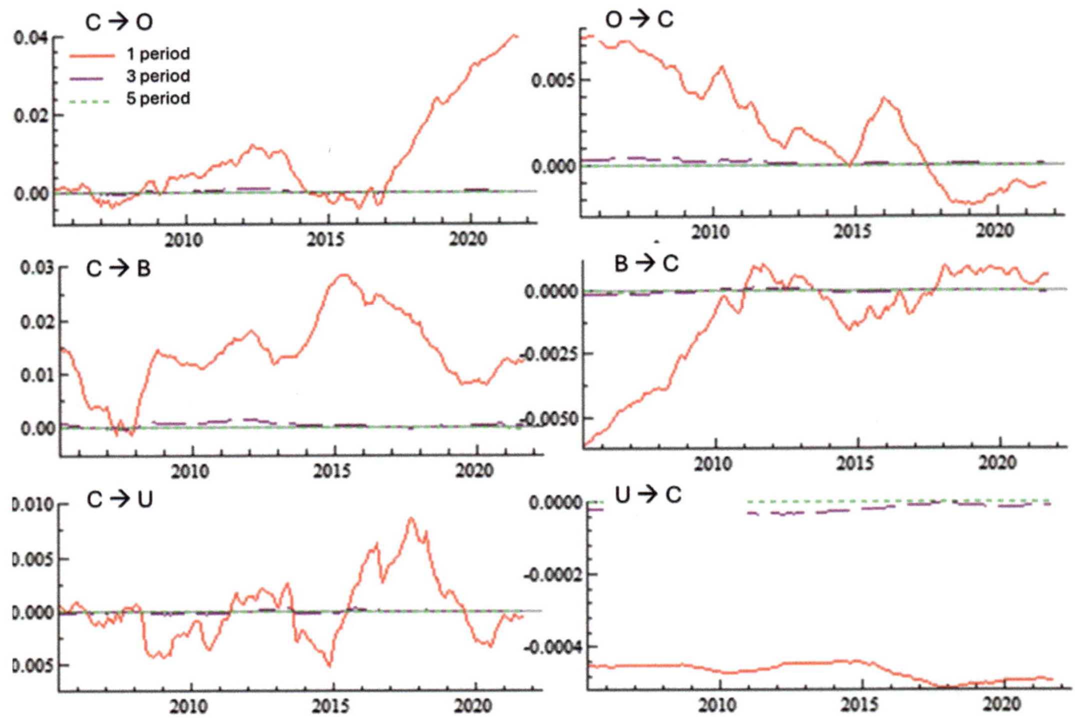

Fig. 9.4 Time-varying impulse response functions over time

Moreover, we identify risk contagion in carbon finance. Despite the absence of a globally integrated carbon market, we observe that its risk contagion with other financial markets has become apparent. There is a significant risk transmission from carbon finance to the oil market, notably from carbon price volatility to oil price volatility. Moreover, shocks in the oil market have immediate repercussions on the carbon financial market, which then impacts the stability of the dollar's value and leads to a volatility offset in the bond market.

Based on the findings above, some policy implications emerge that could inform future regulatory and economic strategies.

- Green Finance Integration: The financialization of the carbon market, tied closely with green finance awareness, underscores the necessity for policymakers to foster an environment conducive to green finance. Policy initiatives could include incentives for investment in green assets and the development of benchmarks for green finance products, enhancing the appeal and stability of carbon finance.
- Carbon-Oil Relationship: The significant correlation between carbon finance and oil prices suggests a need for policies that manage the transitional risks associated with decarbonization, particularly in the energy sector. Policymakers might consider crafting transition roadmaps for industries heavily reliant on fossil fuels, promoting investment in clean technologies, and establishing clear guidelines for carbon pricing.
- Monetary Policy Influence: The observed impact of monetary policy on carbon finance indicates that central banks should consider the implications of their policies on carbon markets. This might involve assessing the unintended consequences of interest rate adjustments on carbon pricing and integrating carbon market stability as a factor in monetary decision-making processes.

- Market-Specific Policies: Given the regional fragmentation of carbon markets, policies tailored to the specific characteristics of regional markets may be more effective than a one-size-fits-all approach. Regional policies could address market liquidity, cross-border carbon trading, and harmonization of standards to ensure the efficient functioning of carbon markets.
- Risk Management Frameworks: The evidence of risk contagion between carbon finance and other financial markets, particularly the oil market, highlights the need for robust risk management frameworks. Policymakers could work toward developing such frameworks to monitor and mitigate systemic risks, ensuring that carbon finance contributes to financial stability rather than exacerbating volatility.
- Cross-Sectoral Collaboration: The interplay between carbon finance and other economic sectors warrants enhanced cross-sectoral coordination. This could involve the creation of inter-agency task forces that include financial regulators, environmental agencies, and industry representatives to ensure cohesive policy development.
- Information Transparency: Enhancing transparency and the availability of market data can help market participants make more informed decisions and assess risks more accurately. Policy initiatives may include mandating the disclosure of carbon-related financial risks and fostering the development of carbon market analytics.
- Strategic Reserves: In light of the significant influence carbon prices can have on other markets, strategic reserves and intervention mechanisms might be necessary to prevent and address excessive price volatility.

In conclusion, a holistic and dynamic approach to policy development is needed, taking into consideration the nuanced and evolving relationships between carbon finance and other financial and commodity markets. Such policies should aim not only at enhancing the efficiency and stability of carbon markets but also at advancing the broader goals of climate policy and sustainable economic development.

References

Hu, Q., Li, T., Li, X., & Dong, H. (2021). Dynamic characteristics of oil attributes and their market effects. *Energies, 14*(13), 3927.

Lo, A. Y. (2013). Carbon trading in a socialist market economy: Can China make a difference? *Ecological Economics, 87*, 72–74.

Rizvi, S. K. A., Naqvi, B., Boubaker, S., & Mirza, N. (2022). The power play of natural gas and crude oil in the move towards the financialization of the energy market. *Energy Economics, 112*, 106131.

Wang, D., Sun, Y., & Wang, Y. (2024). Comparing the EU and Chinese carbon trading market operations and their spillover effects. *Journal of Environmental Management, 351*, 119795.

Zhai, D., Zhang, T., Liang, G., & Liu, B. (2024). Quantum carbon finance: Carbon emission rights option pricing and investment decision. *Energy Economics, 134*, 107628.

Zhang, Y.-J., & Wei, Y.-M. (2010). The crude oil market and the gold market: Evidence for cointegration, causality and price discovery. *Resources Policy, 35*(3), 168–177.

Zhao, Z., Lau, C. K. M., Soliman, A., & Farhani, S. (2023). Energy commodity and stock market interconnectedness: Evidence from carbon emission trading system. *Technological Forecasting and Social Change, 194*, 122669.

Part II
Policies

This Part of this book focuses on the policy responses necessary to harness finance as a constructive tool in addressing systemic, geopolitical, and environmental challenges. It emphasizes the need for advanced monetary policy tools and robust financial infrastructure to support economic resilience, stability, and international cooperation. The chapters in this section propose targeted policies, combining theory with case studies to showcase finance's capacity for positive transformation when aligned with well-designed institutional frameworks.

The first theme, "Monetary Policy," examines innovative approaches to improve the reach and impact of central banking tools. Chapter 10 introduces the medium-term rate as a novel policy instrument, illustrating how it enables more stable economic guidance than traditional short-term rates. This chapter highlights China's experience, where a focus on medium-term lending rates has proven effective in managing growth and controlling inflation. Chapter 11 expands on international currency circulation, proposing it as a policy target to support currency stability and reduce dependency on dominant foreign currencies. In a globalized market, the ability to circulate currency internationally strengthens domestic economies while promoting sustainable cross-border trade. Chapter 12 discusses the concept of currency flowback, emphasizing how it supports financial stability by ensuring that foreign-held domestic currency assets return to the issuing economy, thus mitigating risks associated with currency internationalization.

The second theme, "Financial Infrastructure," addresses the structural foundations needed to maintain financial stability and facilitate market integration, with a particular focus on innovative technology. Chapter 13 explores asset tokenization, highlighting how Distributed Ledger Technology can modernize Financial Market Infrastructure by enabling transparent, secure, and efficient asset management. Tokenizing traditional assets like bonds simplifies cross-border transactions and reduces reliance on intermediaries, paving the way for inclusive financial markets. Chapter 14 evaluates the treasury bond market as critical financial infrastructure, comparing China's Transparent Holding System with the US's multi-tiered Indirect Holding System. The analysis suggests that China's transparent, direct holding approach offers stability and resilience, particularly valuable as the nation opens its treasury market to global investors.

The insights presented in this Part emphasize how monetary policy and financial infrastructure, when strategically structured, contribute to a resilient, stable financial system capable of addressing global economic challenges. The proposed tools and policies highlight finance's potential to promote inclusive growth, support sustainable development, and foster international financial cooperation. Together, these chapters align with the book's theme of finance as a constructive force, illustrating that, with innovative policy responses, finance can be a powerful driver of sustainable economic progress.

Monetary Policy

Theme D is dedicated to exploring various monetary policy instruments and their applications in addressing modern economic challenges. It highlights how strategic adjustments to interest rate mechanisms, currency flow, and currency repatriation can enhance financial stability and support sustainable economic growth.

Chapter 10 introduces the concept of a medium-term rate, used as a stable benchmark to guide lending rates across China's financial markets. The chapter finds that medium-term rates, anchored in China's Loan Prime Rate, enable more effective monetary policy transmission than short-term adjustments, as they align closely with market conditions.

Chapter 11 examines international currency circulation as a policy target. Through the bond market, ICC can reduce exchange rate volatility and support economic stability by managing the flow of a country's currency abroad. The analysis shows that effective ICC mechanisms can strengthen a currency's global presence while fostering resilience within the domestic market.

Chapter 12 introduces currency flowback, or the repatriation of foreign-held currency assets, as a policy mechanism to maintain liquidity and control capital movement. By ensuring a balanced return of RMB assets to China, currency flowback mitigates risks associated with currency internationalization and promotes market stability.

Together, these chapters show how monetary policy can serve a constructive role by adapting to the complexities of global financial markets. Through enhanced tools and thoughtful mechanisms, central banks can foster a stable financial environment, aligning with the book's theme of finance as a driver of sustainable economic growth.

10 Medium-Term Rate as a Policy Instrument

Abstract

We evaluate China's 2019 reform that installed the Loan Prime Rate (LPR)—anchored by the Medium-term Lending Facility (MLF)—as the nation's principal lending benchmark. Two questions guide the analysis: Has the LPR strengthened monetary policy transmission, and does it satisfy international criteria for a reliable benchmark? Using term-structure models and cross-market comparisons with the US secured overnight financing rate and other global yardsticks, we test how effectively LPR movements pass through to loan pricing and how closely the rate tracks underlying funding conditions. Results indicate that the LPR's medium-term tenor transmits People's Bank of China signals more smoothly than prior short-term references, giving policymakers finer control over credit costs. The rate meets most Bank for International Settlements standards—transparency, representativeness, and robustness—yet its stability would improve with deeper derivative markets and a wider set of quoted maturities. Aligning the LPR with MLF operations lets the PBoC manage interest rate expectations in a manner analogous to the Federal Reserve's use of SOFR. Policy recommendations are threefold: reinforce the LPR's benchmark status to sharpen monetary precision; foster derivatives linked to the LPR to enhance risk management; and extend the curve to longer tenors to channel finance to sectors requiring patient capital. Properly nurtured, the LPR can promote inclusive growth and resilient financial infrastructure.

Keywords

Monetary policy · Medium-term rate · Loan prime rate

Classification

SDG9

10.1 Introduction

In August 2019, a pivotal moment unfolded in China's financial landscape as the PBoC ushered in a significant evolution. With the official announcement of the LPR by the National Interbank Funding Center, the stage was set for a paradigm shift in the country's financial infrastructure. This milestone not only introduced the 1-year and 5-year LPR interest rate swap contracts but also witnessed a flurry of 20 transactions totaling a nominal principal of 2.98 billion yuan.

Just nine days later, on August 29th, another crucial announcement echoed through the financial corridors with the National Interbank Funding Center's addition of interest rate swap contracts, with LPR as the focal point, to the X-Swap system. Spanning maturities from 6 months to 10 years, this expansion significantly bolstered

D. Guo and P. Zhou, *Beating Financial Swords into Developmental Plowshares*, Sustainable Development Goals Series, https://doi.org/10.1007/978-981-95-5152-1_10

the liquidity of interest rate swaps, underlining China's commitment to fostering a robust financial ecosystem.

At the heart of this transformation lies the benchmark interest rate, a cornerstone of financial markets globally. Determined by the interplays of supply and demand, the benchmark serves as the foundational reference point for pricing various financial assets. The emergence of the LPR, endorsed by the PBC, coupled with the dynamic development of related derivatives, further solidifies its benchmark status, wielding profound influence over asset pricing mechanisms.

As the LPR interest rate swap market continues to burgeon, it holds the promise of sculpting a comprehensive benchmark yield curve. Such a curve would not only wield significant implications for asset pricing dynamics within the financial sphere but also play a pivotal role in shaping the transmission of financing costs throughout the real economy. In essence, the evolution of the LPR ecosystem stands poised to reshape the financial landscape of China, casting ripples that extend far beyond its borders. This chapter studies the features of LPR and the transmission efficiency of monetary policy.

10.2 Literature

We review existing research on dynamics among benchmark interest rates, monetary policy transmission, and the emergence of medium-term policy rates as central bank benchmarks. Drawing on a rich tapestry of research, we focus on three dimensions.

10.2.1 Evolution of Benchmark Interest Rates

The evolutionary trajectory of benchmark interest rates unfolds against the backdrop of dynamic shifts in global financial markets. From the historical dominance of risk-free rates typified by the US treasury benchmark to the prominence of inter-bank offered rates exemplified by the LIBOR, the journey of benchmarks has been marked by transformation and reform. The seminal work of Wooldridge (2001) elucidates the dependence of market participants on government yield curves, while McCauley (2001) underscores the phenomenon of benchmark tipping, where shortcomings in existing benchmarks prompt the adoption of superior alternatives. Kreicher et al. (2014) shed light on market preferences for non-treasury bond interest rates, signaling a departure from traditional benchmarks. As the literature evolves, the call for benchmark interest rates grounded in actual transactions, as advocated by the BIS, emphasizes the imperative of stability in interbank liquidity.

10.2.2 Monetary Policy Transmission

Interest rate liberalization emerges as a linchpin in enhancing the efficacy of monetary policy transmission mechanisms. Yi (2018) points out the pivotal role of interest rate liberalization in recalibrating the price formation mechanism of financial factors. Mishkin (2018) highlights the importance of benchmark interest rates in transmitting policy signals to the market. Estrella & Estrella & Mishkin (1997) empirically demonstrate the impact of the Fed's monetary policy on short-term interest rates, elucidating the interactions between policy benchmarks and market dynamics. Moreover, Stock & Watson (1993) underscore the predictive power of benchmark interest rates in guiding economic indicators, albeit acknowledging the challenges of smooth transmission in the Chinese financial context, as in Liang (2018).

10.2.3 Medium-Term Policy Rates

A nuanced examination of medium-term policy rates reveals their pivotal role in calibrating economic growth and inflation targets. Woodford (2003) unpacks the smooth path of central banks in adjusting policy rates to achieve optimal economic outcomes, while Sun (2016) highlights the constraints posed by imperfect financial markets on transmission efficiency. In the Chinese context, the selection of 1-year and 5-year MLF as anchor rates for the LPR mechanism reflects empirical alignment with theoretical frameworks, as elucidated by Guo (2019). This strategic alignment underscores the PBC's concerted efforts to navigate interest rate liberalization while mitigating the negative effects of credit constraints and asset-liability management. Drawing on international standards and experiences, the paper evaluates the benchmark status of the LPR and forecasts the future development trend of the new benchmark rate. Through this analysis, the study aims to answer the following two research questions:

- RQ1: Has the new LPR mechanism improved the transmission efficiency of monetary policy?
- RQ2: Does the LPR meet the conditions for a benchmark rate?

This chapter makes the following contributions in several key areas. First, it integrates interest rate benchmark characteristics into the analysis of the monetary policy transmission mechanism, emphasizing the pivotal role of benchmark features in gauging the efficacy of policy transmission. This approach represents a novel theoretical and empirical advancement in the field. Second, the paper introduces the ideal benchmark standard set by BIS in evaluating the LPR mechanism. By leveraging insights from financial history and international benchmark trends, the study offers recommendations to fortify the LPR benchmark and shape future benchmark curves, thereby fostering the ongoing reform of interest rate liberalization in China. Moreover, the research outcomes provide actionable suggestions for the implementation of medium-term policy interest rates by the PBoC, while also serving as a valuable reference for the theoretical and empirical development of the LPR benchmark and benchmark curve construction.

10.3 Theoretical Basis

When adjusting policy interest rates, central banks can opt for either short-term or longer-term rates, a decision closely linked to the maturity of the host country's financial market. Countries with highly mature and efficient financial markets typically adopt a standard monetary policy framework, with central banks like the Fed favoring short-term policy rates. In contrast, financial markets in other countries, such as the Eurozone, exhibit imperfections due to varying national debt market development, complicating the efficacy of market-oriented manipulations akin to those of the Fed. To elucidate this, we begin with the well-known Taylor rule adopted by central banks in developed economies:

$$i_t = i_t^* + \rho_\pi\left(\pi_t - \pi_t^*\right) + \rho_Y\left(y_t - y_t^*\right)$$

In this equation, i_t is the nominal short-term interest rate (e.g., Fed Fund Rate or FFR in the US, Bank of England base rate in the US), i_t^* is the equilibrium interest rate determined by the real side of the economy. π_t^* is the inflation target (usually 2%), and y_t^* is the (log) equilibrium output level. Therefore, the Taylor rule states that the short-term interest rate is in equilibrium only if there is no inflation gap $\pi_t - \pi_t^* = 0$ or output gap $y_t - y_t^* = 0$. If inflation is higher than the target $\pi_t - \pi_t^* > 0$ or if output is higher than the equilibrium $y_t - y_t^* > 0$ (overheated), then the central bank will raise the short-term interest rate to reduce π_t and y_t by a higher financial cost to households and firms. If inflation is lower than the target $\pi_t - \pi_t^* < 0$ or if output is lower than the equilibrium $y_t - y_t^* < 0$ (recession), then the central bank will reduce the short-term interest rate to stimulate π_t and y_t by a lower financial cost to households and firms.

However, inconsistencies exist between the variables on the two sides of the Taylor rule. While inflation and output are medium to long-term variables, the nominal interest rate represents short-term policy rates. Consequently, the transmission of short-term rates to medium and long-term rates hinges on financial market maturity and transmission efficiency. Linear transmission, ideal for medium and long-term rates, is rare; nonlinear relationships often prevail, complicating interest rate rules. Monetary policy transmission issues can invalidate short-term rate adjustments, necessitating a shift toward medium and long-term yield curves in mature financial markets.

In comparing financial market perfections, stark differences emerge between China and the US. While the RMB's internationalization is underway, it has yet to attain the status of the USD. Furthermore, China's bond market, though sizable, suffers from investor structure and derivatives market deficiencies, hampering policy transmission. Consequently, the PBC cannot solely rely on adjusting short-term rates according to the Taylor rule's linear response function. Regarding medium-term policy interest rates, scholars have provided insights. The "two-sector mechanism" among Chinese commercial banks underscores the direct transmission of policy rates to the real economy through medium and long-term lending facilities. Moreover, a general equilibrium framework confirms the efficacy of medium-term policy rate regulation in stimulating lending and reducing interest rates.

Evaluating benchmark rates entails comprehensive considerations. Benchmarks must provide stable, accurate rates unaffected by market manipulation, with pricing capabilities extending beyond the money market. Additionally, benchmark rates should align closely with financing rates to facilitate benchmark-based lending and financing. The BIS has proposed rigorous standards for inter-bank benchmark rates, emphasizing market stability, pricing functionality, and service provision in financial contracts. Compliance with these standards ensures benchmark acceptance and adoption, vital for benchmark rate efficacy in financial markets.

10.4 Empirical Precedents

In the evolution of the benchmark interest rate curve within the US capital market, two key curves have emerged with significant implications. The first is the US treasury yield curve, while the other is the interest rate swap curve based on LIBOR. These two curves have historically served as benchmark interest rate curves in global capital market pricing. Their transactional convenience and low costs have been facilitated by a relatively balanced and competitively structured financial environment. However, a pivotal moment occurred with the initial benchmark tipping in modern financial history. Before the 1990s, the benchmark yield curve of treasury bonds held sway. Yet, with the advancement of interest rate liberalization and derivatives markets, the interest rate swap curve based on LIBOR gradually supplanted the US treasury yield curve, assuming a paramount position.

US treasury bonds boast the world's largest bond market and are renowned for their activity. These factors underpin the US treasury interest rate as a risk-free benchmark. Additionally, the complete maturities of treasury bonds facilitate the formation of a benchmark yield curve. Furthermore, the diverse investor base, including individual investors, mutual funds, and monetary authorities such as the Fed, contributes to market stability and prevents abrupt price drops. Notably, a significant portion of US treasury bonds held abroad serves both to stabilize the market and to engage investing countries in the US economic ecosystem. Leveraging treasury bonds as pledged assets in money market and derivatives transactions has further solidified their benchmarking role, facilitating the construction of a comprehensive US bond yield curve. This curve offers advantages such as complete maturity coverage, uniformity, ample stock, and high liquidity, positioning US treasury bonds as crucial collateral in financial markets and enabling effective policy transmission by central banks.

In the 1980s, as the interest rate market burgeoned and financial products like interest rate swaps and currency derivatives gained traction, the need arose for a common interest rate measure in global financial transactions. Thus, the British Bankers' Association (BBA) introduced LIBOR as the benchmark interest rate in international financial markets for an extended period.

The rise of the LIBOR benchmark stemmed from limitations of US treasury bonds. Challenges in constructing a benchmark yield curve for treasury bonds, coupled with constraints on bond supply and the failure of the benchmark curve during economic crises, prompted the need for an alternative. LIBOR's interest rate swap curve addressed these drawbacks. Offering greater convenience, stability, and alignment with market needs, LIBOR facilitated transactions across various financial institutions and entities. Its credit risk and pro-cyclical nature provided consistency with market cycles and the credit bond market, overcoming deficiencies in the treasury benchmark, and ensuring effective monetary policy transmission.

Following the global financial crisis, the LIBOR scandal erupted, exposing conflicts of interest and regulatory lapses within the benchmark system. The loss of confidence in LIBOR spurred resistance, leading to the development of risk-free alternative rates for the USD. Ultimately, the Alternative Reference Rate Committee (ARRC), led by the Fed, endorsed the Secured Overnight Financing Rate (SOFR) as the definitive alternative rate.

The construction of SOFR is grounded in its close association with money market interest rates, offering wide coverage and liquidity. Its gradual adoption in derivatives transactions and asset pricing, coupled with the establishment of contracts for floating rate notes (FRNs) and syndicated loans, underscores its growing prominence in financial markets. However, challenges persist, with SOFR's reliance on US treasury bonds as collateral introducing constraints on the benchmark interest rate. Fluctuations in treasury bond supply and demand can impact SOFR, potentially leading to divergences among benchmark interest rates and necessitating ongoing market monitoring and adjustment (Fig. 10.1).

10.5 Analysis

10.5.1 Evolution of the New LPR Mechanism

The LPR introduced by the PBoC represents a significant shift in China's monetary policy. This market reference rate, tied to the MLF, combines features of both treasury bond benchmark rates and LIBOR. The MLF transactions, which require collateral financing such as treasury bonds, resemble the setup of SOFR. While the LPR currently meets the three standards set by the BIS for benchmark rates, further development is needed for it to become an ideal market benchmark.

The LPR's anchor rate, the MLF interest rate, serves as a crucial tool in the inter-bank money market (Fig. 10.2). However, MLF transactions

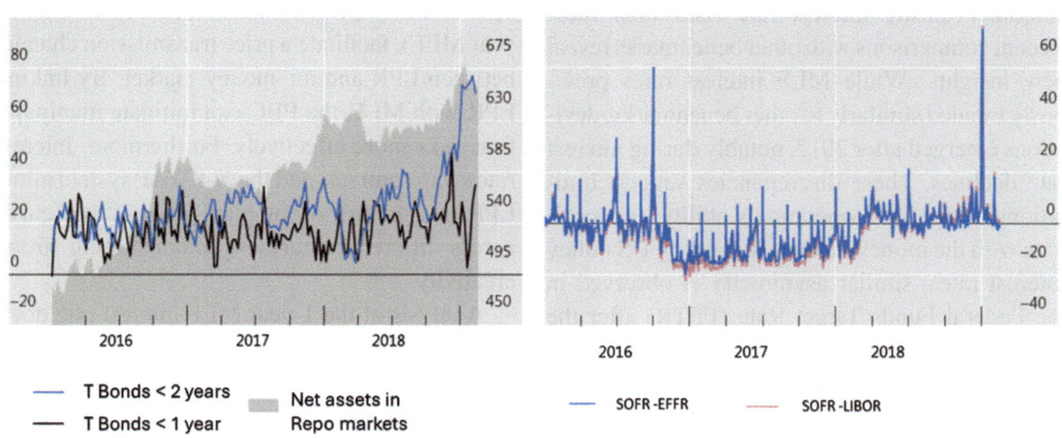

Fig. 10.1 Treasury bond markets (unit: $billion) and SOFR spread (unit: basis point)

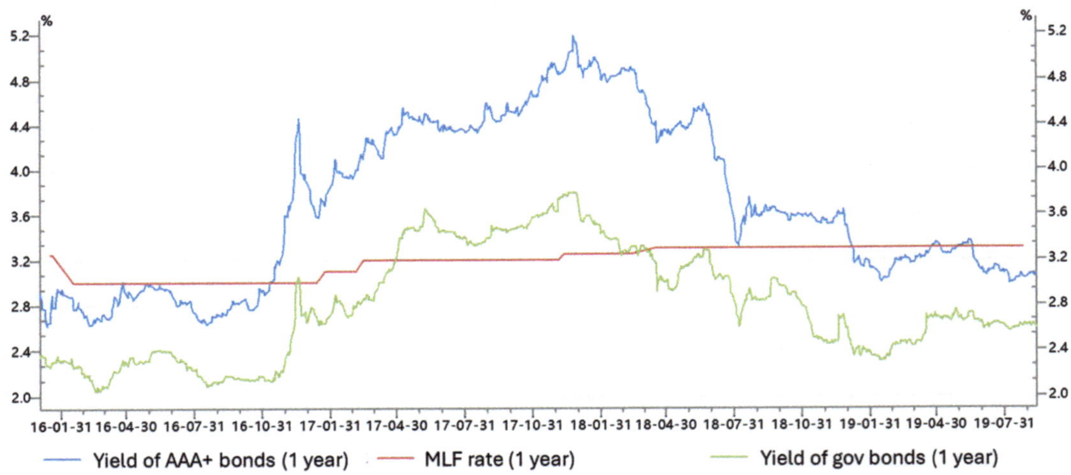

Fig. 10.2 Differences between the MLF rate and market benchmarks

are subject to strict constraints. First, only qualified primary dealers in the money market can engage in MLF operations, mainly commercial banks. Second, transaction timings are limited by counter-cyclical regulations, favoring less frequent transactions to minimize interest rate fluctuations. These constraints distinguish MLF from benchmarks like SOFR and LIBOR. Consequently, PBoC opts to quote LPR monthly, aligning with China's other macroeconomic indicators.

An important consideration in meeting the BIS standard is the asymmetric transmission of the MLF interest rate in the LPR anchor rate. Studies have identified asymmetry in the benchmark MLF of the LPR rate, with policy transmission being smoother during interest rate rises than falls. Recent comparisons with other benchmarks reveal new insights. While MLF interest rates previously trended similarly to other benchmarks, deviations emerged after 2017, notably during interest rate declines. These discrepancies suggest limitations in the MLF operation's ability to coordinate with the money market. Regarding US policy interest rates, similar asymmetry is observed in the Federal Funds Target Rate (FFTR) after the financial crisis. Such deviations pose challenges in pricing financial products and managing assets and liabilities. Additionally, LPR carries credit risks, adding heterogeneity that complicates the benchmark yield curve and is difficult to mitigate through derivative products.

10.5.2 Development of the LPR Benchmark Curve

The National Interbank Funding Center, authorized by the PBoC to announce the LPR, has introduced interest rate swap contracts using 1-year and 5-year LPR rates. These developments lay the groundwork for constructing the LPR yield curve. As LPR uses MLF as the anchor rate, aligning with international trends in benchmark interest rates, the conception of the future LPR benchmark curve is explored. LPR quotations, now based on the open market operation interest rate (primarily 1-year MLF), facilitate a price transmission channel between LPR and the money market. By linking LPR with MLF, the PBC can mitigate manipulation risks more effectively. Furthermore, interest rate swap contracts and the X-SWAP system allow LPR to establish a complete interest rate curve across different maturities, demonstrating strong creativity.

Analysis of the 1-year MLF interest rate deviation and the reference rate of the credit bond market reveals LPR's inherent relationship with the real economy. Quotations of LPR support the PBC's goal of reducing financing costs for the real economy and establishing an effective monetary policy transmission mechanism. Additionally, LPR and MLF interest rates are quoted with a relatively fixed spread, consistent with global interest rate liberalization trends. PBC's monetary policy regulations and the supply and demand dynamics of MLF collateral can influence the LPR benchmark curve. Similar to SOFR and treasury bonds, MLF collateral impacts the repo market's interest rates. Consequently, changes in collateral supply and demand can lead to fluctuations in the LPR benchmark interest rate.

The divergence between benchmark rates in different markets poses challenges in asset-liability management and increases mismatched risks for market participants. Existing interest rate swap transactions do not hedge differences in benchmarks effectively. Moreover, a lack of derivative trading mechanisms further complicates the elimination of benchmark rate divergences. Enhancements in the future LPR benchmark yield curve should consider requirements for basis trading, drawing from experiences with transactions like TED transactions, LIBOR, and OIS transactions.

10.6 Conclusion

Drawing from international comparisons, this study establishes an evaluation framework and a reference system to assess the policy transmission efficiency, new benchmark features of the LPR mechanism, and the prospective benchmark curve. The conclusions drawn from this analysis are as follows:

First, integrating the MLF as the anchor rate in the new LPR mechanism enhances the transmission of monetary policy to the real economy. The reform and theoretical underpinnings of the LPR address gaps in both theoretical and empirical research on China's medium-term policy interest rate transmission mechanism. The proposed approach by Guofeng Sun presents practical value, applicable across both immature and mature markets, even in times of crisis. This new mechanism has significant political implications, suggesting that insights from China's medium-term policy interest rate can offer guidance for the Fed's conventional policy framework.

Second, the LPR adopted by the PBoC demonstrates benchmark characteristics, with the MLF interest rate offering forward-looking guidance. While the LPR aligns well with the BIS standard market features, its pricing and service features require further development. In comparison to the well-established SOFR, the LPR still has some gaps in benchmark features. Challenges in market pricing and asset-liability management stem from the lack of price discovery and speculative mechanisms in derivative trading. However, an analysis indicates a convergence trend in the deviation between the LPR benchmark and the benchmark interest rate in the credit bond market, contrasting with the divergence of risk-free interest rates among banks.

Third, constructing the LPR benchmark yield curve can enhance the efficiency of monetary policy transmission. The evolution of international benchmarks informs us of the optimization of the new benchmark curve in the market. Leveraging MLF open market operations and future LPR interest rate swaps, the new benchmark curve should exhibit creativity akin to SOFR, avoiding manipulation and offering stable duration and robust external supervision conditions. This aligns with market trading and risk management needs. Expectation guidance from the MLF interest rate on the market interest rate helps mitigate market deviations caused by risk-free interest rates and counter-cyclical policy adjustments. Extending the yield curve across various maturities aligns with the real economy's need for diverse-term funds to yield policy dividends.

References

Estrella, A., & Mishkin, F. S. (1997). The predictive power of the term structure of interest rates in Europe and the United States: Implications for the European Central Bank. *European Economic Review, 41*(7), 1375–1401.

Guo, D. (2019). Comparison of LPR mechanisms between US and China. *China Finance, 17*, 42–46.

Kreicher, L., McCauley, R. N., & Wooldridge, P. D. (2014). Benchmark tipping in the global bond market. *BIS Quarterly Review, 10*(1), 466.

Liang, S. (2018). Transmission mechanism of monetary policy in the context of interest rate marketization. *Financial Regulation Research, 7*, 82–92.

McCauley, R. N. (2001). Benchmark tipping in the money and bond markets. *BIS Quarterly Review, 3*(1), 39–45.

Mishkin, F. S. (2018). Improving the use of discretion in monetary policy. *International Finance, 21*(3), 224–238.

Stock, J. H., & Watson, M. W. (1993). A simple estimator of Cointegrating vectors in higher order integrated systems. *Econometrica, 61*(4), 783–820.

Sun, G. (2016). Paradigm shift in monetary policy and development of financial markets in China. *Tsinghua Finance Review, 1*, 30–33.

Woodford, M. (2003). Optimal interest-rate smoothing. *The Review of Economic Studies, 70*(4), 861–886.

Wooldridge, J. M. (2001). Applications of generalized method of moments estimation. *Journal of Economic Perspectives, 15*(4), 87–100.

Yi, G. (2018). Review and outlook of monetary policy. *China Finance, 13*, 90–91.

11 International Currency Circulation as a Policy Target

Abstract

We examine how an International Currency Circulation (ICC) framework anchored in domestic treasury bond markets can reduce liquidity risk as economies promote their currencies abroad. Using an agent-based model that replicates heterogeneous investors, we test the effect of monetary policy stances, foreign participation, and sentiment shocks on bond prices under various ICC designs. Three results emerge. First, policy tightening calms prices quickly, whereas easing delays yet amplifies movements; a neutral stance yields the smoothest path. Second, overseas investors deepen liquidity and curb volatility—unless the market depends excessively on speculative flows, which can intensify downturns. Third, sentiment proves nonlinear: optimism supports stability, but pessimism can trigger abrupt sell-offs. Policy lessons follow. Authorities should calibrate easing cycles, pace market opening, and strengthen disclosure to temper speculative waves. Sentiment management through clear guidance further safeguards the ICC channel. By embedding these measures, treasury bond markets serve as safe conduits for currency internationalization, advancing inclusive growth, resilient infrastructure, and effective institutions.

Keywords

International currency circulation · Monetary policy

Classification

SDG17

11.1 Introduction

In the contemporary landscape of global finance, the internationalization of local currencies stands as a pivotal yet intricate challenge for monetary policymakers. Amidst this pursuit, the establishment of an efficient international currency circulation (ICC) mechanism is of paramount importance to address liquidity risks inherent in the internationalization process. As scholars and policymakers grapple with the complexities of currency circulation, a central problem emerges: how can an effective ICC mechanism be established to navigate the risks associated with the internationalization of local currencies in the inter-bank treasury bond market?

To contextualize this question, it is crucial to review the existing literature that has laid the foundation for understanding ICC. Existing scholarly works have primarily concentrated on two critical aspects: the crises arising from currency internationalization and the selection

D. Guo and P. Zhou, *Beating Financial Swords into Developmental Plowshares*,
Sustainable Development Goals Series, https://doi.org/10.1007/978-981-95-5152-1_11

of safe assets for ICC. Scholars have meticulously examined the mechanisms driving currency crises within the international monetary system. Simultaneously, a substantial body of literature, pioneered by Kindleberger and Krugman, emphasizes the geopolitical and economic dimensions influencing the choice of financial vehicles for ICC. Notably, the prominence of US treasury bonds in this role, as highlighted by Krishnamurthy and Milbradt, underscores the interconnectedness of economic power, trade dynamics, and the selection of safe assets.

Against the backdrop of this existing literature, this article contributes a novel perspective by employing an Agent-Based Model (ABM) to construct a computational framework for analyzing the impact of risk in the inter-bank treasury bond market. ABM, historically underutilized in financial analysis, provides a unique avenue to simulate the actions and interactions of autonomous agents, thereby offering a nuanced understanding of complex economic phenomena. Grounded in the insights from Behavioral Finance, our research aims to address the research question by exploring the dynamics of ICC and the implications on the stability of the treasury bond market. This simulation-based research seeks to enhance the understanding of policymakers, investors, and academics in implementing monetary policy in the form of treasury bonds.

11.2 Literature

Establishing an ICC mechanism can effectively address liquidity risks arising from the internationalization of local currencies, thereby fostering the comprehensive development of local currency internationalization (Guo & Zhou, 2021). Existing literature on ICC primarily centers on two key aspects: causes of currency crises and identification of safe assets.

The first body of literature concentrates on crises stemming from currency internationalization. Scholars such Filardo et al. (2016) examine the mechanisms of currency crises within the international monetary system. They highlight the liquidity issues in the international monetary system, as evidenced by historical events like the conflict between the British pound and the US dollar, leading to the collapse of the gold standard and the Bretton Woods system. Additionally, Bernanke and Eichengreen argue that the internal tensions within the dollar double-linked system contribute to the "Triffin's dilemma" within the Bretton Woods framework (Bernanke, 2005; Eichengreen & Kawai, 2014; Eichengreen & Lombardi, 2017; Eichengreen & Mathieson, 2000). This dilemma arises as the US, through trade imbalances, provides liquidity and foreign exchange reserves to the world, ultimately resulting in the breakdown of the monetary system.

The second strand of literature focuses on the selection of safe assets for ICC. Currency circulation can involve goods, technology, services, or financial assets, as discussed by Feng et al. (2023). Among these, a substantial body of literature analyzes financial vehicles based on international reserve assets. Scholars like Kindleberger and Krugman argue that the choice of financial vehicles for ICC is not merely a financial matter but is intricately linked with economic and trade power, as well as military and diplomatic hegemony, considering the functions of money, war, and financial crises. He et al. (2016) contend that US treasury bonds serve as the world's safe assets, supporting the USD international recycling mechanism and facilitating US expansionary economic policies.

When comparing the internationalization efforts of the USD and the JPY, along with the opening of the treasury bond markets in the US and Japan, a notable distinction emerges. The US actively promotes both the internationalization of the USD and the opening of its treasury bond market, whereas Japan's government did not actively champion the internationalization of the yen and the establishment of the currency circulation system. In terms of the choice of circulation vehicles, the USD opted for the onshore treasury bond market, while the JPY commenced with the construction of an offshore market.

To elaborate on the internationalization policy of the JPY, it underwent phases of negative, passive, and active policies (Zhang et al., 2016). In the evolution from a "trade yen" to an "investment yen," Japan's bond market, particularly the treasury bond market, lags behind in terms of internationalization (Xie & Lin, 2019). Therefore, it holds greater significance for China to take the US treasury bond market as the benchmark. Additionally, the dollar crisis in 1970s resulted from poor ICC, triggering the collapse of the Bretton Woods system. To overcome this crisis and promote the opening of the treasury bond market, the US balanced the ICC by holding overseas US treasury bonds. This approach not only solidified its world currency status but also serves as a reference point for other countries.

Due to data availability, research on ICC beyond USD is constrained. Existing literature predominantly explores the impact of overseas holdings of US treasury bonds on macro variables (Beltran et al., 2013), the micro-mechanisms of foreign investors' participation in primary and secondary markets (Fabozzi & Jones, 2019), motivations for other countries to invest in US treasury bonds, and the support of overseas holdings of the USD. Moreover, Wu and Li (2018) analyze the crucial role of US treasury bonds in the ICC, emphasizing their anchoring effect. Guo (2019), based on information from the US government's website, identifies the gradual non-market opening-up process of the US treasury bond market through political, military, and diplomatic means. Based on existing literature, the timeline, approach, and nature of the US treasury bond market's opening can be summarized in Table 11.1.

This chapter takes a novel approach to address the question. ABM serves as a computational model designed to simulate the actions and interactions of autonomous agents. ABM is not the dominant analytical method. The mainstream approaches are still VAR and DSGE models. However, ABM has significant advantages in analyzing complex economic issues, as it can flexibly incorporate behavioral finance insights into economic models, especially agent heterogeneities and herding behaviors. These rich features are important to financial markets but difficult to be incorporated in traditional models like VAR and DSGE.

11.3 Model

To conduct an economic simulation of transactions in the treasury bond market, we have developed a heterogeneous investor model within the Netlogo system. The research framework is illustrated in Fig. 11.1, which outlines our approach to analyzing investor heterogeneity.

11.3.1 Rules and Mechanisms Settings in the Inter-bank Market

Treasury bonds and policy financial bonds serve as benchmark products for interest rates in the inter-bank market and exhibit a high correlation. For simplicity, we assume that treasury bond transactions occur exclusively between banks, considering their significant trading volumes. We establish both transaction price and volume mechanisms, alongside a transaction monitoring mechanism.

11.3.1.1 Transaction Price Mechanism

We assume a single transaction type for the treasury bonds. The net price, initialized at 100, is chosen as the treasury bond market price based on market supply and demand principles. The current treasury bond price (P_t) is determined by the demand for treasury bonds, represented by the formula: $P_t = \alpha P_{t-1}$. Here, α is the lag coefficient, influenced by the difference (ΔQ_t) between the current supply (Q_t^s) and demand for treasury bonds (Q_t^d). When $\Delta Q_t > 0$, $\alpha > 1$ leading to a rise in treasury bond prices. Conversely, when $\Delta Q_t < 0$, $\alpha < 1$, resulting in a decrease in treasury bond prices. If $\Delta Q_t = 0$, $\alpha = 1$, and the treasury bond price remains constant.

Table 11.1 The gradual opening process of the US treasury bond market

Market types	Illiquid treasury bond market			Treasury bond market		Medium- and long-term treasury bond market		
Foreign subjects	Foreign currencies denominated		USD denominated	Official	Private	Petroleum country	Private	Official
	Official	Bank	Official					
Opening times	1961–1979	1978–1983	1963–2012	1970–present	1982–present	1974–present	1984–present	1990s–present
Main events	Lisa bond	Carter bond	Industrial countries + three Latin American countries	the eve of the collapse of the Bretton Woods system	Oil crisis	Oil crisis	Oil crisis	Global imbalance of payment + financial crisis
Main mechanism	Directed sale			Money market fund + the Eurodollar market		Foreign official additional issuance + full opening		
Opening types	Government-driven			External demand pulled		Government-driven + external demand pulled		

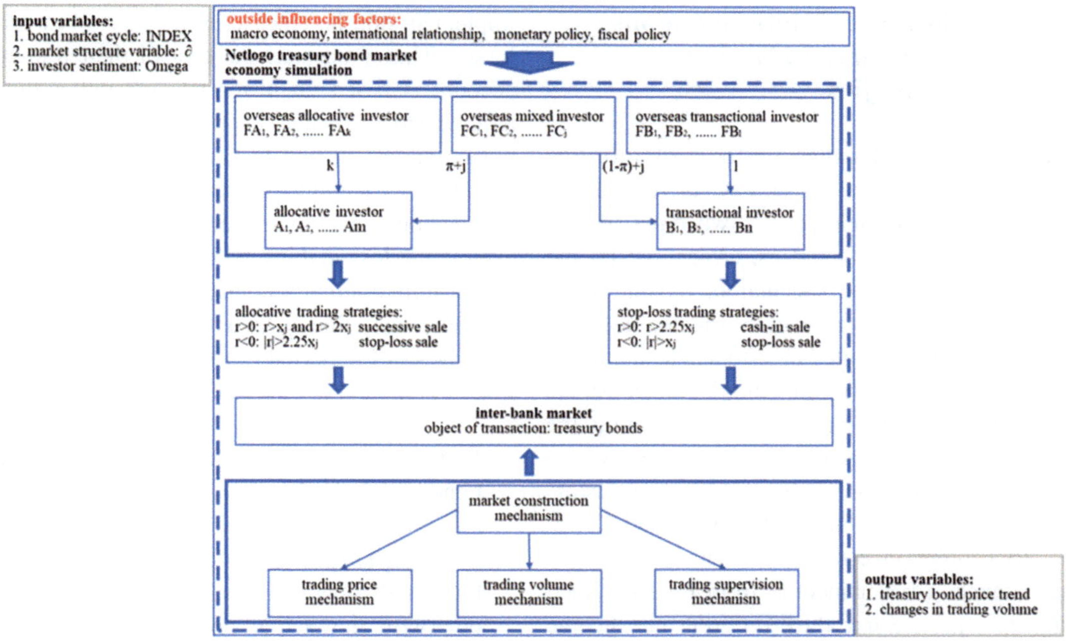

Fig. 11.1 The research framework for analyzing investor heterogeneity

11.3.1.2 Transaction Volume Mechanism

Market participants are categorized into three groups based on the trading strategy: long-selling, short-selling, and holding. The difference between supply and demand (ΔQ_t) is determined by the formula:

$$\Delta Q_t = \frac{Q_t^{long} - Q_t^{short}}{Q_t^{long} + Q_t^{short} + Q_t^{hold}}$$

Here, Q_t^{long}, Q_t^{short}, and Q_t^{hold} represent the numbers of long traders, short sellers, and holders, respectively. Depending on the relationship between Q_t^{long} and Q_t^{short}, the market position is either buying long, selling short, or at a stalemate.

While market activity is typically analyzed based on absolute and relative transaction volumes, the inter-bank market experiences less frequent transactions compared to the stock market. Therefore, we opt for analyzing the decisive volume of trading volume to measure market activity. The formula for current trading volume is given by:

$$Q_t^{trade} \equiv Q_t^{long} + Q_t^{short}$$

11.3.1.3 Transaction Monitoring Mechanism

We introduce a regulatory intervention into the research framework, wherein a circuit breaker is triggered to halt trading if bond prices rise or fall excessively. This aligns with real-world scenarios where governments intervene during abnormal market fluctuations or severe attacks, resorting to measures such as market closure. The circuit breaker mechanism is represented by:

- Circuit breaker of bull market: $P_t > \overline{P}$, stop trading at $t + 1$.
- Circuit breaker of bear market: $P_t < \underline{P}$, stop trading at $t + 1$.

11.3.2 Settings of Heterogeneous Investors and Trading Strategies

In line with the classification for stock investors by Da Costa et al. (2013), we categorize investors in the inter-bank market into two types: disposition effect type investors (Agent_DEI) and stop-loss effect type speculators (Agent_STP). These correspond to allocation-oriented investors and transaction-oriented investors in actual transactions. Additionally, our simulation considers domestic and foreign investors, extending the framework to an open-economy context, where the ICC mechanism involves foreign investors increasing their holdings of treasury bonds.

To capture investor heterogeneity based on preferences for net income from treasury bond transactions, we introduce different net income rates in the ABM. The net income rate (r_t) is calculated as the natural logarithm of the current price (P_t) minus the natural logarithm of the previous period's price (P_{t-1}).

Furthermore, we assume different institutions possess varied expected returns (X_i), where $i = 1,2,3,\ldots,N$ and N represents the number of all participants in the inter-bank market. We set $X_i > 0$, designate X_{max} as the maximum expected rate with a normal distribution. When simulating actual trader behavior, the probability distribution for buying and selling behaviors aligns with Da Costa et a. (2013)'s approach.

Allocative Investors

Allocative investors, in contrast to transactional investors, exhibit a stronger inclination toward long-term bond investments and a robust willingness to hold them. Their trading habits reflect disposition effects, meaning they tend to cash in returns when the portfolio has a positive return and exhibits a low risk tolerance. Conversely, in the face of losses, allocative investors are more likely to compensate by extending the waiting period for positions, indicating a higher risk tolerance for losses.

Some banks in the inter-bank market have lower profit targets. They cash in profits but do not implement stop-loss measures promptly in case of losses. This is because the cost of their trading account is based on historical cost rather than adjusting to timely market prices. Based on performance appraisal, unsold bonds do not result in actual losses, leading to a strategy of waiting for a price rebound over time to compensate for losses, even if the loss-making bonds are transferred to longer-term holding accounts.

Thus, we define r_{it}^{DEI} as the return of allocative investor i at period t, assuming all allocative investors share the same trading strategy:

1. If there is a positive return, sell part of the bonds when $r_{it}^{DEI} > X_i$, or sell all bonds when $r_{it}^{DEI} > 2X_i$.
2. If there is a negative return, allocative investors hold onto bonds when $\left|r_{it}^{DEI}\right| < 2.25X_i$; otherwise, they sell all bonds.

Additionally, the trading behavior of allocative investors is characterized by a "herding effect." They are influenced by their local environment and tend to adopt the same trading behavior as other traders. We simulate this "herding effect" based on Netlogo's framework, where each trader corresponds to a patch, and adjacent patches influence each other's transaction activities. Specifically, the buying probability of an allocative investor is directly proportional to the number of surrounding investors choosing to buy.

11.3.3 Estimations of Input Variables and System Parameters

In our simulations, we have three key systemic input variables: the bond market cycle variable (Σ), market structure variable (Θ), and investor sentiment variable (Ω). These variables are adjusted to perform multi-scenario analyses, aiming to understand how these factors influence treasury bond prices and market activity. The estimation approaches for these variables are explained below.

1. **Bond Market Cycle Variable (Σ):** This variable represents the impact of external information on the market, simulating both bull and bear bond markets. Notable events like 9/11 are considered major negative influences, leading to a value within the range $[-\infty, -1]$. To simulate the impact of the current monetary policy on the inter-bank treasury bond market, we opt for a relatively mild range of $[-1,1]$, capturing scenarios of neutral, stable, and loose monetary policy.
2. **Market Structure Variable (Θ):** This variable indicates the proportion of trading investors to total traders. Assume an initial wealth of 100 for each trader and consistent numbers of investors and the proportion of their bond holdings at the beginning. Commercial banks, city commercial banks, insurance institutions, and similar entities are categorized as allocative investors. On the other hand, brokers and funds fall under the transactional investor category. While the actual proportion of allocative investors in bond custodian institutions is around 10%, the proportion of bond trader institutions is closer to 20%.
3. **Investor Sentiment Variable (Ω):** We use the parameter to measure investor overconfidence, reflecting market sentiment. A higher Ω value implies more active participation and frequent transactions in the market. We set the desirable range of Ω as (0,10], where 0 signifies minimal market activity, and values exceeding 10 suggest extremely active investor participation.

Additional parameter settings include: $\overline{P} = 200$ and $\underline{P} = 50$ in the circuit breaker mechanism, $\delta \sim Uniform(0{,}0.2)$, the maximum expected return $X_{max} = 20$ and $X_i \sim Uniform(0{,}0.2)$. The upper limit of the total number of simulated periods is set to 1500 ticks, where a tick is the time unit in Netlogo, differing from actual trading time.

With these settings, snapshots of the inter-bank national debt market at time points 100 ticks and 500 ticks are presented under the initial state ($\Sigma = 0$, $\Theta = 0.1$, $\Omega = 1$). Blue patches denote long trading, red patches represent short trading, and white patches signify a holding state (Fig. 11.2).

11.4 Results

11.4.1 Simulation of Monetary Policy Effect

Currently, the primary cause of fluctuations in treasury bond prices within the inter-bank market is the liquidity tightness in the money market. Guo (2019) underscores the strong correlation between monetary policy and the treasury bond market, emphasizing the market's weak efficient state. In our ABM, we introduce the adjustable bond market cycle variable (Σ). $\Sigma = 0$ signifies neutral monetary policy. $\Sigma = -1$ represents a contractionary monetary policy, with the central bank reducing money supply or increasing policy interest rates. $\Sigma = 1$ indicates expansionary monetary policy, with the central bank injecting money or lowering policy interest rates. $\Sigma = 0.02$ reflects a prudent monetary policy, showcasing a central bank adopting a cautious monetary policy with an appropriate and loose policy orientation. Importantly, we deviate from traditional volume-price policies and adopt more structural monetary policies and forward-looking guidelines (Fig. 11.3).

In the case of neutrality ($\Sigma = 0$), the treasury bond price exhibits a mean-reverting trend, hovering in a small range above 100. The frequency of fluctuations is low. The market tends to be stable, with the price determined by market supply and demand.

In the case of monetary tightening ($\Sigma = -1$), the treasury bond price experiences a downward trend, aligning with the market rule under tight monetary policy where yield to maturity rises, causing bond prices to fall. The closing price at the end of the simulation is 89.2, with a maximum decrease of 14.2% (85.8). Time-varying features are evident, showing significant declines in the early period, with two distinct price jumps. The second jump indicates substantial stop-loss activity by transactional investors,

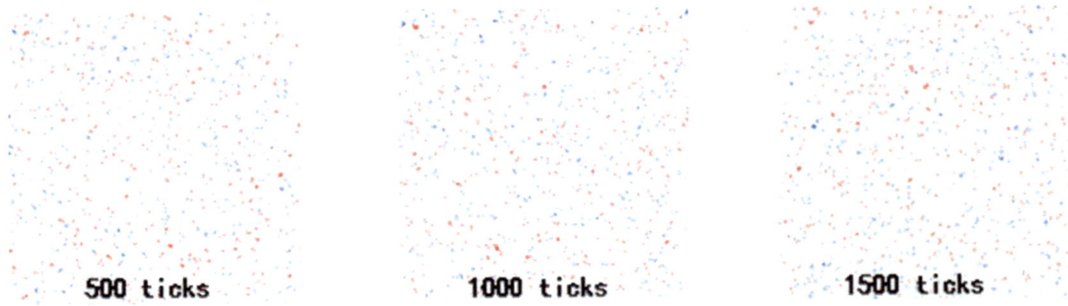

Fig. 11.2 The overall view of treasury bond market observations

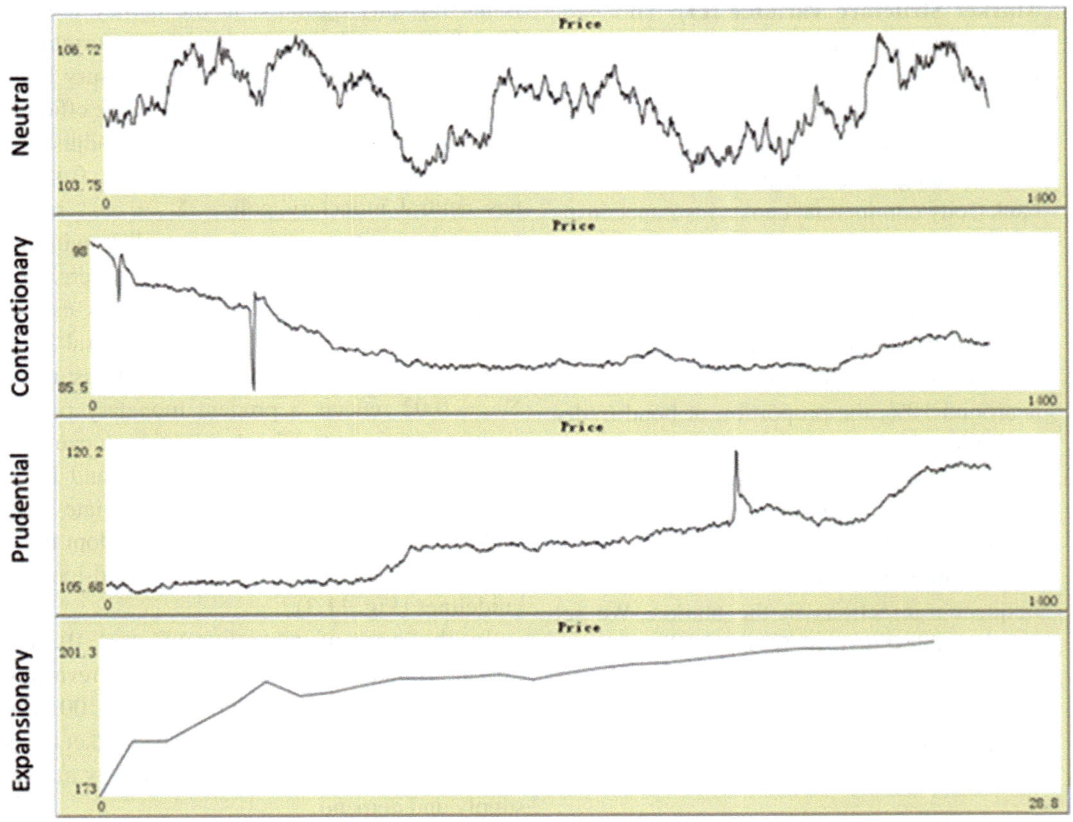

Fig. 11.3 Impacts of monetary policies on treasury bond price

followed by a subsequent price rebound as allocative investors hold low-priced bonds to reduce position costs. The impact of the tight monetary policy persists for an extended period due to the rigidity of treasury bonds' bottom price. The herding effect influences allocative investors' holding reduction, affecting bond trading activity.

In the case of quantitative easing ($\Sigma = 1$), the bond price rises to over 170 by the end of the simulation period. A ceiling is set at 200 as the upper limit price, triggering a halt in trading once reached. Trading volume significantly increases in the initial observation period, reaching 16,500, but experiences a sharp decline after hitting the upper limit price. Asymmetric effects are observed, with tightening policies having decreasing convergence and easing policies displaying divergent characteristics with greater lag effects. Adjusting

Σ to 0.02 results in a treasury bond price fluctuating between 105 and 118, similar to $\Sigma = -1$ but with distinct time-varying characteristics in the price trend. During the early period (400 ticks), the policy's price effect is not significant. The first price jump occurs after 450 periods (110). After the first jump, the market enters a new price range, witnessing large trade volumes and a significant jump shock near 920 ticks. Allocative investors achieve their profit targets, selling bonds for income realization. The price recovers quickly after allocative investors' sales, with speculative investors pushing the price to the third jump at 1200 ticks.

11.4.2 Simulation of Overseas Holdings Effect

In the context of RMB internationalization, the surge in RMB is anticipated to boost the holding ratio of foreign investment institutions. In alignment with the categorization of domestic investment institutions, we classify overseas holders into allocative investors and transactional investors. Examining the impact of increased overseas holdings on the treasury bond investor structure, we distinguish three distinct scenarios:

- Conservative Change: Overseas holdings alter the proportion of institutional investors, accounting for 10% of the total market structure.
- Moderate Change: Overseas holdings include a higher percentage of transactional investors, constituting 15% of the trading type.
- Aggressive Change: Transactional investors in overseas holdings gradually increase, reaching a substantial 40%.

Conservative Market Structure. The simulation in Fig. 11.4 primarily focuses on the impact of increased overseas holdings during a bear market, which is crucial for risk prevention. Setting $\Sigma = -1$ as the initial state of the bear market aligns with recent practical experiences, where the bull-bear market in the inter-bank sector is driven by monetary policy. Despite the change in foreign investor structure, the increased overseas holdings do not alter the price trend of the original market, maintaining similarity to the monetary tightening scenario in Fig. 11.3.

Moderate Market Structure. Due to the rise in overseas holdings, the investor structure shifts, assuming a 15% increase in the proportion of transactional investors. This leads to enhanced price stability. The closing price at the end of this period is 98.3, higher than the conservative scenario's 12.5, with the most significant drop of 8%, nearly 5% lower than the conservative market. The price curve experiences a relatively smooth decline in the early stage, transforming the original two price jumps into a "slow decline and rapid rebound" pattern. This shift can be attributed to the increased proportion of overseas transactional investors, improving the market structure and boosting treasury bond market price stability.

Aggressive Market Structure. Assuming increased overseas holdings results in an aggressive change in market structure, setting the transaction to stop when the price falls to 50. The treasury bond price exhibits a gradual decline at the beginning of the bear market, differing from the previous two situations. Following the drop, there is no direct rapid decline jump; instead, a price recovery occurs at the observation period of 35 ticks, followed by a stable period lasting more than 100 ticks. A cliff-like drop emerges in the observation period of 140 ticks, corresponding to a sharp increase in transaction volume to 13,000. Subsequently, the lower limit is reached during the observation period of 184 ticks, resulting in the stagnation of repeat transactions. This scenario mirrors the reality in emerging markets, where foreign capital influxes during the boom of emerging markets contribute to transactional investment, providing stability for a certain period. However, a swift exit of funds leads to a rapid collapse in market prices.

11.4.3 Simulation of Investor Sentiment Effect

In our simulation, the parameter Ω serves as a measure of changes in investor sentiments

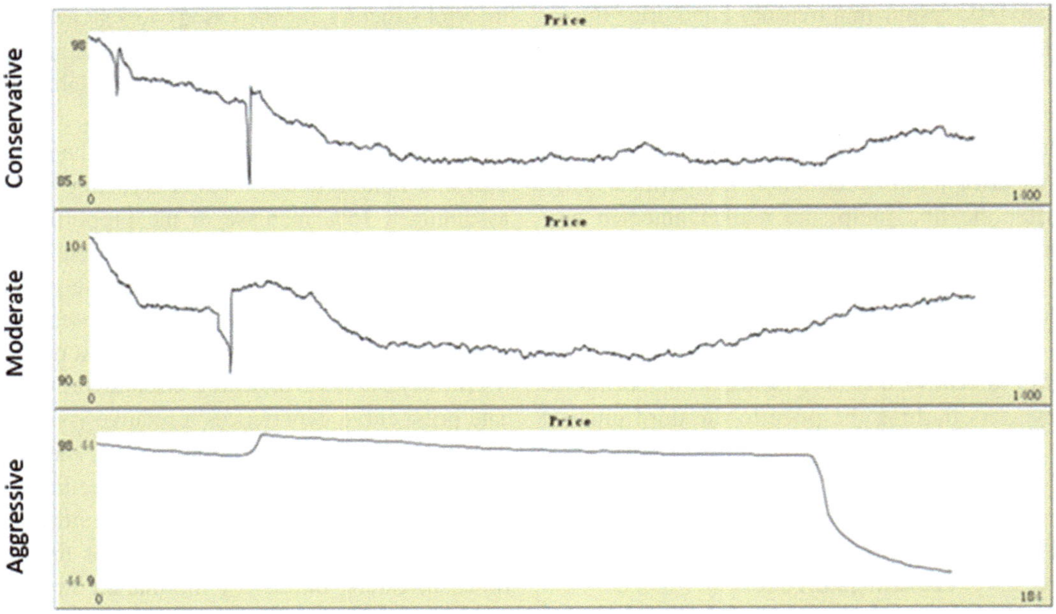

Fig. 11.4 Impacts of increased overseas holdings on treasury bond price

regarding treasury bonds. A higher Ω value indicates stronger sensitivity to market information. Specifically, Ω set at 0 suggests investors' emotional numbness, reflecting insensitivity to market information. As Ω increases beyond 0, investor sentiments become more influential, leading to price fluctuations (Fig. 11.5).

The simulation analyzes four scenarios based on different Ω values:

Hearding Emotions ($\Omega = 1$). Investors follow rational economic assumptions, making expectations based on macroeconomic and monetary policy changes. This reflects a stable market period where investors' expectations align, minimizing drastic fluctuations due to overly pessimistic or optimistic emotions. Tight monetary policy signals a bear market, but investors navigate the short-term policies without panic.

Positive Expectations ($\Omega = 2$). Investor sentiment sensitivity is slightly higher than following emotions, leading to increased trading adjustments. Despite heightened sensitivity, the downward price trend slows, and the early stage price jumps decrease. The overall treasury bond price curve shifts upward, especially during ticks 500–800, exceeding 100 at its highest point, reflecting investors' optimistic expectations. Volatility induced by positive expectations benefits transactional investors in band operations, supporting market activity during the bear market.

Negative Expectations ($\Omega = 5$). With a significant increase in sentiment sensitivity, the price curve shows a distinct trend. In the early bear market stage, bond prices exhibit a gentle, continuous decline, with two small fluctuations before tick 1024. A sudden "crash" occurs at tick 1025, reaching the lower limit of suspension (50), indicating the destructive impact of investor pessimism. The slow downward trend in the early stage resembles the aggregation process of negative expectations, and the abrupt crash has a devastating effect on the market. The simulation results affirm the nonlinear relationship between investor sentiment and treasury bond prices. This nonlinearity complicates the monitoring and prevention of risk factors in treasury bond prices. Despite less sensitivity in price fluctuation than investors with a low Ω, a slow decline in negative expectations can lead to a disastrous impact in the later stages, highlighting the complexity of assessing and mitigating risk in treasury bond prices.

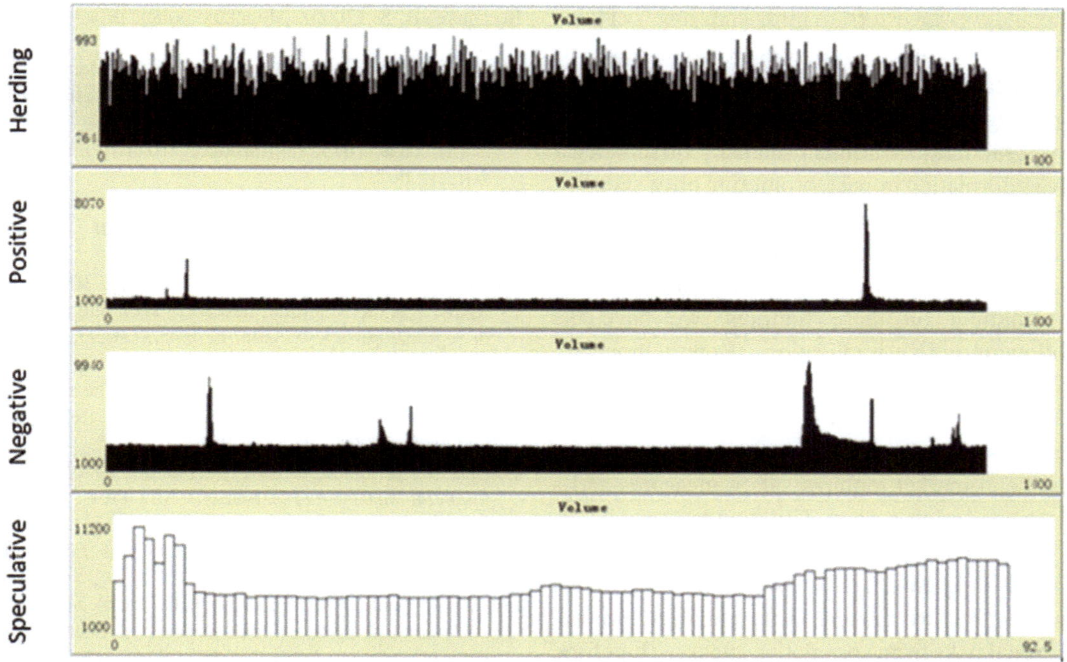

Fig. 11.5 Impacts of investors' sentiment on treasury bond trading volume

Speculative Sentiment ($\Omega = 10$). This scenario represents an extreme state where investor sentiments act as amplifiers of market information, with significant impacts on prices. Without setting a lower limit, the treasury bond price could converge to 0, emphasizing the extreme nature of speculative sentiment. A lower limit of 50 halts transactions at tick 87, depicting a rapid price decline and significantly higher trading volume compared to other scenarios. The simulation mirrors the phenomenon of overseas holdings rapidly withdrawing when expecting treasury bond depreciation, demonstrating theoretical significance. While the speculative sentiment scenario holds theoretical significance, the practical relevance lies in negative expectations for studying overseas holdings' fleeing during a treasury bond market downturn. The simulation outcomes provide valuable insights into the intricate dynamics of investor sentiments and their consequential effects on market behavior.

11.5 Conclusion

Our ABM simulations offer insights into various factors influencing the treasury bond market and the transmission effects of potential risks in the ICC. Three key conclusions emerge. First, monetary policy serves as a pivotal tool for stabilizing the treasury bond market. Counter-cyclical regulations have asymmetrical effects in the weak efficient inter-bank bond market. Maintaining market stability requires a neutral monetary policy. Tight policies exhibit convergent characteristics, while expansionary policies show a lagged amplification effect. Second, introducing overseas institutions for ICC optimizes the onshore market structure. Overseas holdings contribute to market stability, offering investment proceeds. Simulations reveal that transactional investors can enhance market liquidity and treasury bond price stability, but an excessive level can lead to increased price fluctuations, especially with the presence of speculative investors. Third, the link between investor sentiment and treasury bond prices is nonlinear. Investor sentiment, often seen as a price signal amplifier, exhibits a nuanced relationship. Moderate sentiment intensity offsets negative information impact, promoting price stability. However, elevated sentiment intensity poses a risk of price collapse after accumulation, emphasizing the nonlinear nature of this relationship.

Building on these findings, we have the following policy implications. Robust monetary policy is crucial, with a focus on mitigating hidden risks associated with the lag effect of quantitative easing. Moreover, the gradual opening of the bond market requires safety measures and a risk monitoring system. Utilizing treasury bonds for ICC enhances market efficiency and stability. Establishing an effective risk monitoring system with safety parameters is essential to prevent external risks from speculative attacks. Therefore, it is advisable to strengthen information disclosure systems and regulate intermediary services to curb market manipulation. Given the influences of market sentiments, measures should be taken to improve rational judgment, foster transaction activity, and instill market confidence.

References

Beltran, D. O., Kretchmer, M., Marquez, J., & Thomas, C. P. (2013). Foreign holdings of U.S. Treasuries and U.S. Treasury yields. *Journal of International Money and Finance, 32*, 1120–1143.

Bernanke, B. S. (2005). Monetary policy in a world of mobile capital. *Cato Journal, 25*, 1.

Da Costa, N., Goulart, M., Cupertino, C., Macedo, J., and Da Silva, S. (2013). The disposition effect and investor experience. *Journal of Banking & Finance, 37*(5), 1669–1675. https://doi.org/10.1016/j.jbankfin.2012.12.007.

Eichengreen, B., & Kawai, M. (2014). Issues for renminbi internationalization: an overview. *ADBI Working Papers*, 454.

Eichengreen, B., & Lombardi, D. (2017). RMBI or RMBR? Is the Renminbi destined to become a global or regional currency? *Asian Economic Papers, 16*(1), 35–59.

Eichengreen, B., & Mathieson, D. J. (2000). The currency composition of foreign exchange reserves: Retrospect and prospect. *IMF Working Paper*.

Fabozzi, F., & Jones, F. (2019). *Foundations of global financial markets and institutions*. MIT Press.

Feng, L., Le, D. T., & Yuan, F. (2023). Inclusion of the RMB in SDRs and the impossible trinity in China. *Economic Systems, 47*(2), Article 100941.

Filardo, A., Genberg, H., & Hofmann, B. (2016). Monetary analysis and the global financial cycle: An Asian central bank perspective. *Journal of Asian Economics, 46*, 1–16.

Guo, D. (2019). Evolution of the US external debt monetization. *China Finance, 17*, 83–85.

Guo, D., & Zhou, P. (2021). The rise of a new anchor currency in RCEP? A tale of three currencies. *Economic Modelling, 104*, Article 105647.

He, Z., Krishnamurthy, A., & Milbradt, K. (2016). What makes US government bonds safe assets? *American Economic Review, 106*(5), 519–523.

Wu, S., & Li, D. (2018). New measurement of currency internationalization—Analysis based on the perspective of international financial investment. *Economic Dynamics, 2*, 146–158.

Xie, Y., & Lin, S. (2019). Experience of opening the Japanese bond market. *China Finance, 9*, 40–42.

Zhang, Z., Makin, A. J., & Bai, Q. (2016). Yen internationalization and Japan's international reserves. *Economic Modelling, 52*, 452–466.

12 Currency Flowback as a Policy Mechanism

Abstract

We analyze the phenomenon of "currency flowback"—the return of offshore renminbi (RMB) to China's financial system—as a channel linking the currency's internationalization with domestic stability. A DSGE model embedding flowback mechanisms and foreign bond portfolios simulates bond market liberalization, external investment, and macro-financial shocks, asking whether balanced flowback can widen the RMB's global role while safeguarding the home economy. Results show that gradual opening of the onshore Treasury market raises demand for RMB assets, deepens liquidity, and narrows exchange rate swings, strengthening the currency's attractiveness as a settlement unit. Moderate foreign holdings dampen the transmission of interest rate or crisis shocks, bolstering capital account resilience; however, excessive concentrations heighten exposure to abrupt reversals. Thus, flowback is stabilizing only up to a threshold. Policy recommendations are threefold: expand bond market access while capping single-class foreign concentrations; establish a monitoring framework for flowback volumes and maturity profiles; and integrate flowback metrics into People's Bank of China policy rules, especially during stress episodes. Managed wisely, flowback can advance efficient capital formation, robust financial infrastructure, and balanced integration into global markets.

Keywords

Currency flowback · Monetary policy · RMB internationalization

Classification

SDG9

12.1 Introduction

The internationalization of the RMB has emerged as a focal point in discussions surrounding global financial markets and economic dynamics (Guo & Zhou, 2021). As China's economic influence continues to expand, facilitated by its robust trade relationships, burgeoning foreign investments, and ambitious financial reforms (Wei et al., 2023), the question of the RMB's role on the international stage becomes increasingly pertinent. Central to this discourse is the phenomenon of currency flowback, which encapsulates the movement of RMB back to China's domestic financial system after being utilized abroad.

Currency flowback represents a multifaceted process shaped by a myriad of economic, financial, and policy factors. It reflects the interaction between domestic and international market forces, impacting exchange rates, monetary policies, and capital flows. Understanding the dynamics of currency flowback is crucial for policymakers, economists, and market participants seeking to

D. Guo and P. Zhou, *Beating Financial Swords into Developmental Plowshares*, Sustainable Development Goals Series, https://doi.org/10.1007/978-981-95-5152-1_12

comprehend the evolving landscape of global finance and China's position within it.

This article aims to investigate the relationship between currency flowback and the internationalization of the RMB. By examining empirical evidence, theoretical frameworks, and case studies, we endeavor to shed light on the mechanisms driving currency flowback and its implications for the RMB's internationalization agenda. Furthermore, we seek to identify challenges, opportunities, and policy implications arising from the nexus between currency flowback and the RMB's global aspirations.

The structure of this article is organized as follows. First, we provide a comprehensive review of the literature on currency flowback and the internationalization of currencies, with a specific focus on the RMB. Next, we present an analytical framework, a Dynamic Stochastic General Equilibrium model, for understanding the drivers and determinants of currency flowback by empirical evidence and model simulation. Finally, we discuss policy implications and avenues for future research, aiming to contribute to the scholarly discourse on currency internationalization and global finance.

12.2 Literature Review

Currency flowback, also known as repatriation or repatriation flow, has garnered increasing attention in the realm of international finance and monetary economics. This phenomenon, which pertains to the movement of a currency back to its country of origin after being utilized abroad, holds significant implications for the internationalization of currencies, including the RMB. In this literature review, we explore key themes, theories, and empirical findings related to currency flowback and its intersection with the internationalization of currencies.

Currency internationalization refers to the process by which a currency gains acceptance and usage beyond its domestic borders. It encompasses various dimensions, including trade invoicing, international reserves, capital markets, and financial transactions. The seminal work of Cohen (2012) provides a comprehensive framework for analyzing currency internationalization, distinguishing between "usage" and "issuance" dimensions. According to Cohen, the internationalization of a currency involves not only its use in transactions but also its adoption as a reserve currency and its issuance in international financial markets.

Several factors drive currency flowback, spanning economic, financial, and policy domains. Economic fundamentals, such as trade balances, investment returns, and interest rate differentials, influence the demand for a currency and, consequently, the propensity for repatriation. Moreover, changes in investor sentiment, geopolitical developments, and macroeconomic policies can trigger shifts in capital flows, leading to currency flowback (Antonio-Ocampo, 2017).

Empirical studies have examined the determinants and patterns of currency flowback across different currencies and regions. Research by Camanho et al. (2022) finds that currencies of countries with large external imbalances are subject to higher repatriation flows, reflecting investors' risk aversion and concerns about exchange rate volatility. Similarly, Gopinath et al. (2020) document significant variations in currency flowback across emerging market economies, driven by changes in global risk appetite and monetary policy divergence among advanced economies.

The internationalization of the RMB has emerged as a focal point in China's economic and financial reforms. Scholars have explored various dimensions of RMB internationalization, including its role in trade settlement, offshore financial markets, and central bank reserves. Wang (2015) highlights the importance of currency convertibility, financial market development, and policy coordination in advancing the RMB's internationalization agenda. Moreover, the establishment of offshore RMB centers, such as Hong Kong and Singapore, has facilitated the offshore use of the RMB and contributed to its global acceptance (Cheung, 2023).

The interplay between currency flowback and RMB internationalization is complex and dynamic. On the one hand, repatriation flows reflect investors' confidence in the stability and prospects of the RMB, bolstering its international standing. On the other hand, currency flowback may exert pressure on domestic monetary conditions and exchange rates, posing challenges for policymakers seeking to manage capital flows and maintain financial stability (Chinn & Ito, 2007).

The opening of bond markets plays a pivotal role in facilitating currency flowback and promoting the internationalization of currencies, including the RMB. Bond market liberalization allows foreign investors greater access to domestic debt securities, fostering cross-border capital flows and increasing the demand for the domestic currency. China's gradual opening of its bond market to foreign investors, through initiatives such as the Bond Connect program and inclusion of Chinese bonds in global indices, has led to increased foreign participation in its bond market (Walker et al., 2021). Empirical evidence suggests that the opening of bond markets can spur currency flowback by attracting foreign capital seeking higher returns and portfolio diversification. Research by Wu et al. (2017) finds that the liberalization of bond markets in emerging economies leads to greater inflows of foreign capital, contributing to currency appreciation and repatriation flows. Moreover, the integration of domestic bond markets with global financial markets enhances the liquidity and depth of the bond market, making it more attractive to foreign investors (Claessens & Schmukler, 2007).

The opening-up of China's bond market has been instrumental in advancing the internationalization of the RMB. By allowing foreign investors greater access to Chinese bonds, policymakers aim to promote the use of the RMB in international transactions, enhance its status as a reserve currency, and integrate China into the global financial system. The inclusion of Chinese bonds in major global bond indices, such as the Bloomberg Barclays Global Aggregate Index and the FTSE World Government Bond Index, reflects China's efforts to increase the visibility and acceptance of the RMB in international capital markets (Frankel, 2012). Furthermore, the opening of China's bond market facilitates the offshore use of the RMB, particularly in offshore bond issuance and settlement. Offshore RMB bond markets, such as the Dim Sum bond market in Hong Kong, provide foreign investors with opportunities to invest in RMB-denominated assets outside mainland China, thereby promoting the international use of the RMB (Chey et al., 2019).

The interplay between bond market opening, currency flowback, and RMB internationalization underscores the complex dynamics shaping China's financial integration with the global economy. The liberalization of China's bond market attracts foreign capital inflows, contributing to currency appreciation and repatriation flows. These repatriation flows, in turn, reinforce the internationalization of the RMB by increasing its use in cross-border transactions and enhancing its attractiveness to global investors. However, policymakers must navigate challenges associated with capital mobility, exchange rate volatility, and financial stability in the process of opening bond markets and promoting currency internationalization. Effective coordination of monetary policy, capital account management, and financial market regulation is essential to mitigate risks and ensure the orderly integration of domestic bond markets into the global financial system.

In conclusion, the opening of bond markets plays a crucial role in facilitating currency flowback and advancing the internationalization of currencies, including the RMB. By attracting foreign investors and promoting the use of domestic currencies in international transactions, bond market liberalization contributes to the integration of domestic financial markets with the global economy. Understanding the interplay between bond market opening, currency flowback, and RMB internationalization is essential for policymakers and market participants navigating the complexities of China's financial reforms and its evolving role in the global financial system. The following DSGE model incorporates the bond market opening into the financial system.

12.3 Model

Building on the review, we develop an open DSGE model with currency flowback mechanisms following the real business cycle paradigm (Canova & Ubide, 1998; Zhang & Zhou, 2021). Throughout this chapter, variables with superscript d are the domestic demand for domestic products/bonds (e.g., C^d, B^d), and those with superscript f are the domestic demand for foreign products/bonds (e.g., C^f, B^f). All variables with a star $*$ indicate the foreign counterparts (e.g., $C_t^*, i_t^*, s^*, \gamma^*$). The timing convention is such that the subscript t means the variable is determined at t or during period t (between $t-1$ and t), but it can take effect in period $t+1$ as a state variable (e.g., K_t).

Consumer: The representative consumer maximizes her expected lifetime utility:

$$\max_{\left\{C_t, C_t^d, C_t^f, N_t, L_t, Z_t, B_t, B_t^f\right\}_{t=0}^{\infty}} \mathbf{E}_t \sum_{t=0}^{\infty} \beta^t U(C_t, L_t)$$

We assume a time-separable isoelastic utility function similar to McCallum and Nelson (2000), where θ is the relative utility weight of leisure (L_t) and ϵ_t^L is an exogenous preference shock with respect to leisure ($\epsilon_t^L > 0$ means leisure is more desirable).

$$U(C_t, L_t) = \ln C_t + \theta e^{\epsilon_t^L} \ln L_t$$

Furthermore, to introduce open economy, the composite consumption C_t is an aggregator between domestic and foreign products, where γ is the relative utility weight for imported foreign product $C_t^f \equiv M_t$ and ϵ_t^M is the exogenous preference shock with respect to C_t^f ($\epsilon_t^M > 0$ means imported foreign product is more desirable than usual), and s is the elasticity of substitution. Note that in steady state ($\epsilon_t^M = 0$), the utility weights of the domestic and foreign products are respectively equal to $\frac{1}{1+\gamma}$ and $\frac{\gamma}{1+\gamma}$.

$$C_t \equiv \left[\left(\frac{1}{1+\gamma e^{\epsilon_t^M}}\right)^{\frac{1}{s}} \left(C_t^d\right)^{\frac{s-1}{s}} + \left(\frac{\gamma e^{\epsilon_t^M}}{1+\gamma e^{\epsilon_t^M}}\right)^{\frac{1}{s}} \left(C_t^f\right)^{\frac{s-1}{s}}\right]^{\frac{s}{s-1}}$$

There are three constraints restricting the optimization process. First, time endowment is split between labor (N_t), financial activities (Z_t) such as working in the banking sector, and leisure (L_t).

$$N_t + Z_t + L_t = 1$$

Second, after a lump-sum tax T_t (net of any transfer payment) the dispensable income (including labor income at the rate of w_t, financial income at the rate of ω_t, and the dividend income per capita Π_t) is spent on consumption and financial investment (on both domestic and foreign bonds). The domestic bonds issued by the home country can be held by both domestic and foreign investors. The ratio held by foreign investors is set to be fixed at μ, so the ratio held by domestic investors is $1-\mu$. Here, the relative prices of financial assets are normalized to 1, so we need to interpret B_t^d and B_t^f as quantities (net holdings) respectively denominated by domestic and foreign output units. Moreover, the real exchange rate χ_t is needed to account for the value difference between domestic and foreign output units (1 unit of foreign output is equal to χ_t units of domestic output). The world interest rate i_t^* is exogenous.

$$\begin{aligned} C_t^d + \chi_t C_t^f + (1-\mu)\left[B_t^d - (1+i_{t-1})B_{t-1}^d\right] \\ + \chi_t B_t^f - \chi_t\left(1+i_{t-1}^*\right)B_{t-1}^f \\ = w_t N_t + \omega_t Z_t + \Pi_t - T_t \end{aligned}$$

Firm: The representative firm maximizes the sum of discounted future profit flows. The discount rate is equal to the market (real) interest rate $r_t = i_t$ and the discount factor $D_t = \frac{1}{(1+i_0)\ldots(1+i_{t-1})}$ for $t \geq 1$ and $D_0 = 1$. The output sector and the financial sector are consolidated to one composite firm, but this setup is equivalent to the decentralized two-sector model according to the First Fundamental Theorem of Welfare Economics.

$$\max_{\{Y_t, K_t, I_t, N_t, Z_t\}_{t=0}^{\infty}} \mathbf{E}_t \sum_{t=0}^{\infty} D_t (Y_t - I_t - w_t N_t - \omega_t Z_t \equiv \Pi_t)$$

There are four constraints. The first is the production function of the aggregate output Y_t, with A_t being the Harrod neutral (or labor augmenting) technology and α being the income share of labor. The advantage of this specification is well documented that the growth rate of output is equal to the growth rate of technology in the balanced growth path.

$$Y_t = (A_t N_t)^{\alpha} K_{t-1}^{1-\alpha}$$

The second is to endogenize technological progress by financial depth in a similar way to other endogenous growth models (e.g., human capital, Lucas, 1988; knowledge capital, Romer, 1990). This feature makes the firm's optimization problem dynamic because the decision today (on Z_t) affects both the present and the future. A quadratic feature of the relationship between technological growth (g_A) and financial depth ($\tilde{F}_t$) is supported by empirical evidence and corporate finance theory (explained in the market clearing subsection). Given that our model follows a neoclassical paradigm, the contribution of capital (including financial capital) is diminishing. This is the fundamental reason for this observed inverted-U relationship in data. $\tilde{F}_t \equiv F_t / Y_t$, a standard measure of financial depth, is defined as the ratio between the total financial capital and GDP, delineating the relative abundance of financial instruments to facilitate the real economy. ϵ_t^A is an exogenous productivity shock.

$$g_{At} \equiv \frac{A_t}{A_{t-1}} - 1 = a_0 + a_1 \tilde{F}_t + a_2 \tilde{F}_t^2 + \epsilon_t^A$$

The third constraint describes the financial capital production function. In the light of the evidence, the financial depth is determined by both financial labor input and the previous relative financial capital in a similar fashion to the aggregate output production function. The difference is that we do not restrict it to constant returns to scale, so $\phi_1 + \phi_2$ can be greater than 1.[1] ϵ_t^F is an exogenous productivity shock specific to the financial sector.

$$\tilde{F}_t = \Phi_0 \tilde{F}_{t-1}^{\phi_1} Z_t^{\phi_2} e^{\epsilon_t^F} \Leftrightarrow \ln \tilde{F}_t \approx \phi_0 + \phi_1 \ln \tilde{F}_{t-1} + \phi_2 \ln Z_t + \epsilon_t^F$$

Finally, the law of motion for physical capital is specified below. We grant the ownership of capital is to firms rather than household, but according to the Coase theorem, whoever owns the capital does not make any difference if there is no transaction cost.

$$K_t - (1 - \delta) K_{t-1} = I_t$$

Government: The government finances its expenditure G_t by a lump-sum tax T_t and government bond B_t (G1), while the expenditure is a fraction (ζ) of GDP disturbed by a fiscal policy shock ϵ_t^G.

$$G_t = T_t + B_t^d - (1 + i_{t-1}) B_{t-1}^d$$

$$G_t = (\zeta Y_t) e^{\epsilon_t^G}$$

Rest of the World: The equations below describe the balance of payment, i.e., current account surplus (trade balance + factor income) on the left-hand side of the equation is equal to capital account deficit on the right-hand side. Note that the current account and capital account consider bond holdings between domestic $(1 - \mu)$ and foreign (μ) investors. Import and export being derived from consumer's marginal conditions by symmetry:

$$\left[(X_t - \chi_t M_t) + \chi_t i_{t-1}^* B_{t-1}^f - \mu i_{t-1} B_{t-1}^d\right] = \chi_t \left(B_t^f - B_{t-1}^f\right) - \mu \left(B_t^d - B_{t-1}^d\right)$$

$$M_t \equiv C_t^f = \left(\frac{\gamma e^{\epsilon_t^M}}{1 + \gamma e^{\epsilon_t^M}}\right)^{-\frac{1}{s-1}} \left(1 + \frac{\chi_t^{s-1}}{\gamma e^{\epsilon_t^M}}\right)^{-\frac{s}{s-1}} C_t$$

$$X_t = \left(\frac{\gamma^* e^{\epsilon_t^X}}{1 + \gamma^* e^{\epsilon_t^X}}\right)^{-\frac{1}{s^*-1}} \left(1 + \frac{(1/\chi_t)^{s^*-1}}{\gamma^* e^{\epsilon_t^X}}\right)^{-\frac{s^*}{s^*-1}} C_t^*$$

[1] The estimated equation based on the US data is: $\ln \tilde{F}_t = \underset{(2.1344)}{0.8162} + \underset{(0.0543)}{0.9061} \ln \tilde{F}_{t-1} + \underset{(0.5165)}{0.1571} \ln Z_t$. We will use the estimates to calibrate ϕ_1 and ϕ_2. It turns out that the financial capital production function is very close to constant returns to scale ($\widehat{\phi}_1 + \widehat{\phi}_2 = 1.0632$).

Note that the first order conditions for C_t^f and C_t^d are used to obtain the M_t equation. Also, χ_t is reversed in the X_t equation because the real exchange rate facing the rest of the world is the reciprocal of that facing the domestic consumers. Moreover, ϵ_t^X is the exogenous preference shock with respect to domestic output in the world market ($\epsilon_t^X > 0$ means the exported domestic output is more desirable). It is a common modeling choice to include a preference shock as such in the literature of international business cycles to match the persistence observed in the data (Rothert, 2020). C_t^* is the exogenous world consumption per capita, which is the counterpart of C_t.

Market Clearing: The clearing conditions hold for output markets, labor markets, capital markets, and financial markets, both domestically and internationally. The two domestic labor markets (in the financial sector and non-financial sector) are competitive, and the two wages are equalized. Since capital is owned by firms, the cost of investment is internalized and there is no explicit capital market. Note that the consumer's budget constraint, the definition of the firm's profit, the government's budget constraint, and the balance of payment imply the domestic output market clearing condition $Y_t = C_t^d + I_t + G_t + X_t$. Moreover, under the small open-economy assumption, the international output and financial markets are exogenous so the demand and supply can always meet. The only relevant market clearing condition is therefore the domestic financial market:

$$F_t = \left(St_t + B_t^{pr} + Cr_t\right) + B_t^d$$

The left-hand-side F_t is the total domestic financial capital produced and maintained by the financial sector, and the right-hand-side includes the external finance demanded by the firm (St_t: stock market capitalization; B_t^{pr}: private bond; Cr_t: bank credit/loan) and the public bond demanded by the government (B_t^d). According to the corporate finance literature (e.g., trade-off theory and pecking order theory), the demand for external finance $\left(St_t + B_t^{pr} + Cr_t\right)$ is a result of optimization leading to a ratio of the total capital (K_t). Panel data evidence (Rajan & Zingales, 1995) shows that this optimal ratio ranges from 20% in the US, 30% in Canada, 36% in the UK to 50% in Japan. In our data, this ratio (κ) of external finance is derived to be 25.88%. The financial market clearing condition can be rewritten as:

$$F_t = \kappa K_t + B_t^d$$

The bottom line is that this system consists of $N_n = 21$ endogenous variables, $N_x = 8$ exogenous variables (i.e., stochastic shocks) and the same number of innovations. Mathematically, there is no technical difference between endogenous and exogenous variables, so let's group them together into a 29-by-1 vector $\mathbf{x}_t$. The 8 innovations are grouped into an 8-by-1 vector $\boldsymbol{\eta}_t$. The structural form of the equation system can be summarized as:

$$\mathbf{E}_t\left[f\left(\mathbf{x}_t, \mathbf{x}_{t-1}, \mathbf{x}_{t+1}, \boldsymbol{\eta}_t | \boldsymbol{\theta}\right)\right] = 0, \text{where } \boldsymbol{\theta} \in \Theta.$$

12.4 Results

The model that is estimated and calibrated to match the data features is then solved and simulated using the perturbation method. Our analysis of the model will focus on the relationship between FD and growth rate. Table 12.1 summarizes implied steady states of the endogenous and exogenous variables. A particularly interesting implication is that the long-run steady state of FD level ($\overline{F} = 1.596$) is lower than the turning point of the quadratic equation, i.e., $-\frac{a_1}{2a_2} = 2.4$. In other words, the social welfare maximizing solution is different from the growth maximizing solution, under which the maximum growth rate is 6.75%, greater than the steady state growth rate 2.62%. To understand this difference, remember that the equilibrium FD level is derived to maximize the consumer's utility, rather than to maximize the growth rate. Therefore, to maximize a different objective function, the FD level needs to deviate from the welfare-maximizing level. An economy can grow faster if the financial depth is distorted to a higher level at the cost of the social welfare.

One example is China, which experienced an unprecedented financial development and high

Table 12.1 The calibrated parameters and steady states of the baseline model

	Meaning	Calibration			Meaning	Steady state	
θ	relative utility weight of leisure	4.492	D	$\overline{C}$	aggregate consumption	0.656	E
β	subjective discount factor	0.989	D	$\overline{C}^d$	domestic goods	0.513	D
γ	relative weight of foreign goods	0.279	D	$\overline{N}$	non-financial labor	0.197	E
s	elasticity of substitution	1.200	F	$\overline{Z}$	financial labor	0.014	E
α	income share of labor	0.737	D	$\overline{B}^d$	domestic bonds	0.360	E
a_0	constant term	–0.298	D	$\overline{B}^f$	foreign bonds	0.000	F
a_1	linear term	0.304	D	$\overline{K}$	physical capital stock	4.779	D
a_2	quadratic term	–0.063	D	$\overline{I}$	investment	0.210	E
ϕ_0	constant term	0.712	D	$\overline{Y}$	output	1.026	E
ϕ_1	income share of $\tilde{F}_{t-1}$	0.906	E	$\overline{g}_Y$	growth rate of output	0.026	D
ϕ_2	income share of Z	0.157	E	$\overline{A}$	labor-augmented productivity	2.929	D
δ	capital depreciation rate	0.019	D	$\overline{g}_A$	growth rate of A	0.026	D
ζ	share of G	0.134	D	$\overline{F}$	financial depth	1.596	E
κ	optimal external finance rate	0.259	D	$\overline{\Pi}$	economic profit	0.000	F
ρ_A	AR(1) coefficient	0.815	E	$\overline{T}$	tax revenue	0.138	D
ρ_F	AR(1) coefficient	0.063	E	$\overline{G}$	government expenditure	0.134	D
ρ_L	AR(1) coefficient	0.063	F	$\overline{X}$	export	0.143	D
ρ_X	AR(1) coefficient	0.063	F	$\overline{M}$	import	0.143	E
ρ_M	AR(1) coefficient	0.063	F	$\overline{w}$	real wage	3.737	D
ρ_G	AR(1) coefficient	0.885	F	$\overline{i}$	interest rate	0.038	D
ρ_{i*}	AR(1) coefficient	0.683	E	$\overline{\chi}$	real exchange rate	1.000	F
$i*$	steady state $i*$	0.038	E	$\overline{C}^*$	world consumption	0.656	F
ρ_{C*}	AR(1) coefficient	0.441	E	$\overline{i}^*$	world interest rate	0.038	E
g_{C*}	steady state growth rate of $C*$	0.026	E	$\overline{\epsilon}_A$	productivity shock	0.000	F
σ_A	standard deviation	0.066	E	$\overline{\epsilon}_F$	financial shock	0.000	F
σ_F	standard deviation	0.038	E	$\overline{\epsilon}_L$	leisure preference shock	0.000	F
σ_L	standard deviation	0.100	F	$\overline{\epsilon}_X$	export preference shock	0.000	F
σ_X	standard deviation	0.090	E	$\overline{\epsilon}_M$	import preference shock	0.000	F
σ_M	standard deviation	0.090	E	$\overline{\epsilon}_G$	government expenditure shock	0.000	F
σ_G	standard deviation	0.024	E				
σ_{i*}	standard deviation	0.023	E				
σ_{C*}	standard deviation	0.016	E				

Notes "E" stands for estimated from data by GMM regression (with lagged endogenous variables as instruments), "F" stands for fixed based on the empirical DSGE literature (Zhang & Zhou, 2021), and "D" stands for derived from the equation system

economic growth over the last three decades. In 2016, the financial sector in China already accounts for over 10% of its GDP, much higher than 6.5% in the US. This is obviously a distortion of the economy, leading to higher risks of financial bubbles and a loss of welfare (Sun et al., 2020). This dynamic stochastic equation system can be solved and simulated using the perturbation method.

The *long-run* properties of the model can be analyzed by the variance decomposition. Figure 12.1 compares the contributions of the

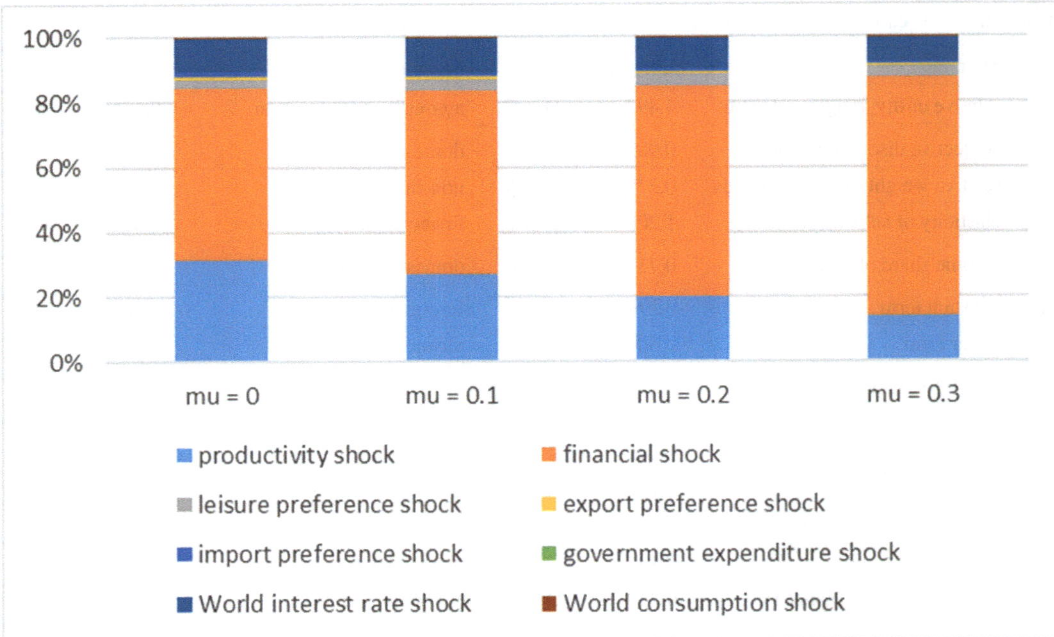

Fig. 12.1 Variance decomposition of output growth under different foreign holding

eight shocks to the variance of output growth under the four foreign holding ratios of domestic bonds (μ). It shows that as more bonds are held by foreign investors, the contributions of domestic productivity shock and world interest rate shock decrease, while the contribution of domestic financial shock rises.

The *short-run* properties of the estimated model are summarized by impulse response functions. The following three figures show the responses of output growth (g_Y) after productivity shock (η^A), financial shock (η^F), world interest rate shock (η^{i*}), and export preference shock (η^X) respectively. As the foreign holding ratio of domestic bonds (μ) rises, the effects become smaller because the shocks are absorbed by foreign economies.

The four impulse responses of Fig. 12.2 focus on the financial depth (F) after the three shocks. Similar to output growth, the financial depth also undergoes smaller effects if the foreign bond holdings (μ) increase. Due to the dampening effects, the speed of convergence is also shorter. Moreover, it is also shown that the convergence speed of financial depth is generally slower than that of output growth by comparing the horizontal axes of Figs. 12.1 and 12.2. This is because financial depth is a stock while output is a flow. It takes longer time for a stock variable to adjust due to the accumulated deviations. Thus, opening up the bond markets to foreign investors can substantially improve the stability of domestic financial markets (Fig. 12.3).

12.5 Conclusion

This chapter has provided valuable insights into the drivers and determinants of currency flowback, as well as its implications for the internationalization of the RMB. Currency flowback, as the movement of a currency back to its country of origin after being utilized abroad, reflects a complex interplay of economic, financial, and policy factors. The literature suggests that economic fundamentals, including trade balances, investment returns, and interest rate differentials, are key drivers of currency flowback. Changes in investor sentiment, geopolitical developments, and macroeconomic policies also influence repatriation flows, highlighting the dynamic nature of capital movements in the global economy.

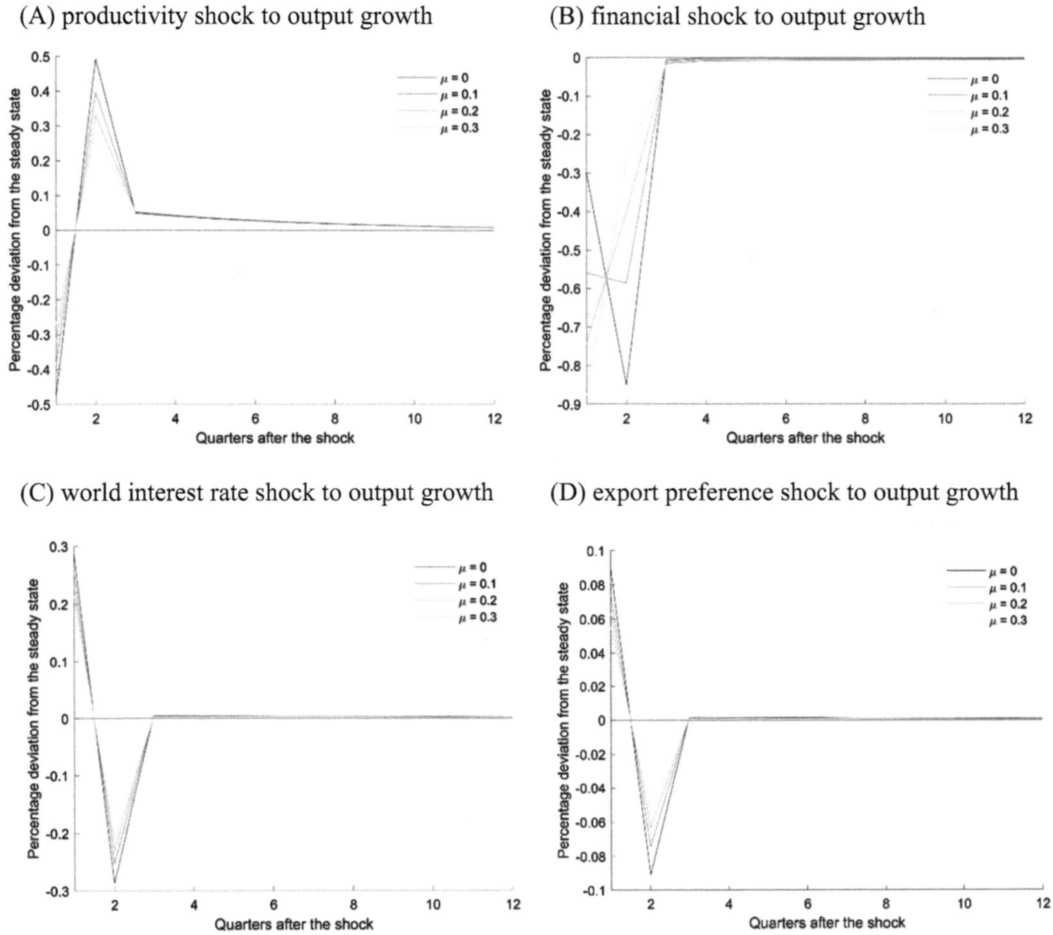

Fig. 12.2 Impulse response functions of output growth

Specifically, the opening of bond markets has emerged as a significant factor in facilitating currency flowback and promoting the internationalization of currencies. By attracting foreign investors and increasing the liquidity of domestic bond markets, bond market liberalization contributes to capital inflows and enhances the attractiveness of domestic currencies, such as the RMB, on the global stage.

We have developed an open-economy DSGE model with currency flowback mechanisms via the bond market. It is shown that the opening-up of the domestic bond market can improve financial stability and economic resilience when exogenous shocks hit the economy. Nevertheless, our simulations are done under a moderate foreign holding ratio (less than 30%), which is close to the ratio of the US-issued bonds. Our conclusion may not hold if there is an excessive foreign holding ratio of domestic bonds due to monopsonic power of the big buyers and importation of external shocks. That is also why the holding ratio in all developed economies is kept at a moderate level.

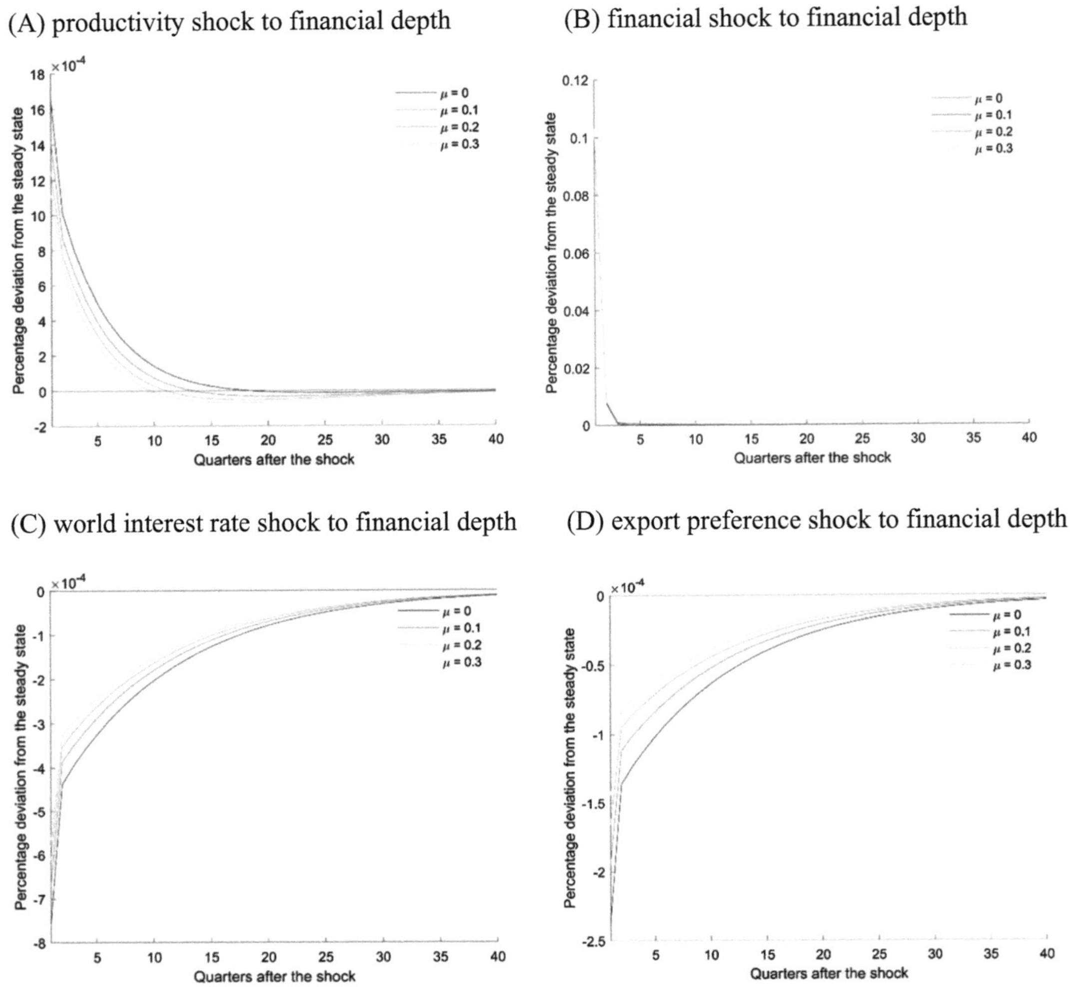

Fig. 12.3 Impulse response functions of financial depth

References

Antonio-Ocampo, J. (2017). *Resetting the international monetary (non) system*. Oxford University Press.

Camanho, N., Hau, H., & Rey, H. (2022). Global portfolio rebalancing and exchange rates. *The Review of Financial Studies, 35*(11), 5228–5274.

Canova, F., & Ubide, A. J. (1998). International business cycles, financial markets and household production. *Journal of Economic Dynamics and Control, 22*(4), 545–572.

Cheung, Y.-W. (2023). A decade of RMB internationalisation. *Economic and Political Studies, 11*(1), 47–74.

Chey, H.-K., Kim, G.-Y., & Lee, D. H. (2019). Which foreign states support the global use of the Chinese renminbi? The international political economy of currency internationalisation. *The World Economy, 42*(8), 2403–2426.

Chinn, M. D., & Ito, H. (2007). Current account balances, financial development and institutions: Assaying the world "saving glut." *Journal of International Money and Finance, 26*(4), 546–569.

Claessens, S., & Schmukler, S. L. (2007). International financial integration through equity markets: Which firms from which countries go global? *Journal of International Money and Finance, 26*(5), 788–813.

Cohen, B. J. (2012). The benefits and costs of an international currency: Getting the calculus right. *Open Economies Review, 23*(1), 13–31.

Frankel, J. (2012). Internationalization of the RMB and historical precedents. *Journal of Economic Integration, 27*(3), 329–365.

Gopinath, G., Boz, E., Casas, C., Díez, F. J., Gourinchas, P.-O., & Plagborg-Møller, M. (2020). Dominant currency paradigm. *American Economic Review, 110*(3), 677–719.

Guo, D., & Zhou, P. (2021). The rise of a new anchor currency in RCEP? A tale of three currencies. *Economic Modelling, 104*, Article 105647.

Lucas, R. E. (1988). On the mechanics of economic development. *Journal of Monetary Economics, 22*(1), 3–42.

McCallum, B., & Nelson, E. (2000). Monetary policy for an open economy: An alternative framework with optimizing agents and sticky prices. *Oxford Review of Economic Policy, 16*(4), 74–91.

Rajan, R. G.; & Zingales, L. (1995). What Do We Know about Capital Structure? Some Evidence from International Data. *The Journal of Finance, 50*: 1421–1460. https://doi.org/10.1111/j.1540-6261.1995.tb05184.x.

Romer, P. M. (1990). Endogenous technological change. *Journal of Political Economy, 98*(5, Part 2), S71–S102.

Rothert, J. (2020). International business cycles in emerging markets. *International Economic Review, 61*(2), 753–781.

Sun, P., Tan, Y., & Yang, G. (2020). Export, FDI and the welfare gains from trade liberalization. *Economic Modelling, 92*, 230–238.

Walker, T., Zhang, X., Zhang, A., & Wang, Y. (2021). Fact or fiction: Implicit government guarantees in China's corporate bond market. *Journal of International Money and Finance, 116*, Article 102414.

Wang, Y. D. (2015). Convertibility restriction in China's foreign exchange market and its impact on forward pricing. *Journal of Banking & Finance, 50*, 616–631.

Wei, H., Tu, Y., & Zhou, P. (2023). Technical barriers to trade and export performance: Comparing exiting and staying firms. *Economic Modelling, 126*, Article 106439.

Wu, M., Huang, P., & Ni, Y. (2017). Capital liberalization and various financial markets: Evidence from Taiwan. *The Quarterly Review of Economics and Finance, 66*, 265–274.

Zhang, B.; & Zhou, P. (2021). Financial development and economic growth in a microfounded small open economy model. *North American Journal of Economics and Finance, 58*, article number: 101544. https://doi.org/10.1016/j.najef.2021.101544.

Asset Tokenization as Financial Infrastructure

13

Abstract

We assess Distributed Ledger Technology (DLT) as a modernization path for financial-market infrastructure (FMI)—the payment, clearing, and settlement rails that keep markets running. Drawing on recent advances in bond tokenization, the chapter maps three trends: (i) migration from manual workflows to digital, centralized platforms; (ii) a fresh move toward decentralized records via DLT; and (iii) regulatory adaptation to safeguard stability amid big-data and blockchain tools. We show that permissioned DLT raises transparency, trims settlement-cycle risk, and supports programmable asset tokenization, yet fully open networks carry operational and supervisory hazards. For bond markets, a "heterogeneous consortium" design—where selected banks and official nodes validate transactions—balances decentralization with oversight. Policy guidance is as follows. First, embed bond tokenization inside existing legal frameworks to digitize assets without fracturing liquidity. Second, involve regulators and diverse intermediaries as consortium validators to maintain trust. Third, roll out cross-border DLT links incrementally, allowing standards to mature alongside technology. A stepwise strategy converts blockchain from a disruptive weapon into constructive market infrastructure, reinforcing resilience while widening access to capital.

Keywords

Financial market infrastructure · Distributed ledger technology

Classification

SDG9

13.1 Introduction

Financial Market Infrastructure refers to the most fundamental back-end systems, processes, and institutions that facilitate the functioning of financial markets, such as the payment and settlement systems, exchanges, and central counterparties (Panagariya, 2022). It provides the foundation for trading, clearing, and settling financial transactions and is critical to the stability and efficiency of the financial system (Berndsen et al., 2018). The evolution of FMI has been shaped by both technological advancements and regulatory changes. Before 2008, FMIs have become more digitalized, centralized, and integrated, leading to increased efficiency, reduced settlement times, and improved risk management. The advent of the internet and advancements in information technology have also enabled new ways of trading and settling financial transactions, such as electronic trading platforms and digital payment systems. Nevertheless, the global financial crisis of 2008 brought increased attention to the flaws of centralized financial systems and prompted regulatory

D. Guo and P. Zhou, *Beating Financial Swords into Developmental Plowshares*,
Sustainable Development Goals Series, https://doi.org/10.1007/978-981-95-5152-1_13

reforms aimed at improving their stability and resilience (Li & Perez-Saiz, 2018). These reforms, such as the implementation of central clearing for certain types of derivatives and the creation of a new type of central counterparty, have further entrenched the role of FMI.

The rise in DLT, especially blockchain, has provided new opportunities for innovative solutions to FMI, which we term as DLT-FMI. But these developments have also raised questions about the balance between innovation and regulation, as well as the implications for market structure and the role of intermediaries. Blockchain technology has the potential to disrupt FMI by enabling faster, more secure, and more transparent transactions and settlements (Frizzo-Barker et al., 2020). One of the key benefits of blockchain technology is its decentralized architecture, which eliminates the need for intermediaries and increases transparency and security in financial transactions. For example, blockchain-based payment systems can allow for real-time, cross-border transactions without banks. This can significantly reduce transaction costs and increase the speed of payments (Chang et al., 2020). Another potential use of blockchain technology in finance is the creation of new digital assets, such as cryptocurrencies and non-fungible tokens, which can be used as an alternative to traditional fiat currencies and assets. This can lead to the creation of new financial instruments and markets and can challenge the dominance of traditional financial institutions (Chen et al., 2023). Blockchain technology can also be used to improve efficiency and reduce the risk of the back-end systems that support financial transactions. For example, blockchain-based settlement systems can enable faster and more secure settlement of trades, reducing the risk of failed trades and increasing overall market efficiency (Kowalski et al., 2021). Nevertheless, the widespread adoption of blockchain in the financial sector will depend on various factors, such as regulatory clarity, security, scalability, and interoperability (Ahluwalia et al., 2020). The financial industry will need to evaluate these challenges carefully to determine the most effective and efficient ways of DLT-FMI. Given the importance of FMI and DLT, this chapter aims to bridge the two strands of literature to answer the following research questions (RQs).

RQ1: How does FMI evolve over time and across countries?
RQ2: What is the emerging trend of FMI development?
RQ3: How does DLT contribute to FMI?
RQ4: What is the optimal mechanism design of DLT-FMI in bond markets?

We first examine FMI from an evolutionary perspective based on the historical development experiences of three major economies (RQ1). The trend from centralized digitalization to decentralized tokenization has been identified as a response to the trust crisis of centralized monetary authorities and financial intermediaries since 2008 (RQ2). Blockchain technology offers a promising solution to mitigate the agency problem and trust issues in traditional centralized FMI. We then explore the details of how DLT-FMI can be designed in general (RQ3) and specifically in the context of bond market tokenization (RQ4). We suggest that a gradual, incremental innovation approach should be followed, rather than a disruptive revolution. A balance between decentralization and centralization is necessary to develop DLT-FMI. We propose a solution in the form of a heterogeneous consortium blockchain. Next, we use China's bond market as a context to conduct an in-depth case study.

13.2 An Evolutionary Perspective

According to the Principles for Financial Market Infrastructures (PFMI) published by the Committee on Payment and Settlement Systems (CPSS) and the International Organization of Securities Commissions (IOSCO) in 2012, FMI is defined as "*a set of systems, entities, rules, procedures and standards that support the functioning of financial markets by facilitating the exchange of financial assets, including payment and settlement systems, central securities depositories, central counterparties, trade repositories and other similar systems.*" PFMI provides a comprehensive framework for the oversight and regulation of FMI, with a focus on ensuring the safety, efficiency, and stability of these critical components of the financial system. The principles cover a wide range of issues, including governance, risk management, and operational efficiency, and provide guidance for regulators to promote market confidence and stability. The aim of PFMI is to promote the safe and efficient functioning of financial markets by ensuring that FMI has robust governance and risk management frameworks in place and by promoting the adoption of common standards and practices across different markets.

To gain a better understanding of the current structure of FMI (RQ1) and predict its future trends (RQ2), it is necessary to extract the patterns from its historical development. In the following subsections, the evolution of FMI in three major economies, the US, Europe, and China, are reviewed.

13.2.1 US

The evolution of FMI in the US has gone through several significant changes over the past several decades. It can be roughly divided into five historical phases.

(1) **Pre-1970s**. The FMI in the US was less developed and less sophisticated compared to today's standards. During this period, financial markets in the US were primarily based on manual systems, with limited use of technology. The discrepancy between the surging demand for transactions in exchanges and the limited capacity of the manual trading system eventually led to the "Paper Blizzard" crisis in 1960s. Overall, the FMI in the US before the 1970s was characterized by limited use of technology, slow and manual processes, and a fragmented structure.
(2) **1970s**. The introduction of electronic trading systems in the 1970s marked the beginning of the modern era of FMI in the US. During this period, the first automated trading systems were introduced, and exchanges began to transition from manual open outcry systems to electronic trading platforms.
(3) **1980s–1990s**. The 1980s and 1990s saw the growth of over the counter (OTC) financial markets, which added a new layer of complexity to the financial system. The use of OTC derivatives and other complex financial instruments increased during this period, and regulators began to focus on improving the transparency and stability of these markets.
(4) **2000–2008**. The 2000s saw significant changes in the regulation of FMIs in the US, as regulators responded to increasing concerns about systemic risk in the financial system. During this period, the Federal Reserve established the Continuous Linked Settlement (CLS) system, which aimed to reduce settlement risk in forex markets.
(5) **Post-2008**. The 2008 global financial crisis highlighted the importance of strong and effective FMI in ensuring stability and confidence in financial markets. In response to the crisis, regulators in the US and around the world took steps to strengthen FMIs and reduce systemic risk. In the aftermath of the 2008 crisis, the US implemented a number of reforms aimed at improving the stability and resilience of the financial system. These reforms included the Dodd-Frank Wall Street Reform and Consumer Protection Act, which established the Financial Stability Oversight Council (FSOC) to oversee FMIs and promote stability in the financial system. The Total Holding System becomes a centralized solution to clearing bond markets.

Today, the FMI in the US is highly developed and has been shaped by a combination of technological advancements, increased globalization, and regulatory initiatives. It has resulted in a sophisticated and integrated infrastructure that supports the efficient functioning of financial markets and enhances the stability and confidence of the financial system (Zhang & Zhou, 2021). It features mature clearinghouses, payment systems, capital markets, and regulatory framework.

First, The US has a number of clearinghouses, such as the Depository Trust Company, which play a key role in reducing settlement risk and enhancing the efficiency of financial markets. Clearinghouses act as intermediaries between buyers and sellers of securities and are responsible for maintaining the integrity of the settlement process. Second, The US has several high-speed payment systems, such as the Fedwire Funds Service, which is used for large-value inter-bank payments, and the Automated Clearing House network, which is used for small-value retail payments. These payment systems aim to improve the efficiency and stability of the payment system in the US. Third, The US has a well-developed capital market infrastructure, with several large stock exchanges, including NYSE and NASDAQ, and a number of other financial markets, such as the bond market and the derivatives market. Fourth, The FMI in the US is subject to a robust regulatory framework, which aims to ensure stability and efficiency of financial markets. This includes regulations such as the Dodd-Frank Wall Street Reform and Consumer Protection Act, which was implemented in response to the financial crisis of 2008, and the Securities and Exchange Commission (SEC), which is responsible for enforcing securities laws and regulations.

13.2.2 Europe

The evolution of PMI in Europe has been shaped by a number of key factors, including technological advancements, increased globalization, and regulatory initiatives. Here are some of the key stages of the evolution of FMI in Europe:

(1) **Pre-1990s**. Before the 1990s, the FMI in Europe was fragmented, with different countries having different systems and processes for clearing and settling financial transactions. There was also limited use of technology in the financial sector, and manual processes were still widely used.
(2) **1990s–2008**. During this period, Europe experienced a significant expansion of its financial markets, and there was a growing need for a more integrated and efficient FMI. In response, the EU launched the Single European Payments Area (SEPA) project, which aimed to create a single market for euro payments within the EU.
(3) **2008–2010s**. The financial crisis of 2008 had a significant impact on the FMI in Europe and led to increased regulatory scrutiny and a greater focus on stability and resilience in the financial system. This led to the development of the EU's Capital Markets Union (CMU) initiative, which aims to create a single market for capital in Europe.
(4) **2020s**. In recent years, the FMI in Europe has continued to evolve, with a focus on improving the efficiency and stability of financial markets. This has included the development of new technology such as blockchain and increased regulatory oversight, including the implementation of the EU's MiFID II directive, which aims to enhance the transparency and efficiency of financial markets.

Overall, the evolution of the FMI in Europe has been shaped by a combination of technological advancements, increased globalization, and regulatory initiatives, and has resulted in a sophisticated and integrated infrastructure that supports the efficient functioning of financial markets and enhances the stability and confidence of the financial system. The focus is on improving the efficiency and stability of financial markets by centralized settlement systems, payment systems, capital markets, and regulatory framework.

First, one of the key features of the FMI in Europe is the use of centralized settlement systems, which aim to reduce settlement risk and enhance the efficiency of financial markets. For example, the European Central Securities Depository Regulation (CSDR) requires that all securities transactions in the EU be settled through a central securities depository. Second, The FMI in Europe includes several high-speed payment systems, such as the TARGET2 system, which is used for large-value inter-bank payments in the EU. These payment systems aim to improve the efficiency and stability of the payment system in Europe. Third, Europe has a well-developed capital market infrastructure, with a number of stock exchanges, including the London Stock Exchange and the Euronext exchange. In addition, the EU has implemented a number of initiatives aimed at enhancing the integration and efficiency of its capital markets, including the CMU project. Finally, The FMI in Europe is subject to a robust regulatory framework, which aims to ensure the stability and efficiency of financial markets. This includes regulations such as the EU Market Abuse Regulation, which aims to prevent market abuse, and the EU MiFID II directive, which aims to enhance the transparency and efficiency of financial markets.

13.2.3 China

The FMI in China has undergone significant development and evolution since late 1970s, as the country has transformed into one of the world's largest economies.

(1) **1970s–1980s**. During this period, the Chinese government started to reform the country's financial system and opened up the economy to foreign investment. This helped to lay the foundation for the development of the FMI in China and paved the way for the growth of the stock market and other financial markets in the years to come.
(2) **1990s**. China established its first stock market, the Shanghai Stock Exchange, in 1990, and later established the Shenzhen Stock Exchange. These stock exchanges have grown rapidly in size and importance, and now rank among the largest in the world.
(3) **2000s**. The first decade of the twenty-first century saw continued growth and development of the FMI in China, as the country became an increasingly important player in the global financial system. The Chinese stock market continued to grow. The banking sector underwent significant reforms, but many shadow banking activities were developed as the transition took place (Wang et al., 2021). New payment systems were developed to support the growth of electronic commerce.
(4) **2010s**. During this decade, the FMI in China experienced rapid expansion and growth, as the government continued to support the development of key financial institutions and infrastructure. The bond market grew rapidly, becoming one of the largest in the world and providing an important source of financing for the government and for corporations. Additionally, the regulatory framework for the FMI in China was strengthened, helping to reduce systemic risk and improve market efficiency.
(5) **2020s**. In recent years, the FMI in China has continued to evolve and mature, as the government has implemented new reforms and initiatives to support the growth of the financial markets. This has included measures to promote green bonds (Guo & Zhou, 2021), increase market transparency, reduce systemic risk, as well as efforts to encourage the use of new technologies, such as blockchain. Specifically, PBoC developed and launched the first central bank digital currency e-CNY in 2020. In the meantime, blockchain technology is also applied to solving traditional finance problems such as cross-border payments, supply chain finance, and bond issuance (tokenization).

Overall, the evolution of the FMI in China has been shaped by a combination of government support, market forces, and technological advancements, and has helped to position the country as a key player in the regional trade and global financial system. The FMI of China has developed its own characteristics in the following building blocks.

First, China has two major stock exchanges, the Shanghai Stock Exchange and the Shenzhen Stock Exchange, which rank among the largest in the world by market capitalization. The Chinese stock markets provide a venue for companies to raise capital and for investors to trade and invest in stocks. Second, the banking sector in China is dominated by a few large state-owned banks but also includes a growing number of smaller private banks and other financial institutions. The banking sector has undergone significant reforms and consolidation in recent years, improving the stability and efficiency of the sector. Third, China has a number of modern and efficient payment systems, including the China National Advanced Payment System, which allows for real-time interbank transfers and helps to improve the efficiency of the payment system in the country. Fourth, China has a large and rapidly growing bond market, which provides an important source of financing for the government and for corporations. The bond market has been supported by the development of key institutions and infrastructure, such as the China Securities Depository and Clearing Corporation and consortium blockchain. Finally, the regulatory framework for the FMI in China is overseen by the People's Bank of China (PBoC), the country's central bank, which has been instrumental in guiding the development of the FMI in recent years. The PBoC has been focused on improving market efficiency, reducing systemic risk, and protecting the interests of investors.

13.2.4 Trend Analysis

Based on the evolutionary paths of US, Europe, and China, we summarize the following dimensions of modern FMI: stock market, bond market, banking system, payment system, and regulatory framework. Each of these FMI components plays a crucial role in maintaining the stability and efficiency of financial markets, and they work together to facilitate the smooth functioning of financial markets.

Table 13.1 compares the FMIs of the US, Europe, and China. It shows that the US has been at the forefront of FMI development, with a mature and comprehensive financial foundation. The US was the first economy to digitalize its FMI, and after the financial crisis of 2008, the focus shifted to regulation. Europe followed in the US's footsteps in terms of digitalization and regulation, but with a unique emphasis on integration among different members of the region. The issuance of the Euro currency helped unify the monetary system but also led to debt issues. The current focus in Europe is on regulation and the adoption of new technologies. China lagged behind until the 1990s but has since seen the fastest development due to its ability to adopt and adapt to existing models. The transition costs for adopting new technology in China are lower, and the country has been at the forefront of blockchain technology adoption, as it benefits the most from the decentralization feature of the technology. Conversely, the US, as the established center, is more cautious about blockchain technology, as the essence of decentralization is to challenge the market power of the center.

The comparison of FMIs of the three major economies has revealed three key trends in the development of FMI. First, *digitalization* has been accelerating, leading to streamlining of processes, improved efficiency, increased transparency, cost savings, and reduced risk. This trend started in the US in the 1970s and has spread to all fields of FMI such as the stock market, bond market, banking, and payment systems. The result of digitalization is a highly centralized system, which is subject to the principal-agent problem eventually leading to the global financial crisis in 2008. Second, *tokenization* has emerged as a new form of FMI, where traditional financial assets are converted into digital assets, often referred to as tokens. Tokenization has the potential to revolutionize the way financial assets are traded and settled, offering increased efficiency and accessibility, as well as transparency and decentralization through blockchain solutions. Finally, *regulation* has been evolving in tandem with the development of new technologies like big data, AI, and blockchain, becoming increasingly important to ensure an orderly financial market. Regulations set the rules within which market participants can play and need to evolve with the new challenges posed by the development of these technologies.

Table 13.1 Comparison of FMIs of US, Europe, and China

	US	Europe	China
Pre-1970s	Manual exchanges (open cry and paper based); intermediaries (broker-dealer); fragmented payment systems	Fragmented, mainly manual (paper based)	No exchange; command economy without financial markets; cash-based and stamp-based payment system
1970s	Electronic trading system introduced		
1980s	OTC introduced		Reform and open-up
1990s	Financial derivatives developed, regulation developed to ensure transparency and stability	Digitalized system introduced to improve efficiency	Stock exchanges established
2000–2008	Regulation developed to reduce settlement risk in forex market (e.g., CLS)	Integrated monetary, banking, and payment system (e.g., SEPA, Euro)	Banking sector reformed to be market-based, digitalized system introduced
2008–2010s	Regulation developed to reduce systemic risk (e.g., FSOC), Total Holding System in bond market	Regulation developed to improve stability and resilience (e.g., CMU)	Bond market developed for both companies and governments, digital payment system
2020s	Regulation developed for blockchain-based finance (e.g., SEC)	New technology adoption such as blockchain (e.g., MiFID II)	Blockchain, e-CNY, regulation developed to reduce systemic risk, Transparent Holding System (THS) in bond market

13.3 DLT as FMI

Blockchain technology is the most famous DLT thanks to the hype of blockchain-based cryptocurrencies like Bitcoin and Ethereum. As argued earlier, the incorporation of DLT into FMI or DLT-FMI provides an innovative solution to payment and settlement. We introduce the technical framework of DLT and its novel features as FMI (RQ3) and analyze the practicality of DLT-FMI in bond market (RQ4).

13.3.1 Technical Framework

As illustrated in Fig. 13.1, the issuer of assets (e.g., bond) tokenizes its assets into tokens and sells it to the public. Ownership is recorded in distributed ledgers verified by validators using a certain consensus mechanism such as proof of stake. After the issuance, transactions between two parties, A and B can be done without a trusted third party. A sends its tokenized assets to the blockchain via its own node, which is received by the node of B. This transaction is broadcast to the entire blockchain, where validators verify the transaction and encapsulate the data into the new block. In some blockchains, auditors exist to review the accuracy and integrity of transaction records, verify the authenticity of smart contracts, and ensure the security of blockchain networks. The defining feature of DLT is decentralization structure, which enhances trust among market participants without a trusted authority or intermediary.

There are many ways that DLT (blockchain in particular) can be used as an FMI. First, it improves transparency. Blockchain's decentralized and transparent ledger can provide a clear and reliable record of transactions and ownership, which can improve the transparency of the financial market and increase trust among market participants. Second, it reduces settlement risk. Blockchain's real-time transaction processing and automatic reconciliation features can reduce the time required to settle trades, which can help to reduce settlement risk and improve market efficiency. Third, it enhances security. Blockchain's decentralized and secure nature can help to reduce the risk of cyberattacks and fraud, which are major concerns in the financial market. Fourth, it increases interoperability. Blockchain's interoperable nature can help to connect different financial

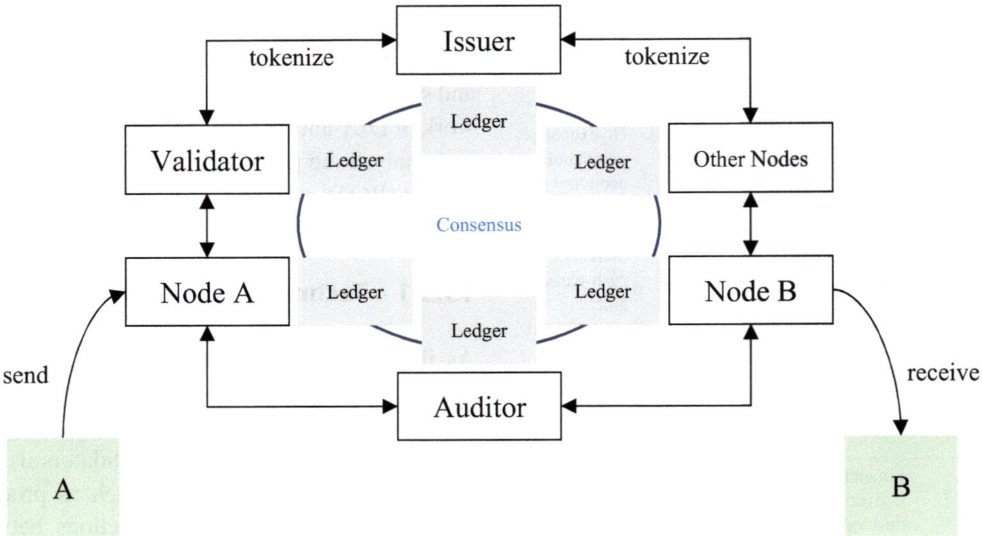

Fig. 13.1 The technical framework of DLT

market infrastructures and reduce the barriers to entry in the financial market, which can increase competition and promote innovation. Finally, it tokenizes assets. Blockchain's ability to tokenize assets, such as bonds and securities, can provide a new and more efficient way to manage and trade these assets, which can increase market liquidity and reduce the costs of trading.

To make use of these features, the integration of DLT to existing FMI can be either partial or complete. We can unify consensus mechanism, cryptographic algorithm, and smart contracts into one integral piece, resulting in a complete DLT-FMI solution. Alternatively, partial integration models can serve ad hoc contexts such as central securities depository (CSD) and payment systems (PS), leading to DLT-CSD and DLT-PS. Therefore, the decision of blockchain adoption is not only a matter of yes or no (extensive margin), but also a matter of degree (intensive margin).

Table 13.2 examines the differences in permission of access, operation, restrictions on participation, role of nodes, and consensus mechanisms in DLT-FMI. At one end, Plan A is a traditional centralized FMI, and at the other end, Plan D is a pure public blockchain. The former has a proven history of high agency costs, while the latter inevitably leads to high regulatory risks. The eclectic Plans B and C are more likely to be implemented in practice because they strike a good balance between innovation and regulation. In other words, an incremental innovation is preferred to disruptive innovation.

13.3.2 Bond Market

We focus on the risks of DLT-FMI in a particular context, bond market, which plays a critical role in FMI. It provides a platform for issuers to raise capital and for investors to access a diverse range of fixed income investments. Bond market is also likely to be the first financial market to adopt tokenization (bond tokenization) to promote efficiency, transparency, security, and accessibility.

- Technical risk. The implementation of DLT-based FMI in bond markets is still a relatively new concept, and there are concerns about the stability, security, and scalability of blockchain technology. There is also a risk of system failures and technical glitches that can disrupt the functioning of the bond market.
- Regulatory risk. DLT- FMI operates in a decentralized manner, which raises concerns about the lack of central control and oversight. This

Table 13.2 Different types of DLT-FMI

	Plan A	Plan B	Plan C	Plan D
Permission	Permissioned	Permissioned	Permissioned	Permissionless
Operation	Centralized	Decentralized	Decentralized	Decentralized
Restriction	Restricted	Restricted	Restricted	Unrestricted
Node's role	Heterogenous	Heterogenous	Homogenous	Homogenous
Consensus	Single	Single/Multiple	Multiple	Multiple

can result in difficulties for regulators in monitoring and enforcing regulations, leading to regulatory risks.

- Market risk. The use of DLT in the bond market may also result in new types of market risks, such as liquidity risks, as well as increased risks related to the transfer and custody of securities.
- Operational risk. The implementation of DLT-based FMI in the bond market requires significant changes to existing systems and processes, and there is a risk of operational disruptions and inefficiencies during the transition.
- Legal risk. The use of DLT in the bond market may raise legal and contractual issues related to the ownership and transfer of securities, which can result in disputes and legal challenges.

Overall, the incorporation of DLT-FMI in the bond market presents a number of risks that must be carefully considered and managed in order to ensure its success. The key to overcoming these risks is to strike a balance between the benefits offered by DLT and the need for stability, security, and regulatory compliance in the financial market.

To address the specific risks in the bond market, a gradual or "incremental innovation" approach is suggested for blockchain adoption. We define two types of DLT-based digital bonds. One is "tokenized bonds," which are issued, registered, managed, and transacted on blockchains throughout the entire lifecycle of bonds. The other is "bond tokenization," which aims to use on-chain counterparts to represent off-chain bonds (partly or entirely). It facilitates rather than replaces traditional issuance, registration, management, and transaction of bonds. Rather than jumping into issuing pure tokenized bonds (Plan D), the emphasis should initially be on tokenizing existing bonds (bond tokenization). This creates a new form of existing assets rather than creating new assets, as the market needs time to build trust in disruptive technologies and regulations need time to mature. Hence, the transition from digitalization to tokenization should begin with the traditional financial and regulatory framework, augmented with the benefits of DLT-FMI.

Furthermore, it is recommended that consortium blockchains (Plans B and C) should be utilized instead of public blockchains (Plan D) for the incremental innovation of bond tokenization. A key characteristic of consortium blockchains is their diverse nodes. Allocating varying powers and responsibilities to different nodes strikes a balance between decentralization and centralization benefits. Unlike a homogenous mechanism (Plan C), a consortium blockchain with heterogeneous nodes (Plan B) can reduce the risks of financial instability and the "51% attack."

13.4 Case Study: Bond Market in China

The size of China's bond market is one of the largest in the world and the FMI development in China is at the forefront of major economies. We use China's bond market as a case study to draw some policy implications on DLT-FMI. On the one hand, a "disruptive innovation" on existing FMI is not suitable in the Chinese context. The FMI of China's bond market has a fast follower's advantage. China's bond market plays a leading role in developing a Transparency Holding System (THS), which is a more reliable design compared to the US's Indirect Holding System (IHS) and disruptive DLT-FMI. On the other hand, an "incremental innovation" of FMI incorporating selected benefits of DLT is more appropriate. In fields like cross-market bond settlements and cross-border bond issuance, blockchain technology can play an important role, but the incorporation should be gradual. The two policy implications are analyzed in the following subsections.

13.4.1 Why Not Disruptive Innovation

DLT-FMI is regarded as a disruptive solution to the traditional indirect holding system of bonds. For example, the IHS in the US assigns bond ownership to intermediaries at the cost of investor's legal ownership. Moreover, the investors undertake the credit risks of intermediaries, especially when intermediaries run into bankruptcy. In this case, legislation generally does not prioritize the investors' claims of their own bonds. In addition, intermediaries can misuse the bonds held by them. These drawbacks of IHS are resolved by the THS adopted by countries like China, Greece, and Scandinavian countries. In the THS, intermediaries hold rather than own bonds for the investors. In other words, the trust issues are already solved by THS without resorting to DLT-FMI solutions.

In terms of financial regulations, CNY-denominated bond markets have a significant fast follower's advantage in developing their FMI. THS provides a transparent mechanism for regulation as well as an efficient solution for transactions, which are supposed to be the benefits of DLT-FMI. For example, the inter-bank bond market in China adopted a centralized and digitalized processing system, which can achieve a T + 0 settlement since 2004. This efficiency is significantly higher than the counterpart in the US. The US model (IHS) is essentially a multi-level custodian system, which forms a pyramid structure. The efficiency of the system depends on the level with the lowest efficiency, and the security of the system also depends on the level with the lowest security. In 1995, the SEC revised the legislation to reduce the settlement duration from T + 5 down to T + 3. Only in 2017 has the settlement duration reduced to T + 2, which is still significantly longer than the THS in China.

Therefore, the existing FMI in China's bond markets (especially the inter-bank bond market) have already achieved the desired efficiency in operation and transparency in regulation. The centralized FMI also has a mature legal framework and FinTech toolbox, which are superior to the immature, unstable DLT-FMI solutions.

13.4.2 Why Incremental Innovation

China's bond market is large, but it is still in its infancy stage of an emerging economy. Internationalization of CNY and marketization of CNY-denominated bonds have encouraged foreign holdings of Chinese government bonds. It is an embodiment of the strong confidence of the world in the Chinese economy, but international hot money also inflicts a security threat to the government bond market. Since COVID-19, the global economy has been flooded with excessive liquidity due to QE and low interest rates. Unconventional monetary policies impose unbalanced threats and risks to emerging economies, because they lack flexibility in the capital market. To avoid such crises, bond market in China needs to take an incremental innovation to gradually incorporate DLT into the existing FMI.

13.4.2.1 Heterogeneous Consortium Blockchain

The DLT-FMI in the bond market should start with a heterogenous consortium blockchain. In the status quo, there are two bond markets in China: one is inter-bank bond market, and the other is open exchange market. The two-tier bond market structure is entrenched by three back-end institutions: China Securities Depository and Clearing Corporation (CSDC), China Central Depository & Clearing Company (CCDC), and Shanghai Clearinghouse (SHCH). Among the three organizations, only CSDC and CCDC have developed a collaboration mechanism which only focuses on custodian and exchange of selected government bonds. Most bonds are not tradable in different locations.

Specifically, CCDC has been leading the digitalization strategy of China. A national blockchain-based FMI pilot project has been successfully launched in 2022, and the first industrial standard and connection regulation of blockchain-based bond issuance will be published in 2023. Other breakthroughs in FMI include digitalization of bond market disclosure using the Extendable Business Reporting Language (XBRL), maturity structure management of local government bonds using automated models, and reduction of financing cost. CCDC follows five philosophies in their development of FMI, i.e., innovation, coordination, green, open, and sharing. In contrast, SHCH does not run any business on government bonds, resulting in a dual platform. The government bond market is managed by CSDC as an order keeper in cross-market exchanges. However, there have been many inefficient arrangements and double bookkeeping due to the lack of direct information sharing between CSDC and other exchanges. Information systems of different exchanges vary substantially with some even lack of digitalization. Inconsistencies and human errors are likely to occur.

To address these issues, an obvious solution is to develop a centralized FMI. According to historical experience in the US, a central custodian trustee is established to bridge the other local exchanges. In the 1980s, there were seven custodian trustees, but now they have been merged into one centralized custodian—Depository Trust & Clearing Corporation (DTC). There are about 40 electronic bond exchanges in the US, all of which have direct connection with DTC to enable easier access to the bond market. Another example is the EU, where cross-border bond markets are directly connected with a centralized trustee in each country. For example, client platforms like MTS, Tradeweb, Bloomberg, and Euroex Bond are directly linked with the central trustee in German, making it convenient to engage in international investment on cross-border bond markets.

In China's context, it is difficult to directly adopt the international experience without adaption. To enhance the connectivity of existing FMI without a disruptive innovation, a heterogeneous consortium blockchain strikes a good balance between regulation and innovation. The basic idea is to maintain procedures and frameworks of existing FMI, but it is augmented with and connected by a cross-city blockchain. CSDC and CCDC are major market participants with heterogeneous responsibilities and powers. They can validate transactions and form new blocks in the chain. This eclectic approach is an example the Plan B in Table 13.2, which is an incremental innovation of DLT-FMI.

13.4.2.2 Regulation Framework

It is essential to protect financial stability by online and offline monitoring of national and international fund flows. The regulation framework must be adjusted to supervise the heterogenous consortium blockchain in the following three aspects.

The first is to make regulators key market participants on the blockchain. Consortium blockchains are featured with permissioned access to mitigate risks of permissionless, unregulated public blockchains. The ledgers on the consortium blockchain are validated by key market participants (e.g., CSDC and CCDC) rather than any participants. The differences in market power and responsibilities make it a heterogenous consortium blockchain. In this way, regulatory bodies such as PBoC can also act as key market participants to authorize transactions. It therefore combines the benefits of DLT-FMI with the need for regulation.

Second, regulations must be adapted to accommodate foreign market participants. The onshore bond markets in China are bound to link with FMIs in other countries to enable international investment, but the connection must be selective and prudential. If foreign institutes are admitted to the consortium blockchain, the regulation framework and market rules should be based on the paradigm in China (e.g., THS). This is to avoid malicious attacks and to maintain financial stability. Nevertheless, non-essential elements should be flexible to promote mergers between domestic and international standards and rules. The goal is to build a global FMI with the help of DLT without sacrificing financial stability and security.

Finally, regulations should be adapted to join foreign DLT-FMI to issue new tokenized bonds in offshore bond markets. At present, the World Bank and central banks in many countries (e.g., Australia and Singapore) have developed blockchains for issuing tokenized bonds. To make full use of the global financial market, China should actively join foreign DLT-FMI and revise regulations accordingly. It is unlikely for China to issue tokenized bonds in offshore blockchains in the short run, but participation in foreign DLT-FMI can accumulate relevant knowledge based on international experience.

13.4.2.3 Bond Tokenization

According to the incremental innovation, it is suggested to start the DLT-FMI with tokenization of existing bonds under the current regulation framework ("bond tokenization"), rather than directly issuing new "tokenized bonds." In other words, tokenization should serve the existing bond market in information sharing and trust building, rather than generate new forms of digital assets. In this way, existing legal and regulatory frameworks are still working, so bond tokenization will not disrupt the bond market.

Technically, a heterogeneous consortium blockchain should have the following mechanisms. First, the consensus mechanism should differentiate between fundamental (e.g., voting rights) and transactional validation. Second, an arbitration mechanism should be implemented. The arbitration can either be resolved through decentralized on-chain votes or through a centralized court. Third, a communication mechanism should be implemented. Regular Q&A sessions should be held to ensure transparency and the platform's flexibility to adapt to changing market needs. This feature also calls for a certain degree of centralization to provide incentive of platform administration.

13.5 Conclusion

This chapter reviews the historical evolution of FMI in three major economies (RQ1) and identifies an emerging trend of transitioning from digitalization to tokenization (RQ2). Starting in the 1970s, digitalization has reinforced the centralized power of traditional financial intermediaries. However, the 2008 global financial crisis resulted in a trust crisis for centralized institutions.

To address the principal-agent problem of centralized systems, DLT, particularly blockchain technology, provides a solution to restore trust among market participants by removing the need for a trusted authority or intermediary (RQ3). This trend toward decentralization has resulted in many new forms of FMI based on DLT, which we refer to as DLT-FMI.

Our evidence-based findings on FMI are relevant to policymakers and decision-makers in the financial industry, especially for transition economies like China. Financial stability is crucial for economic reform and development, so a disruptive revolution of DLT-FMI can bring unpredictable turbulence to the financial market and the entire macroeconomy. We analyze the application of blockchain in the bond market and conclude that an incremental innovation with both decentralized and centralized features is more appropriate for blockchain adoption (RQ4). We then propose a heterogeneous consortium blockchain solution to DLT-FMI and suggest that tokenization should start with existing bonds (bond tokenization) to minimize regulatory uncertainties, rather than introducing brand new assets (tokenized bonds).

References

Ahluwalia, S., Mahto, R. V., & Guerrero, M. (2020). Blockchain technology and startup financing: A transaction cost economics perspective. *Technological Forecasting and Social Change, 151*, Article 119854.

Berndsen, R. J., León, C., & Renneboog, L. (2018). Financial stability in networks of financial institutions and market infrastructures. *Journal of Financial Stability, 35*, 120–135.

Chang, V., Baudier, P., Zhang, H., Xu, Q., Zhang, J., & Arami, M. (2020). How Blockchain can impact financial services—The overview, challenges and recommendations from expert interviewees. *Technological Forecasting and Social Change, 158*, Article 120166.

Chen, R. R., Chen, K., & Ou, C. X. J. (2023). Facilitating interorganizational trust in strategic alliances by leveraging blockchain-based systems: Case studies of two eastern banks. *International Journal of Information Management, 68*, Article 102521.

Frizzo-Barker, J., Chow-White, P. A., Adams, P. R., Mentanko, J., Ha, D., & Green, S. (2020). Blockchain as a disruptive technology for business: A systematic review. *International Journal of Information Management, 51*, Article 102029.

Guo, D., & Zhou, P. (2021). Green bonds as hedging assets before and after COVID: A comparative study between the US and China. *Energy Economics, 104*, Article 105696.

Kowalski, M., Lee, Z. W. Y., & Chan, T. K. H. (2021). Blockchain technology and trust relationships in trade finance. *Technological Forecasting and Social Change, 166*, Article 120641.

Li, F., & Perez-Saiz, H. (2018). Measuring systemic risk across financial market infrastructures. *Journal of Financial Stability, 34*, 1–11.

Panagariya, A. (2022). Digital revolution, financial infrastructure and entrepreneurship: The case of India. *Asia and the Global Economy, 2*(2), Article 100027.

Wang, C., Mai Le, V. P., Matthews, K., & Zhou, P. (2021). Shadow banking activity and entrusted loans in a DSGE model of China. *The Manchester School, 89*(5), 445–469.

Zhang, B.; & Zhou, P. (2021). Financial development and economic growth in a microfounded small open economy model. *North American Journal of Economics and Finance, 58*, article number: 101544. https://doi.org/10.1016/j.najef.2021.101544.

Treasury Market as Financial Infrastructure

14

Abstract

We examine China's treasury bond market as a cornerstone of financial stability and renminbi internationalization. It contrasts China's Transparent Holding System (THS) with the US's Indirect Holding System (IHS) across transaction, clearing, and settlement stages. Under the THS, intermediaries never acquire ownership, same-day (T + 0) settlement is routine, and holdings are recorded directly, yielding operational efficiency and lower counterparty risk. The multi-layered US model, by contrast, depends on intermediaries, a T + 2 cycle, and complex custody chains that heighten settlement and transparency risks. Analysis shows that the THS fosters regulatory oversight, supports cross-border investor access, and provides a robust platform for RMB use in trade and investment. Policy recommendations are threefold: (i) preserve and refine THS architecture rather than replicate IHS complexity; (ii) codify transparent, rapid-settlement standards as international benchmarks; and (iii) build RMB-denominated cross-border payment rails independent of legacy networks such as SWIFT. These measures advance financial efficiency, market infrastructure, and institutional trust—transforming the treasury market from a potential point of fragility into a vehicle for global financial resilience.

Keywords

Financial infrastructure · Transparent holding system · Indirect holding system

Classification

SDG9 · SDG17

14.1 Introduction

The stability and growth of treasury bond markets are closely related to both financial stability and economic security (Krishnamurthy & Vissing-Jorgensen, 2015). Given China's leading position in the global bond market and the evident trajectory of RMB internationalization, ensuring the resilience of its financial infrastructure becomes paramount (Green & Gruin 2020). Drawing insights from practices in other nations, this chapter endeavors to offer recommendations for enhancing China's financial infrastructure, particularly within its treasury bond market. Through a comparative analysis of diverse models and systems of financial infrastructure, this study aims to provide valuable insights and strategic guidance for China's financial development.

Figure 14.1 shows four main building blocks of the transaction processes of the US treasury bond market: trading, clearing, settlement, and payment, in which the latter three parts are the core

D. Guo and P. Zhou, *Beating Financial Swords into Developmental Plowshares*,
Sustainable Development Goals Series, https://doi.org/10.1007/978-981-95-5152-1_14

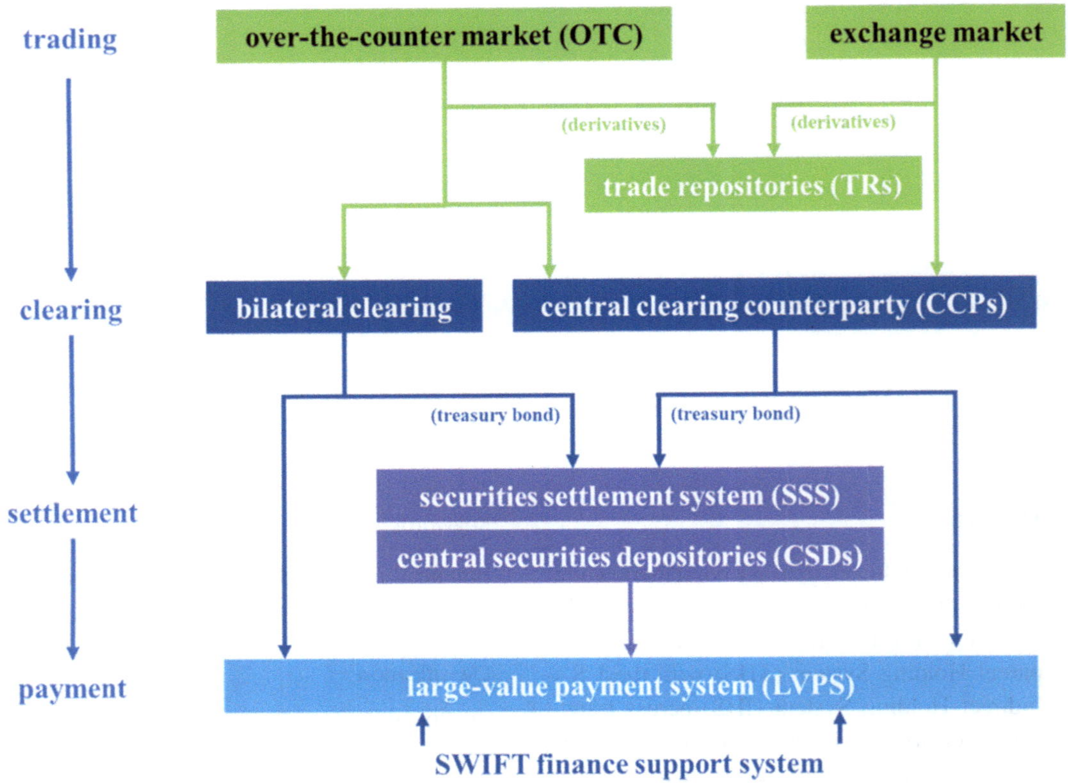

Fig. 14.1 Overview of the US treasury bond market infrastructure

of the financial infrastructure in the US treasury bond market (Hutchison et al., 2016).

Trading. The US treasury bond market comprises both the over the counter (OTC) market and the exchange market, with over 90% of treasury bond transactions occurring in the OTC sector (May, 2010). Participants in the OTC market include commercial banks, foreign banks, securities firms, and institutional investors. The overall framework of the treasury bond financial infrastructure is heavily influenced by the structure and operation of the OTC market, as it dictates the foundational elements of the deposit, settlement, and payment systems. Specifically, the financial infrastructure of the OTC market encompasses an inter-bank broker system, a quotation information system provided by these brokers, and a transaction database. Additionally, the financial infrastructure supporting treasury bond transactions offers database services tailored to the OTC market. These services involve the centralized collection and maintenance of transaction registration information, ensuring transparency regarding risk positions and regulatory requirements. Furthermore, they facilitate risk early warning mechanisms for both market participants and regulatory bodies, ultimately contributing to the stability of financial markets (Yadav, 2021).

Clearing. The clearing process for US treasury bond transactions employs two primary approaches: bilateral clearing and central clearing counterparties (CCPs). The former method resembles the inter-bank bond market in China, while the latter is widely adopted in the US securities and derivatives markets due to its ability to facilitate transactions between treasury bond buyers and sellers with multiple counterparties (Genito, 2019). Specifically, key CCPs operating in the US market include:

- National Securities Clearing Corporation (NSCC): NSCC's primary clearing products encompass stocks, corporate bonds, and municipal bonds.
- Fixed Income Clearing Corporation (FICC): FICC specializes in clearing US treasury bonds and government agency bonds.
- Chicago Mercantile Exchange (CME): CME provides clearing services for futures and options products from both OTC and exchange markets.
- ICE Clear Credit (ICC): ICC primarily clears credit default swaps and similar products.
- London Clearing House (LCH): LCH focuses on clearing interest rate swap products.

These CCPs play a crucial role in facilitating efficient and secure clearing processes for various financial instruments within the US market.

Settlement. The settlement process for US treasury bonds involves the utilization of the securities settlement system and the central securities depository for facilitating ownership transfers and bond payments. Key institutions supporting these functions include Fedwire (also known as Fedwire Securities) and DTC (The Depository Trust Company), with Fedwire operated by the central bank and DTC operated by the Depository Trust and Clearing Corporation (DTCC). Fedwire primarily handles custody and settlement for US government bonds, specific international municipal bonds, and money market instruments. It functions as the electronic transfer system of the Federal Reserve Bank, essential for executing the basic financial functions of "SSS + CSD." The securities settlement systems rely on Fedwire to execute delivery versus payment (DvP), an internationally recognized practice aimed at mitigating settlement risks and disputes. In the US market, DvP is partially guaranteed by the central bank. Moreover, Fedwire plays a crucial role in central settlement, overseeing the delivery of bonds and the payment of funds during the settlement process. The central securities depository is utilized for interest payment purposes. Fedwire not only serves as a bookkeeping system for government bonds but also mandates that participating financial institutions hold Federal Reserve accounts. Only direct customers, brokers, and custodian institutions connected with Fedwire can directly establish primary custodian accounts within it.

Payment. The transaction payment system for US treasury bonds encompasses both the large-value payment system (LVPS) and the retail payment system (RPS). LVPS operates through institutions like the Fedwire Fund and the National Settlement Service (NSS). When collaborating with Fedwire's treasury bond custody function, LVPS can issue vouchers for government bond settlements. Notably, transactions within LVPS become final and irrevocable once funds are transferred, owing to its status as a high-value payment system. On the other hand, RPS involves institutions such as credit/debit card providers. Among the operating entities of RPS, the Fedwire Fund and NSS are notable examples of institutional entities managed by federal banks. Furthermore, it is worth noting that in late 1997, the US transitioned Fedwire's information transmission format to the SWIFT (Society for Worldwide Interbank Financial Telecommunications) format, aligning the US market with international standards. SWIFT serves as a global USD message service network, though it does not function as a payment and settlement system itself. Despite its lack of support for account registration and settlement payments, SWIFT provides essential services for banks and financial market entities, bolstering the USD's status as a global currency. Presently, SWIFT's participating members include major financial institutions and financial market infrastructures engaged in US treasury bond transactions, including the aforementioned US treasury payment system institutions.

14.2 Comparing the US and China

The Chinese treasury bond market's financial market infrastructure (FMI) differs from that of the US in two key aspects: transaction type and institutional model. These disparities contribute to higher efficiency in settlement and payment within China's treasury bond market.

China's treasury bond FMI exhibits two primary distinctions compared to that of the US. Firstly, there exists a divergence in transaction types. The Renminbi (RMB or CNY) treasury bond market is bifurcated into the inter-bank market and the exchange market, with only the former resembling the OTC market for US treasury bonds. Additionally, the registration and trading of RMB treasury bond derivatives are overseen by the China Financial Futures Exchange (CFFEX). While the CFFEX shares some functionalities with US trade repositories (TRs), the latter boasts a more diverse array of major institutions, encompassing DTCC's data service agency, ICE's trading agency, CME's swap data agency, and Bloomberg's swap data service agency.

The second disparity lies in the institutional model. China's bond custody and settlement infrastructure are managed by the China Central Debt Depository & Clearing Corporation Limited (CCDC) and the Shanghai Clearing House (SCH). CCDC oversees government bonds and inter-bank non-government bonds, while SCH handles exchange bonds. Presently, the clearing and settlement mechanisms in China's inter-bank bond market are primarily categorized into two types: full bilateral clearing and net centralized clearing, with the latter adopting CCP. Treasury bonds are managed and settled by CCDC, employing a full settlement approach. Conversely, bonds managed by SCH can be settled via two methods. In instances where treasury bond derivatives transactions necessitate physical delivery, a CCP-like model is facilitated by the China International Capital Corporation (CICC) through CCDC's collateral system.

The FMI of China's treasury bond market demonstrates notable transactional efficiency. Since 2004, the inter-bank bond market has achieved T + 0 settlement through the utilization of a central registration and trusteeship system alongside a modern electronic processing system. This achievement significantly surpasses the settlement efficiency observed in the US treasury bond market. The multi-level trust model employed in the US treasury bond market adopts a pyramid structure, where overall efficiency hinges on the least efficient level and overall safety relies on the lowest level of risk control. In 1995, the US Securities Regulatory Commission implemented the 15C6–1 rule, reducing the settlement period from T + 5 to T + 3. Following the 2008 financial crisis, further efforts were made to shorten settlement times. Subsequently, in September 2017, major financial markets, including the US, transitioned to a T + 2 settlement cycle.

Moreover, the payment mode for RMB treasury bonds in China exhibits greater flexibility and supports cross-border transactions. It accommodates both large-value and retail payments and facilitates cross-border transactions through the RMB Cross-border Interbank Payment System (CIPS). The functionalities of CIPS parallel those of the SWIFT system for cross-border USD payments. In 2018, the operational scope of CIPS was expanded with the introduction of Phase II, extending its operating hours to cover all time zones. Presently, CIPS supports global payment and financial market transactions, with ongoing expansion efforts to enhance its network member coverage.

14.3 Safety Problems

The Indirect Holding System (IHS) serves as an effective remedy for the "paper handling crisis" associated with the Direct Holding System; however, it is not without its shortcomings. In the US treasury bond market, the adoption of IHS post-1960s facilitated "Immobilization" and "Dematerialization" through a multi-tiered holding structure that involved central securities depositories, intermediaries, and actual holders. Nevertheless, following the financial crisis of 2008, flaws within the IHS began to surface, and some argue that they may have contributed to the crisis. One significant drawback of IHS is its potential to enable intermediaries to leverage their clients' assets. Under this system, intermediaries assume legal ownership of securities at the expense of investors, who, in turn, bear the credit risk associated with the intermediary. Legal recourse for investors to reclaim purchased securities in the event of intermediary bankruptcy may be limited. Consequently, investors faced the risk of securities misappropriation by intermediaries, resulting in substantial losses following the crisis.

To mitigate similar issues associated with IHS, reforms within the US treasury bond market are imperative, focusing on simplifying the holding structure, enhancing transparency, and implementing robust supervision mechanisms. Currently, two approaches are being considered to address these concerns: system abandonment and technology-driven restoration. The abandonment of the IHS system in favor of returning to the Direct Holding System (DHS) is one proposed solution. Research in the EU supports this notion, emphasizing the need for data transfer and adherence to transparent legal principles, such as adopting Direct Registration to ensure post-trading transparency in securities transactions.

Alternatively, the restoration of the IHS system through the application of advanced financial technologies is another avenue being explored. Scholars and financial regulators advocate for the establishment of a digital certification management system for securities transactions using blockchain technology, aiming to address systemic defects. While this approach holds promise in resolving existing issues, it also carries the potential for introducing new and possibly greater risks. Moreover, the integration of digital systems into the financial infrastructure is unlikely to yield immediate reforms in the short term.

Since treasury bonds are backed by the state, they possess quasi-monetary attributes and serve as benchmarks. Consequently, the FMI system of China's treasury bond market must address potential issues such as abnormal movements of cross-border capital and economic conflicts, particularly against the backdrop of RMB internationalization and financial market liberalization.

Abnormal movements of cross-border capital typically stem from two primary factors. Firstly, changes driven by the economic cycle play a significant role. Presently, the RMB treasury bond market exhibits characteristics typical of emerging markets, rendering it susceptible to influences from the Federal Reserve's monetary policies. For instance, during periods of global economic downturn, quantitative easing initiatives may lead to a significant influx of cross-border funds. Conversely, as the economy improves and currency conditions normalize, a trend toward capital repatriation may emerge. Secondly, economic conflicts between nations can exacerbate abnormal capital movements. For example, when the US imposes financial sanctions on a country like Russia, it may target ruble-denominated government bonds and restrict US entities from purchasing newly issued Russian government bonds. Such non-economic factors in the treasury bond market can trigger panic among market participants and undermine financial market stability, particularly given the presence of potential "currency blocking" mechanisms.

While economic cycle-driven capital movements exhibit a degree of regularity and are commonplace in emerging markets, financial sanctions represent a more severe form of non-military conflict. Therefore, prior to the implementation of anti-sanctions measures, establishing a transparent regulatory framework is crucial for preemptively identifying potential instances of "currency blocking" and premeditated cross-border flows. Strengthening the regulatory function of the FMI in the treasury bond market necessitates the adoption of a Transparent System, particularly considering China's significant "latecomer advantage" in existing financial infrastructure. China, along with select countries such as Greece and Northern European nations, employs the THS for its FMI, distinguishing it from the IHS utilized in the US. Under the THS, intermediaries are prohibited from assuming the role of investors in holding financial assets, instead solely providing account management services, thereby facilitating multi-level custody services as opposed to multi-level custody.

14.4 Conclusion

Based on the comparative analysis between China's national debt market and that of the US, we propose three recommendations for enhancing the FMI. First, we observe that the complex multi-level holding structure of the IHS used in the US market entails potential risks, whereas China's THS enjoys a distinct follower's advantage. We advise against a hasty transition to the IHS, particularly amidst the ongoing trends of RMB internationalization and treasury bond market opening-up. Furthermore, in the interest of averting financial crises and mitigating economic conflicts, we advocate for the adoption of the THS in China's treasury bond market. Transparent supervision serves as both a prerequisite and a security standard for FMI construction. So, our first suggestion pertains to the formulation and dissemination of Chinese standards through leveraging the advantages of latecomer development. As China's financial market opens up, RMB-denominated treasury bonds are poised to serve as international public goods, necessitating the establishment of an interconnected FMI ecosystem. While China's FMI construction may have commenced later than that of major developed economies, the significant advantages derived from this latecomer status, such as exemplary efficiency in custodian settlement, should be leveraged to promote China's standards and foster innovation.

Second, we stress the importance of implementing transparent supervision in China's onshore treasury bond market to uphold financial stability and ensure that market opening-up remains within the purview of regulatory oversight. Given that China's treasury bond market represents a focal point for overseas institutions to allocate RMB assets, the pursuit of market opening-up presents both development opportunities and potential risks. To address this, it is imperative to align the FMI of China's onshore treasury bond market with the principles of risk prevention and transparent supervision. This entails the adoption of development models and financial technology innovations that adhere to the fundamental requirements of transparent regulatory oversight.

Finally, the advancement of RMB internationalization and the opening-up of the treasury bond market necessitate robust support from a comprehensive cross-border financial infrastructure. As RMB internationalization enters a new phase and China's treasury bonds garner increased attention from overseas investors, the recognition of these bonds as internationally recognized high-quality liquid assets underscores the international reserve function of the RMB. To facilitate the opening-up of the treasury bond market, China must prioritize the development and enhancement of cross-border financial systems, particularly focusing on bolstering the RMB-based Cross-border Interbank Payment System and the RMB Cross-Border Payment & Receipt Management Information System. These initiatives will serve as essential components of the broader effort to support the internationalization of the RMB and facilitate seamless cross-border transactions in the treasury bond market.

References

Genito, L. (2019). Mandatory clearing: The infrastructural authority of central counterparty clearing houses in the OTC derivatives market. *Review of International Political Economy, 26*(5), 938–962.

Green, J., and and Gruin, J. (2020). RMB transnationalization and the infrastructural power of international financial centres. Review of International Political Economy, 28(4), 1028–1054.

Hutchison, N., Squires, G., Adair, A., Berry, J., Lo, D., McGreal, S., & Organ, S. (2016). Financing infrastructure development: Time to unshackle the bonds? *Journal of Property Investment & Finance, 34*(3), 208–224.

Krishnamurthy, A., & Vissing-Jorgensen, A. (2015). The impact of Treasury supply on financial sector lending and stability. *Journal of Financial Economics, 118*(3), 571–600.

May, A. D. (2010). The impact of bond rating changes on corporate bond prices: New evidence from the over-the-counter market. *Journal of Banking & Finance, 34*(11), 2822–2836.

Yadav, Y. (2021). The failed regulation of US treasury markets. *Columbia Law Review, 121*(4), 1173–1250.

General Conclusion

This book provides a comprehensive analysis of monetary-financial systems and policies, and their interplays with broader economic, political, and environmental issues. Based on the evidence, we propose the following actionable implications for policymakers and decision-makers in financial markets.

- **Embrace Financial Sustainability**. The examination of carbon finance's impact on commodity prices suggests that financial policies need to encompass sustainability aspects. This could entail the creation of green financial instruments, such as green bonds and carbon credits, that incentivize investment in sustainable projects and technologies.
- **Promote International Monetary Cooperation**. The significance of monetary policy on carbon finance and commodity prices underlines the necessity for international cooperation. Policymakers should aim to harmonize regulations and create a platform for dialogue to reduce the risk of spillover effects and to enhance the effectiveness of monetary policy globally.
- **Advance Financial Infrastructure Development**. The analysis underlines the importance of developing robust financial infrastructures to support emerging financial sectors such as carbon finance. This could involve regulatory adjustments to foster growth and ensure stability in these markets.
- **Risk Contagion Mitigation Strategies**. The identification of risk contagion between carbon finance and other financial markets warrants the development of mitigation strategies. This could include establishing frameworks for risk assessment and management in financial institutions to preemptively address potential contagion.
- **Policy Support for New Financial Trends**. The recognition that carbon financial effects are becoming a commodity trend characteristic suggests that policy support is crucial for emerging financial trends. Regulators should consider supporting innovative financial markets that align with sustainable development goals. See Chapter

D. Guo and P. Zhou, *Beating Financial Swords into Developmental Plowshares*,
Sustainable Development Goals Series, https://doi.org/10.1007/978-981-95-5152-1

- **Monetary Policy Flexibility**. The effectiveness of different monetary policy tools during rare disasters like pandemics argues for flexible monetary policies. This may involve reevaluating the traditional reliance on interest rates as a policy tool and considering alternative mechanisms that can respond more dynamically to crises.
- **Strengthening Market Resilience**. Given the impacts of financial policy on economic stability, efforts should be concentrated on strengthening market resilience. This includes policies that support diversification, enhance transparency, and encourage responsible-investment practices.
- **Cross-Border Financial Stability Mechanisms**. The research findings indicate the need for mechanisms that can address cross-border financial stability, such as swap lines, regional financial arrangements, and coordinated policy responses to synchronize efforts in mitigating economic shocks.
- **Leverage Technology for Financial Regulation**. We suggest the potential of utilizing disruptive technology, such as distributed ledger technology, to improve financial regulation. Policymakers might encourage innovation in financial services that can lead to more efficient and secure transactions, as well as improved compliance and monitoring.

These evidence-based recommendations can be mapped to the United Nation's SDGs and the 2030 agenda (Table 1).

Furthermore, we synthesize three general principles for the use and policy of finance: (i) dynamic adaptation to systemic changes (**pro-evolution**), (ii) strategic interaction to balance power (**pro-decentralization**), and (iii) proactive adoption of disruptive technologies (**pro-innovation**). We can therefore analyze each piece of advice in terms of the three general principles (Table 2).

Throughout this volume we have shown that finance is a double-edged instrument. Used wisely, it becomes a *wagon* that carries innovation, jobs, and well-being across borders; used recklessly, it turns into a *weapon* that magnifies conflict and scarcity. Short-term rivalries will persist, yet over time every society belongs to the same community of shared destiny. Guided by the enduring insights of thinkers from Aristotle to Confucius, we remain confident that humanity can—and must—*beat financial swords into developmental plowshares.*

Table 1 Mapping the recommendations with SDGs

	Core SDGs	Relevance to the 2030 agenda
Embrace Financial Sustainability	SDG7, SDG9, SDG12, SDG13, SDG17	Green bonds, transition loans, and carbon-credit markets channel capital toward clean energy, resource-efficient production, and climate-mitigation projects, while global disclosure standards hinge on partnerships across public and private actors
Promote International Monetary Cooperation	SDG8, SDG16, SDG17	Coordinated rate setting, swap lines, and joint surveillance curb beggar-thy-neighbor policies, stabilize employment and output, and strengthen rules-based institutions for cross-border liquidity management
Advance Financial Infrastructure Development	SDG8, SDG9, SDG17	Modern payment rails, interoperable clearing systems, and credible benchmark rates lower transaction costs, expand access to finance for firms and households, and enable pooled financing for SDG-aligned investments
Risk Contagion Mitigation Strategies	SDG8, SDG11, SDG16	Integrated stress-testing and macroprudential buffers reduce the likelihood that shocks in carbon or commodity markets cascade into banking and housing systems, protecting livelihoods and urban stability
Policy Support for New Financial Trends	SDG9, SDG12, SDG13, SDG17	Regulatory sandboxes and tax incentives for sustainable derivatives and voluntary-carbon platforms accelerate innovation that prices externalities, nudging consumption and production onto low-carbon paths through multi-stakeholder collaboration
Monetary Policy Flexibility	SDG1, SDG3, SDG8	Counter-cyclical liquidity windows, targeted credit facilities, and temporary yield caps limit job and income losses during pandemics or natural disasters, buffering vulnerable groups and supporting macro-financial health
Strengthening Market Resilience	SDG8, SDG9, SDG11, SDG13	Transparency mandates, diversified collateral frameworks, and responsible-investment codes foster stable capital formation, spur resilient infrastructure, and steer savings away from high-emission assets
Cross-Border Financial Stability Mechanisms	SDG10, SDG16, SDG17	Regional reserve pools, contingent credit lines, and harmonized resolution regimes soften external shocks, narrow inequality between capital-importing and capital-exporting countries, and reinforce cooperative governance
Leverage Technology for Financial Regulation	SDG9, SDG16, SDG17	Distributed ledger settlement, real-time supervisory nodes, and digital-ID based KYC bolster the integrity, efficiency, and inclusiveness of financial services, enabling secure cross-border flows that underpin SDG financing

Table 2 Mapping the recommendations with the three general principles

	Core SDGs	Pro-Evolution	Pro-Decentralization	Pro-Innovation
Embrace Financial Sustainability	SDG7, SDG9, SDG12, SDG13, SDG17	By fostering investments in new technologies, it evolves financial market dynamics	Facilitates the decentralization of investments by promoting diverse, green financial products	Creates avenues for innovative financial instruments like green bonds and carbon credits
Promote International Monetary Cooperation	SDG8, SDG16, SDG17	Facilitates the evolution of global financial systems through collaborative efforts	Promotes a decentralized approach in policymaking through international cooperation	Encourages innovative practices in international policy dialogues and regulatory harmonization
Advance Financial Infrastructure Development	SDG8, SDG9, SDG17	Advances the financial system by integrating modern, robust infrastructures	Supports decentralized financial markets by accommodating diverse financial systems and regulations	Pushes for innovative regulatory adjustments to foster growth in new sectors like carbon finance
Risk Contagion Mitigation Strategies	SDG8, SDG11, SDG16	Promotes the development of evolving risk management practices	Decentralizes risk management by promoting localized strategies tailored to specific market conditions	Introduces innovative assessment and management frameworks to preemptively avoid risk contagions
Policy Support for New Financial Trends	SDG9, SDG12, SDG13, SDG17	Supports the evolution of financial policies to adapt to emerging market trends	Supports decentralized policymaking by accommodating diverse financial innovations and trends	Enables the innovation of financial markets through policy adjustments aligned with sustainability
Monetary Policy Flexibility	SDG1, SDG3, SDG8	Encourages evolving monetary policy tools beyond traditional interest rates	Supports decentralized economic resilience by allowing local economies flexibility in crisis response	Promotes innovative monetary tools that respond dynamically to economic shocks like pandemics
Strengthening Market Resilience	SDG8, SDG9, SDG11, SDG13	Evolves market structures to be more resilient against shocks	Enhances decentralization through diversification and transparency in investments	Drives innovation in market practices that support economic stability
Cross-Border Financial Stability Mechanisms	SDG10, SDG16, SDG17	Enhances the global financial system's evolution to handle economic shocks	Promotes decentralized solutions to cross-border financial stability through coordinated responses	Encourages the innovative use of financial stability mechanisms like swap lines
Leverage Technology for Financial Regulation	SDG9, SDG16, SDG17	Advances regulatory practices through modern technological integration	Promotes decentralization in regulatory processes through DLT, enabling broader oversight	Harnesses innovative technologies like DLT for enhancing financial regulation and compliance

MIX
Papier aus verantwortungsvollen Quellen
Paper from responsible sources
FSC® C105338

If you have any concerns about our products, you can contact us on
ProductSafety@springernature.com

In case Publisher is established outside the EU, the EU authorized representative is:
Springer Nature Customer Service Center GmbH
Europaplatz 3, 69115 Heidelberg, Germany

Printed by Libri Plureos GmbH
in Hamburg, Germany